A S[...] P9-APC-767

TRUE CRIME STORIES

Max Haines was born in Antigonish, Nova Scotia. He is the author of fourteen books, all except one devoted to non-fiction crime. His most recent collection is *Doctors Who Kill*. His earlier work, *The Collected Works of Max Haines*, is considered one of the finest collections of non-fiction crime stories ever produced in Canada.

Crime Flashback is the apt title of Max Haines' newspaper column, which appears twice weekly in *The Toronto Sun*. The column is syndicated across Canada, the U.S., Latin America and Europe, and has been translated into French and Chinese.

A member of Crime Writers of Canada, Mr. Haines resides in Etobicoke, Ont., with his wife Marilyn.

TRUE CRIME STORIES

MAX HAINES

A SIGNET BOOK

NEW AMERICAN LIBRARY

Published in Canada by
Penguin Books Canada Limited, Toronto, Ontario

SIGNET
Published by the Penguin Group
Penguin Books USA Inc., 375 Hudson Street, New York, New York 10014, U.S.A.
Penguin Books Ltd, 27 Wrights Lane, London W8 5TZ, England
Penguin Books Australia Ltd, Ringwood, Victoria, Australia
Penguin Books Canada Ltd, 10 Alcorn Avenue, Toronto, Ontario, Canada M4V 3B2
Penguin Books (NZ) Ltd, 182-190 Wairau Road, Auckland 10, New Zealand

Penguin Books Ltd, Registered Offices: Harmondsworth, Middlesex, England

First published in Canada by the Toronto Sun Publishing Corporation Limited, 1987

Published in Signet by Penguin Books Canada Ltd.

First Printing, 1990
10 9 8 7 6

 REGISTERED TRADEMARK — MARCA REGISTRADA

Printed in Canada

Canadian Cataloguing in Publication Data
Haines, Max
True crime stories

ISBN 0-451-16453-9

1. Murder.   2. Crime and criminals. I. Title.
HV6515.H355 1990   364.1'523   C89-095238-8

Foreword

Did you ever wonder why a sincere and gentle man like Max
Haines would have a burning desire to write about such wicked acts
of crime?

If you read his columns, like many hundreds of thousands do
in the Toronto Sun, you could definitely draw the conclusion that this
fascinating individual would probably be a modern day crimebuster.

I have known Max Haines for about three years, but I feel
that our friendship has existed for many more. My first contact
with him was through his writing at a time when I just started
my career as Chairman of Metropolitan Toronto. Max provided
me, through his columns, with an escape from real life politics,
which is often filled with drama and suspense of its own. I read
almost everything he put to paper about the unsolved murders
as well as the equally intriguing crime stories about the captured
villains.

When you get to know Max, you can not help but like and
admire him. He is warm, humorous, dedicated and always willing to
help if called upon. In fact, Max speaks as well than he writes. I
listened to him recently in Washington, D.C. outlining not only his
career but some of his more interesting stories. He was serious but
humorous. He was direct but warm. He developed, through the
spoken word, a sincere presentation which kept his audience interested
and involved as he does in his written work.

Max started at the Sun a short time after the birth of the
paper but is still considered by many as one of the "founding
fathers".

His popularity, even in the early days, was something to be
envied and as time went by, the Sun's circulation and Max's
fame grew together.

This is his ninth book and I have no doubt that his stories
will, once again, find ways to capture the imagination of his
eager fans.

Paul Godfrey
Publisher
Toronto Sun Publishing Corp.

For
Jay Hudes

Acknowledgments

While gathering the material for this collection of true crime stories, many individuals were consulted who had a first hand connection with the principal characters in the stories.

The late Gordon Sinclair shared the material he had garnered years earlier when he interviewed Kid McCoy. He, more than anyone, enabled me to write the fantastic life of "The Real McCoy".

My thanks also to Jane Stafford, who freely related to me how she had been abused for years, right up until the day she killed her husband beside their Nova Scotia home. Jane's story can be found in "Enough is Enough".

I am deeply indebted to Thurston Fields, the Police Chief of Jewett City, Conn., who willingly escorted me through mud and woods to crime sites where innocent girls met their deaths. His patience contributed in no small measure to "New England Serial Killer".

Det. Insp. Bill McGregor of the Ontario Provincial Police, who has lived for years with the frustrating puzzle of being unable to identify a murder victim, was more than generous in imparting the massive amount of material he has gathered over the years. "Who is the Nation River Girl?" remains one of Canada's most intriguing murder mysteries.

My special thanks to the many police forces, newspapers and librarians who have assisted in finding little known facts, which have helped immeasurably in bringing the various stories to life. In particular, I am indebted to certain members of the Toronto Sun Publishing Corp. Ltd. for their assistance. These include Vince Desai, Joe Marino, as well as Head Librarian Julie Kirsh and her assistants Robert Smith, Glenna Tapscott, Joyce Wagner, Susan Dugas and Katherine Webb-Nelson.

Editors Glenn-Stewart Garnett and Maureen Hudes contributed greatly to the finished product.

As usual, a woman named Marilyn helped too.

— M.H.

Contents

SASSY CASSIE
Cassie pretended to be Carnegie's niece

Some children play doctor or nurse. Others prefer being railway engineers. From childhood Cassie Chadwick played fraud.

Cassie was a rather pudgy, tightlipped lass with no obvious ability or talent. Yet this plain Jane from rural Ontario was able to fleece hard-nosed American bankers out of an estimated $3 million.

Born Elizabeth Bigley in Eastwood, Ont., near Woodstock, in 1857, she displayed a keen but not exceptional mind in school. At the ripe old age of 21, Liz gave the very first inkling of what was to follow. She had pale blue personal cards printed, exclaiming for all the world to see, 'Miss Lizzie Bigley, Heiress to $18,000'.

If anyone questioned Lizzie's claim, she took great glee in displaying a lawyer's letter from England, which explained that she had been left $18,000 by a recently departed uncle. Lizzie was able to purchase several gowns and an organ based on this bogus letter.

When our heroine was unable to pay for any of her purchases, she was arrested and brought to trial. For the very first time, Lizzie displayed her not inconsiderable acting ability. She mimicked the judge, laughed uncontrollably at nothing at all, and sometimes broke into religious hymns. It

1

worked. The judge found the poor girl not guilty, remarking that it was obvious she was insane and should receive some sort of treatment.

After her acquittal, Lizzie took the show on the road. She visited a married sister in Cleveland. Coincidentally, her sister picked that very time to visit the folks back home in Eastwood. While Sis was away, Lizzie mortgaged all her furniture. When Lizzie was unable to pay, the furniture was repossessed. History does not reveal how Sis felt upon returning to an empty home.

Undaunted by this minor setback, Lizzie continued to live by her wits. One of her favorite scams was to pierce her gums with a pin until they bled. In obvious distress she would inform some friend that she required a sum of money for an operation. Lizzie, a keen student of psychology, knew just how much cash she could realistically extract from each mark. Lizzie's gums came to resemble a pincushion.

In 1883 Lizzie, using the name Alice Bastado, entered the blessed state of matrimony. Well, just barely. The marriage lasted for 12 days, which is a quickie even by today's standards. Then again, Lizzie was about 100 years ahead of her time in most things.

She met Dr. Wallace S. Springsteen at a party in Cleveland and quickly let the good doctor know that she was an Irish heiress. At that very moment Dr. Springsteen had need of a cash transfusion to set up his medical practice. He proposed. Lizzie accepted.

Within a week our girl had purchased expensive gowns, rugs, and fine furniture, which was just great with Springsteen, except for one thing. Lizzie neglected to pay for anything. When bill collectors came calling, Lizzie, cool as a cucumber, informed her new husband that the clothing and furniture were little tokens of affection from him to her. The doctor said no way. The bill collectors repossessed everything, including the nuptial bed. Springsteen took to the hills, obtaining a divorce along the way.

Lizzie busied herself for the next two years by marrying an Ohio farmer and taking him for enough cash to set up shop as a clairvoyant in Toledo. She used the name Mme. de Vere. Honest, Lizzie had a crystal ball and everything. She proceeded to successfully shear the sheep who called at her establishment.

One of her sheep, or I should say lamb, because this meek father of five children did have the rather unfortunate name of Joseph Lamb, was shorn of $1500, his entire life's savings. Lamb bellowed. Lizzie assured him that all was not lost. Together they would swindle Richard Brown, a well-known broker, out of a whopping $40,000. The scheme didn't work.

Lizzie and Lamb were both arrested and stood trial. Lamb swore that Lizzie had hypnotized him. Evidently the jury believed him. Lamb was acquitted, but Lizzie drew nine and a half years in the Ohio State Prison. Four years later, Gov. William McKinley granted our Lizzie a pardon.

On the day of her release from prison she headed for Cleveland, changed her name to Mrs. Cassie Hoover, and opened a massage parlor. In walked Dr. Leroy Shippen Chadwick, a prominent Cleveland physician. Dr. Chadwick had lost his wife four years previously and dearly longed for sympathetic female companionship. He also suffered from an extremely painful back condition.

He didn't know it, but he was meeting the only woman in all of Cleveland who could cure both maladies. Cassie proved to be a whiz in the massage parlor, as well as a real charmer in the companionship department. Dr. Chadwick was soon in love.

Now Dr. Chadwick was not Cassie's average choice of husband. No siree, he was a bona fide member of Cleveland society and well-off financially. In short, a fine catch. In 1897, he and Cassie became husband and wife.

It took Cassie about four years of constant spending to decimate the doctor's fortune. Remember, those were the days when a dollar was a hundred cents. It is estimated that Cassie went through a quarter of a million dollars. The Chadwick home was converted into a showcase. Expensive paintings hung on the walls. Fine Persian rugs covered the floors. One Christmas Eve Cassie remodelled the entire house as a surprise for her husband.

In 1902, Dr. Chadwick could take the indiscriminate spending no longer. He closed out his bank account and headed for Europe. Cassie departed for New York, where she pulled off her greatest scam, for which she is remembered to this day.

In order to obtain credit in Cleveland, Cassie told financiers a fantastic tale, which she then proceeded to prove. She told them she was a niece of Frederick Mason, a lifelong associate of multi-millionaire steel magnate Andrew Carnegie. She added that she was heiress to $7 million of Carnegie's securities by virtue of the fact that she was Carnegie's illegitimate daughter. Cassie felt that as Carnegie was getting up there in age, it was time the old boy let her have a few million to come and go on.

Cautious Cleveland bankers decided to check out her story. They suggested that their own lawyer accompany Cassie to the Carnegie estate and have Carnegie sign a few million dollars worth of notes. Cassie thought it a great idea.

A fancy carriage pulled up outside 2 East 91st St. in Manhattan. Cassie suggested that her eccentric millionaire father might not like a lawyer barging in on him unannounced. She would go in, break the ice, and then call for the lawyer. Cassie walked up to the front entrance bold as brass and rang the bell. As the lawyer watched, Cassie chatted with a servant and was then ushered into the mansion.

Fifteen minutes later she reappeared, dejected. Her daddy didn't want to meet any lawyers, but all was not lost. Cassie extracted two $500,000 notes signed by Andrew Carnegie, as well as a wrapped package, which Cassie explained 'held a bunch of bonds'.

Cassie returned to Cleveland, where word of her genuine claim as Carnegie's illegitimate daughter had preceded her. She walked into Cleveland's Wade Park Banking Co., then controlled by Rockefeller interests. Secretary treasurer of the bank, Ira Reynolds, greeted her with open arms. Cassie had two little items with her. She passed Reynolds a promissory note signed by Andrew Carnegie for $500,000 and requested storage space for a package, which she offhandedly remarked contained $5 million in securities. The list of securities was neatly itemized on the outside of the parcel.

Reynolds was delighted to receive the goodies. He suggested that Cassie open an account with his bank in the amount of $50,000, giving her access to pin money. Cassie agreed. As she rose to leave, Cassie stopped short. A smile crossed her face. She wasn't a very astute business person. Shouldn't she get a receipt for the $5 million in stocks and bonds?

"Of course," replied the banker, and hastily signed a receipt listing the securities without ever having opened the package. Cassie had pulled it off. She now had in her possession a legitimate receipt for $5 million in nonexistent securities.

Cassie shifted into high gear. She next appeared in Oberlin, Ohio, where she presented herself to Charles T. Beckwith, president of the Citizens National Bank. Beckwith was stunned at his good fortune. Cassie passed over two half million dollar promissory notes bearing Carnegie's signature. She also showed Beckwith the list of securities being held in trust for her at Mr. Reynold's financial institution.

Small town banker Beckwith had to catch his breath. But wait, there was more. Cassie explained that estate planning was not her long suit. She really needed two intelligent men to handle her affairs. Would Beckwith be interested at $10,000 a year? Beckwith choked on his cigar and jumped at the chance. He offered his head cashier as the second man. It was settled. Cassie walked out of the bank, firmly entrenched as the bank's most prominent customer.

Three weeks later she borrowed $5000. In the succeeding months she borrowed larger amounts. Beckwith was delighted. It wasn't every banker who had Andrew Carnegie's signed notes in his safe.

Within a year Cassie was into the bank for $240,000. Beckwith had forced $102,000 of his own money upon her, in an attempt to pick up the high interest rates, which didn't seem to concern Cassie at all.

Employing much the same scheme, Cassie proceeded to

fleece other financial institutions. She ran up the tab at the Wade Park Banking Co. to $400,000. Elyria Savings Bank coughed up $100,000 and the American Exchange Bank in New York City went to the well for $380,000. The Euclid Avenue Savings Bank was taken for $420,000.

Cassie didn't confine her skullduggery to banks. Dear friend Herbert Newton was swindled out of a whopping $500,000.

What did Cassie do with the veritable Niagara of funds flowing into her coffers? She spent it, that's what she did. It was the turn of the century. A family could live on $9 a week. Cassie gave porters $20 tips. Her home was a showplace, housing objets d'art from around the world. She maintained a stable of servants who jumped to fulfil her every whim and travelled with an entourage to the capitals of Europe. Once, when the mood struck her, she purchased 12 grand pianos and gave them away as gifts. Befitting a woman of her stature, she adorned herself with diamonds worth a king's ransom. Never one to forget those less fortunate, Cassie donated large sums to charity.

The first tiny crack in Cassie's pyramid of subterfuge appeared in 1904 when her good friend, millionaire Herbert Newton, became tired of waiting for Cassie to pay up. He sued her for $190,000. It didn't take long for the house of cards to tumble.

As soon as it became known that Cassie didn't have the ability to pay Newton the relatively small sum of $190,000, the good people of Oberlin, Ohio started a run on the Citizens National Bank. Poor Beckwith had to close the bank's doors. He admitted that the $240,000 owed by Cassie was four times the entire capitalization of the bank.

Reporters reached Andrew Carnegie, who informed the world he not only never had an illegitimate daughter, he had never even heard of Cassie Chadwick.

It was all over. Cassie was arrested in New York. On March 6, 1905, she was brought to trial, charged with forgery and abetting bank officials with misappropriation of funds. Cassie's trial was the most publicized court event in a decade. Carnegie attended the trial and enjoyed it immensely. Charles

Beckwith didn't attend. He died of a heart attack, which many believe was brought on by his personal bankruptcy.

Cassie was found guilty and sentenced to ten years in the Ohio State Penitentiary. Back in prison Cassie's health deteriorated rapidly. In the summr of 1907 she was transferred to the prison hospital, where she died that same year.

In her home town of Eastwood, they still love to relate how Cassie drove up to Carnegie's mansion and was ushered inside by a servant, thereby laying the groundwork for her master swindle. It was easy. Cassie impressed upon the servant her urgent need to use the bathroom. The servant sympathetically obliged.

THE
FIFTY CENT
MURDERS
From counterfeiter to murderer

Not many men have attempted to get rich by counterfeiting 50 cent Canadian coins. Herbert McAuliffe not only attempted the trick but did a fairly good job. Unfortunately, Herbie's rather comical criminal endeavours ended in tragedy when his bungling efforts turned to murder.

Born in North Bay, Ont., Herbie was an above average student during his formative years. He showed a natural mechanical bent and attended a technical school before leaving North Bay for the tobacco belt around Simcoe.

In 1939, together with thousands of other young Canadians, Herbie joined the army. While in the service, he used his mechanical ability to good advantage and quickly rose to the rank of staff sergeant. However, there must have been a little larceny in his heart even then. In 1944, he was dishonorably discharged for stealing money from his comrades.

Herbie gravitated to Windsor, Ont., taking with him one of the army's .45 calibre Thompson sub-machine guns and eight automatic pistols, but we have no reason to believe that he intended to use the army weapons. No, Herbie had other devious plans. He had decided to counterfeit Canadian 50 cent pieces, something never accomplished in this country before.

To facilitate his operation, Herbie rented a double garage

from Germain Noel on London St., using the alias Frank West. Noel listened as Herbie explained that his work was rather noisy and was a top secret government project concerning the invention of a revolutionary new weapon.

Now that his cover was established, Herbie wrote away for books and manuals on coin minting. For weeks he pored over the technical articles. There was one immediate problem — the lack of funds. In order to implement his scheme, he required money to purchase machinery. This minor difficulty was overcome with ease. Herbie became extremely adept at holding up service stations and grocery stores.

Coincidental with his successful robberies, a steady stream of rather sophisticated machinery arrived at the garage on London St. A turret lathe, dies and punch presses worth over $15,000 were delivered to Herbie's factory. A $10,000 hydraulic press for stamping out the coins was installed at the garage. Herbie didn't do things half way.

It was hard work. Herbie carried out his experiments from scratch. He had no assistants and no technical advisors. His painstaking experiments continued for four years, interrupted and financed by his periodic stickups.

At last, his technique was perfected. He had invented his own alloy and was actually able to stamp coins out of cheap metal and coat them with silver in an electro-plating bath. The end result looked perfect. Just for fun, Herbie produced a bucket full.

That same night, Herbie tested his newly minted 50 cent pieces at a gambling joint in Detroit. He knew betting quantities of 50 cent Canadian coins would be unusual and focus attention on him, but he wanted the coins to be examined. If they would be accepted in a gambling den, they would be accepted everywhere. Herbie and his phony fifties passed with flying colors. His coins were identical to the real thing.

Next day, back at the garage, Herbie decided to figure out just how much he would net from his operation. He added up his expenses and was dumbfounded to find out that it cost him 48 cents for every 50 cent coin he produced. If he threw in his own labor he was losing money.

There was a solution. If he had the capital to modernize his plant with new equipment, he could lower costs. Herbie decided that the quickest way to raise capital would be to rob a bank.

In his usual methodical manner, Herbie drove throughout the countryside looking for a suitable bank. He found it in the Imperial Bank of Canada at Langton, Ont. Now, Langton was not a hustling, bustling metropolis. Located about 20 miles from Simcoe, it was not likely that the 250 souls who called Langton home would interfere with Herbie's nefarious scheme.

In preparation for the heist, Herbie stole a car in Windsor. Into it he threw his .45 calibre Thompson sub-machine gun, a Luger and a .45 revolver. He tossed in a brown paper shopping bag to hold his anticipated loot.

Herbie walked up to bank accountant Henry Thompson and announced, "This is a stickup. Listen, chum, if you don't open up the combination on that vault I'll be back tonight to drill you dead." Thompson filled Herbie's paper shopping bag with $22,577 in bills and coins. Herbie waved his gun menacingly and herded 11 customers into the bank vault. He then took off for his waiting car, but in his haste our boy neglected to lock the vault door.

Inside the vault Arthur Lierman, a 31-year-old tobacco farm owner, pushed the door open. As he did so he shouted to William Goddyn, 24, "Come on, Bill, I've got a .22 calibre rifle in my Buick. Let's get him."

Herbie knew he was being followed. A few miles down the road near Frogmore he stopped, took out his sub-machine gun and fired a burst at the pursuing car. Lierman and Goddyn died in a hail of 30 bullets.

Herbie abandoned the shopping bag full of money on the front seat of his stolen car and took off into the bush. Word of the dramatic daylight bank robbery and the murders of two popular citizens of the area spread like wildfire.

The hunt was on. Herbie was headline news across the nation. The largest manhunt in Canadian history up to that time was organized. For three days, Herbie hid out in barns, stole food from farmers and swatted mosquitoes until Graham Haggerty, a 20-year-old farmhand out deer hunting, discovered Herbie in an old shack near Straffordville.

Initially, Herbie was identified as Frank West or George Walker, the two aliases he had used during his years developing fake 50 cent pieces. Eventually his true identity and his counterfeiting career were uncovered and revealed to the public.

Herbie was tried in Simcoe, found guilty of murder and sentenced to death. On Dec. 19, 1950, he was given the last rites of the Catholic church and walked briskly to his death on the scaffold at the Simcoe jail.

So ended the career of Herbert McAuliffe, who will go down in Canadian history as the only man to successfully produce counterfeit 50 cent pieces.

DARLING
MRS. SPARLING
Dr. MacGregor and the farmer's wife

Canada's most infamous medical murderer was Dr. Neill Cream, who took tremendous delight in poisoning unsuspecting ladies before the turn of the century. Less well known but every bit as wicked was London, Ontario's Dr. Robert MacGregor.

By the time he was 30, Dr. MacGregor had left London and set up practice in the village of Ubly in Huron County, Michigan. One January afternoon in 1909, Carrie Sparling, the 45-year-old wife of dairy farmer John Wesley Sparling, walked into the doctor's office with a distressing bit of dust in her left eye.

Although Carrie was the mother of four strapping sons, she had the appearance of a girl of 25. Dr. MacGregor took one look at the bad eye, coughed and said, "Kindly disrobe." The doctor started by staring at Carrie's toes and after several pauses on his way northward finally concentrated on the sore eye. Dr. MacGregor extracted the dust and told his patient that he would drop in on her the next time he was near her farm in Sanilac County, about an hour's buggy drive from Ubly.

Dr. MacGregor was a tall, attractive man. Carrie didn't exactly repulse his advances. The doctor did have a meek, rather ugly wife of his own, who was forgotten from the very day Carrie showed up with that bad eye.

A week after Carrie's visit, Dr. MacGregor travelled to the Sparling farm, where he met big husky, John Wesley and his four sons, Ray, 20, Scyrel, 21, Albert, 23, and Peter, 24.

The doctor thought it best to give Carrie a physical examination. One never knew what damage dust in the eye could inflict. Dr. MacGregor and Carrie were directed to the bedroom by trusting John Wesley. An hour later they emerged and advised Mr. Sparling, "Everything was just fine, even better than we had hoped."

From then on Carrie suffered from a series of minor ailments. The doctor came every second week or so and never failed to cure what ailed her.

After several months had passed, Dr. MacGregor confided to his best friend Xenophon A. Boomhower, who lived in the neighboring village of Bad Axe, that he suspected John Wesley Sparling had Bright's disease. A few months later John Wesley was confined to his bed. Despite Dr. MacGregor's care, the poor man was called to that great dairy farm in the sky.

The doctor, who was now considered a dear family friend by the four boys and something altogether different by Carrie, met with the Sparling family. He advised the boys to take out life insurance. Considering the untimely demise of their father, the four lads thought it good advice. By coincidence, the doctor's father was an insurance agent back in London. He sold them Sun Life of Canada policies.

A year later Dr. MacGregor informed his friend Boomhower that Pete Sparling had acute pancreatitis. Everyone was shocked. Poor Pete. He was laid to rest beside his dad less than a year after the elder Sparling had departed this mortal coil.

Distraught, Carrie decided to sell the farm and purchase a smaller one in Huron County, a stone's throw from Dr. MacGregor's office in Ubly. Coincidental with the Sparlings' move, good friend Xenophon Boomhower was appointed county prosecutor.

The wood was hardly stacked for the winter at the

Sparlings' new farm when Albert took ill. The doctor explained to Boomhower that Albert had lifted a heavy piece of farm machinery and had suffered internal injuries. A few months later Albert joined Pete and John Wesley down at the family plot.

It was vacation time. Dr. MacGregor took his wife on a motoring trip throughout Ontario. While the doctor was away Carrie bought a house in Ubly for investment purposes. It was only a few streets removed from Dr. MacGregor's office. When the MacGregors returned, Carrie suggested that they move out of their present home and rent from her. It seemed like a good idea, and that's how the MacGregors became tenants of Carrie Sparling.

Mrs. MacGregor took ill. Her husband suggested she return to Ontario to visit relatives and rest up. Mrs. MacGregor left the scene. She was no sooner gone than Carrie took to visiting the good doctor. Sometimes she stayed all day. When the fancy struck her she stayed all night. Tongues wagged, but the untimely death of Scyrel Sparling interrupted the gossip.

The death appeared to puzzle Dr. MacGregor. He suggested an autopsy, which he conducted with another doctor in attendance. It was a cursory affair. Dr. MacGregor took one look and said, "Well, well, cancer of the liver." The other doctor agreed without really taking part in the examination. Scyrel joined the other members of his family.

Shortly after Scyrel's tragic passing, a village busybody observed Carrie leaving the doctor's residence at dawn. She informed elderly John Sparling, an uncle of the late John Wesley, who waited until he spied Carrie enter Dr. MacGregor's home. He then climbed up a ladder and peered into the bedroom. Land sakes! The rumors were true. There were Carrie and Dr. MacGregor, coupled.

Things got hot. Old John informed Prosecutor Boomhower, who secretly had Scyrel's body exhumed. Vital organs were sent to the University of Michigan. The university report stated that Scyrel's organs were laced with arsenic. Albert's body was also exhumed. It, too, contained arsenic.

14

When Dr. MacGregor told Boomhower that the one remaining Sparling son, Ray, had taken ill, he knew he had to take immediate action. Unknown to Carrie, he visited the bedridden Ray at the farm and told him the whole sordid story. He advised Ray to pretend to take Dr. MacGregor's medicine but to save it for analysis. The medicine proved to be laced with arsenic.

Dr. MacGregor was taken into custody and charged with Scyrel's murder. Carrie was charged with being an accomplice. During the trial, Prosecutor Boomhower forcefully pointed out that both Albert's and Scyrel's bodies had contained arsenic. Dr. MacGregor was found guilty and sentenced to life in Michigan State Prison. The charges against Carrie were dropped.

As soon as the prison gates closed behind him in 1912, Dr. MacGregor began a campaign of letter writing proclaiming his innocence. One such letter reached Gov. Woodbridge Fuller, who was appalled that testimony concerning Albert's poisoning had been admitted as evidence at a trial which concerned Scyrel's death only. The governor interviewed several members of the jury, who said they would not have found MacGregor guilty if the evidence concerning Albert's death had not been presented.

Gov. Fuller pardoned Dr. MacGregor after he had served four years in prison. Once outside, the doctor was an object of ridicule. Friendless, he applied for the position of physician at Michigan State Prison. The appointment was granted. Dr. MacGregor ministered to the prisoners for 12 years, never leaving the institution until he died within its gray walls in 1928.

THE REAL McCOY
The sad saga of Kid McCoy

Not many men have been welterweight and middle-weight boxing champion of the world, married nine times, and still managed to spend eight years in San Quentin prison for the killing of a prospective tenth bride. Then again, there has never been anyone quite like Kid McCoy.

The Kid's real name was Norman Selby, but he was known for most of his life as Kid McCoy. He fought exactly 200 fights and lost only seven. At the turn of the century he was one of the most famous athletes in the world. McCoy had that quality sometimes called charisma or referred to as showmanship. In any case, he definitely had magnetism in the ring and in the bedroom. Everybody loved the Kid, especially the ladies.

McCoy stood 5 ft. 11 inches, had black wavy hair, and in his prime never weighed over 157 lbs. Let's take a look at his pugilistic career first. We will get to the bedroom soon enough.

In 1896, McCoy beat Tommy Ryan in 15 brutal rounds and captured the middleweight championship of the world. A year later, he purchased a saloon in New York, which became a hangout for the sporting fraternity and actors.

McCoy was so good at his profession that it was difficult for him to find a worthy opponent in his own weight class.

Occasionally a promoter would stage a fight between the Kid and a heavier man. These fights accounted for the Kid's few losses. Gentleman Jim Corbett and Jack Sharkey beat McCoy. Both men outweighed McCoy by over 40 lbs. and both held the heavyweight championship of the world.

One day a drunk sauntered into McCoy's bar and started to verbally abuse McCoy. Someone told the drunk he better watch himself — he was picking on Kid McCoy, welterweight champion of the world. The drunk didn't believe he was in the presence of the champ and continued to berate McCoy. Finally, the Kid lost his patience, and with one punch knocked out the drunk. When the poor man regained consciousness, he rubbed his chin, looked up and said, "That's the real McCoy," and so coined the phrase that is still in use today to denote a genuine article.

In affairs of the heart the Kid answered the bell nine times. All of his wives were good-looking women. Special mention goes to Julia Woodruff Crosselmire, who had three return matches with the Kid, all ending in divorce.

By 1924, the Kid had run through several fortunes and all nine marriages. The black wavy hair was now sparse, and the flat-as-a-pancake midriff had developed an ever so slight bulge. Show business friends from the old days obtained bit parts for him in the movies. In between acting assignments, he was a guard in an airplane factory and had been issued a pistol.

Now 51, the Kid still had that old charisma when it came to the ladies. Theresa W. Mors, wife of wealthy art and antique dealer Albert E. Mors, came under the Kid's spell. Theresa left Albert to live with the Kid. She filed for divorce. Her husband in turn named McCoy as corespondent.

On Aug. 12, 1924, Theresa and the Kid were both hitting the bottle pretty hard. Many believe that McCoy had learned that night that Theresa had decided not to become Mrs. McCoy number ten. That's when the Kid placed his .32 calibre pistol behind Theresa's left ear and shot her dead.

The Kid had a few more blasts of whisky, made out his will and drove to the home of his sister, Jennie Thomas.

McCoy told his sister, "I just had to kill that woman."

Next morning, McCoy was still on the prowl. He made his way to the Mors' antique store on Seventh Ave. He walked inside, where customers William Ross, Sam Stern, and clerk V. C. Emden were passing the time of day. The Kid pulled out his .32 and turned on a music box. He then proceeded to wave his pistol, keeping time to the music. Suddenly he slammed the box shut and robbed the three men of their money. Ross made a sudden motion and the Kid fired, wounding Ross in the leg.

The Kid dashed for the street, where he encountered Mr. and Mrs. Sam Schapp, who owned the store next to the antique shop. Sam knew the Kid. He asked, "Norman, what the hell are you doing?" The Kid answered with two shots. One struck Sam, the other his wife. All three shot that morning by McCoy recovered from their wounds.

Police soon caught up with McCoy and took him into custody. At the time of his arrest he admitted murdering Mrs. Mors. He soon changed his story, claiming that Mrs. Mors had committed suicide.

Attorney Jerry Geisler, who would later gain fame for defending Hollywood stars during their various trials and tribulations, was in the Kid's corner. He did the best he could.

The Kid was convicted of manslaughter in the Mors affair and received from one to ten years in prison. For his early morning shooting spree he received two sentences of one to fourteen years and one sentence of six months to ten years imprisonment.

The Kid was the most popular inmate in San Quentin prison. He received gifts from all over the world. Some of his friends who stuck by him included such public figures as Damon Runyon, Lionel Barrymore, and Sophie Tucker. As a result of the intervention of Henry Ford Sr., McCoy was paroled in 1932 and given employment with the Ford organization.

The Kid lived on for eight years, but suffered bouts of depression from not being in the limelight. In April, 1940, he swallowed a bottle of sleeping pills in a Detroit hotel room. The real McCoy was down for the count.

THE
AMITYVILLE HORROR
A house haunted by tragedy

It is seldom that the by-product of a vicious killing receives more publicity than the actual murder. Everyone remembers Amityville, the small Long Island, N.Y. town which became a household word with the publication of Jay Anson's best-selling book, *The Amityville Horror*.

The book outlined in vivid detail the supernatural phenomena allegedly experienced by George and Kathy Lutz and their family, who purchased a large luxurious Dutch Colonial home in Amityville on Dec. 18, 1975. The Lutz family were driven from their home 28 days later by a series of strange incidents.

They reported that doors had been torn off hinges, strange smells permeated the house, pigs' eyes stared at them through windows and other ghostly happenings occurred. All this was more than the family could take.

Although the supernatural aspects of the Amityville phenomena are now considered to be unfounded, the strange events which took place there stand out from all other haunted house stories because of one undeniable fact. The house at 112 Ocean Ave. was the site of a horrendous multiple murder in 1974.

Prior to that time, there was no talk of the supernatural at the large home on Ocean Ave. It was then occupied by the De Feo family, consisting of Ronald and Louise De Feo and their five children, Ronald, Jr., 23; Dawn, 18; Allison, 13; Mark, 11; and John, 9.

Ronald Sr. was service manager for the family business, the Brigante-Karl Buick agency on Coney Island. Their five bedroom home was complete with swimming pool and boathouse.

Ronnie, who worked for his father at the agency, was later to tell police that he woke up on the morning of Nov. 13, 1974, dressed, and was out of the house at 4:30 a.m. He drove his 1970 Buick Electra to Coney Island, arriving at work shortly after 6 a.m. Ronald Sr. wasn't expected at work that day, as he had an appointment to take Mark to the doctor. Ronnie knew he was in for an easy day.

There was little doubt in Ronnie's mind that his parents considered him the black sheep of the family. They had good reason. Ronnie, a high school dropout, drank heavily, and while not addicted to heroin, was a periodic user. He and his father often had fist fights.

Ronnie was forever getting into trouble. His most serious difficulty had occurred the previous year when he pleaded guilty to stealing several outboard motors. Put on probation, he was often accused by his father of working at the agency only to fulfil the terms of his probation.

Despite the bad blood between father and son, the elder De Feo provided Ronnie with several hundred dollars per week in spending money. Ronnie was in the habit of picking up the tab for his drinking buddies.

Knowing that his father was taking Mark to the doctor and wouldn't be at work, Ronnie hung around the agency only until noon and then took off. He met a friend, Robert Kelske, who mentioned that when he had driven to the De Feo home that morning the two family cars were still in the driveway. This seemed to puzzle Ronnie. He was sure his father was taking Mark to the doctor. At 1:30 p.m. Ronnie visited a girlfriend, where he used the phone to call home. He was surprised to receive no answer.

Later he drove to Robert Kelske's home. He told his friend that he couldn't raise his family on the phone. The two men made a date to meet at Henry's Bar at 6 p.m. Ronnie left Kelske's and went directly to Henry's, where he passed the time by consuming vodka and Seven-Up. He told several customers at the bar that he was concerned at not being able to reach his family all day.

When Kelske showed up at the bar at 6 p.m., Ronnie's first words to him were, "I'm going to have to go home and break a window to get in." He left and returned a short time later shouting, "You got to help me, you got to help me! Someone has shot my mother and father."

Ronnie Kelske, and four other men, dashed to Ronnie's car and drove the half mile to the De Feo home. Ronnie's buddies confirmed that Ronald and Louise De Feo were dead in their bed. Police were called. Officer Kenneth Greguski of the Amityville village police walked through the house. In their room, on twin beds, lay the bodies of Mark and John. Further examination of the sprawling home revealed the bodies of the two De Feo girls, Dawn and Allison. All the victims were found face down in bed. They had been shot to death.

Ronnie cried uncontrollably when he was informed that every member of his family had been slaughtered. When questioned by police, he pulled himself together and told them, "I'll help you in any way I can."

Ronnie proceeded to pinpoint his movements on the day of the tragedy much as they are related here. When police inquired why he had not returned home earlier in the day, he explained that his father had beaten him up once when he had broken a window. He didn't want to risk another beating.

Initially, there was some concern that Ronnie had escaped the murderous attack by chance. Precautions were taken in case the killer was stalking the one remaining member of the De Feo family. That night Ronnie slept on a cot at the police station.

By morning, it was established that eight bullets had been fired. Mr. and Mrs. De Feo had been shot twice, while each of the four children had been shot once. The killer had stood above his victims and fired from a distance of not more than three feet. Only Allison had turned her head to receive a bullet through the left cheek. Ballistics experts determined that all six victims had been killed with a .35 calibre Marlin rifle.

Three rifles were taken from Ronnie's room, but none were Marlins. Ronnie readily admitted owning a fourth rifle, but claimed that he had gotten rid of it. He couldn't remember the calibre. Police didn't believe that Ronnie, a gun buff, would not remember the calibre of a rifle he once owned. He became a prime suspect when detectives found two boxes in his room. One contained a .22 rifle, the other a .35 Marlin.

Under expert questioning, Ronnie's sympathetic and respectful attitude towards the dead members of his family gradually changed. He cursed his father and admitted hating his brothers and sisters. Once it was established that Ronnie had been in the house between 2 a.m. and 4 a.m. when the murders took place, he had difficulty explaining how he didn't hear eight shots being fired. Finally, he admitted to systematically killing his own family, rushing from room to room, slaughtering as he went. In Ronnie's own words, "Once I started, I couldn't stop. It went so fast."

Ronnie directed detectives to a sewer in Brooklyn, where he had disposed of the clothing he had worn while murdering his family. He also told detectives that he had thrown the murder weapon into a canal near his home. On Nov. 15, scuba divers recovered the .35 calibre Marlin.

The motive for the murder was a puzzle. It is believed that the elder De Feo kept large amounts of money in a metal box in his home. This box, which reportedly held as much as $200,000, was found empty. No money has ever shown up.

After he was arrested, Ronnie behaved in an irrational manner, attempting to gain an acquittal by proving insanity. However, psychiatrists testified that, in their opinion, he was malingering.

On Dec. 4, 1975 Ronnie De Feo was found guilty of six counts of murder and sentenced to 25 years to life imprisonment. The sentences are to run concurrently. He will be eligible for parole in 1999, when he will be 48.

D. B. COOPER
A high flying legend

The 37 passengers responded to the announcement that Northwest Airlines Flight 305 was about to take off. Flying time for the 727 between Portland, Oregon and Seattle, Washington was 25 minutes. This flight would take much longer.

It was a trip none of the 37 passengers would ever forget. On that U.S. Thanksgiving evening of Nov. 24, 1971, one of their number would become part of American folklore, as a cross between Robin Hood and Jesse James.

Dan Cooper unobtrusively strolled aboard the aircraft. Stewardesses Florence Shaffner and Tina Mucklow welcomed him aboard. D. B. Cooper, as he came to be known due to a reporting error, took a seat by himself at the rear of the aircraft.

Moments after takeoff, D. B. pressed the button requesting a stewardess' assistance. Miss Shaffner responded. Silently D. B. handed her a folded piece of paper. Miss Shaffner, an attractive brunette, had been approached in many different ways since becoming a stewardess. This was a novel move. She was later to tell authorities, "I thought he was trying to hustle me." Then she read the note.

In simple language it was a demand for 10,000 twenty dollar bills and two sport parachutes. Otherwise the plane, its passengers and crew of six would be blown up. Miss Shaffner gulped as D. B. flipped open his suitcase and revealed two red cylinders attached to coils of wire. To this day no one knows if the contents of D. B.'s briefcase held a real bomb constructed of dynamite or merely highway flares. D. B. closed his briefcase and the contents were never seen by anyone again.

Miss Shaffner walked briskly to the cockpit and passed the note to Captain William Scott. He radioed Seattle for instructions. They, in turn, immediately contacted local police, the FBI and Northwest Airlines president Don Nyrop. Instructions were not long in coming. They were told, "Do whatever he demands."

Scott informed his passengers that there would be a slight delay in landing due to minor mechanical difficulties. Meanwhile, officials on the ground were gathering up and photographing $200,000 in twenty dollar bills.

For three hours, the 727 circled Seattle before beginning its descent. Once on the ground, the passengers were informed of the real cause of the delay. They breathed a collective sigh of relief when D. B. accepted a bag from a Federal Aviation Administration official. The laundry sack contained 21 pounds of twenty dollar bills. D. B. then inspected the two parachutes brought aboard as instructed. Satisfied, he dismissed all passengers and Miss Shaffner with a wave of his hand.

Flight 305 again took to the air. D. B. dictated notes to attendant Tina Mucklow, who passed them on to Captain Scott. Cooper instructed the pilot to head for Reno at an altitude below 10,000 feet, keeping flaps down and cruising at 200 miles per hour. After being assured that his wishes would be carried out to the last detail, D. B. escorted Tina Mucklow to the cockpit and gave firm orders that no one was to leave the cockpit area.

A few minutes, later a red light flashed on Scott's control panel, indicating that the plane's rear boarding ramp had been unlatched. At 8:10 p.m. a second red light indicated that the ramp was fully extended. The aircraft was behaving somewhat erratically due to the extended ramp. Scott, at a loss for words, inquired over the P.A. system, "Anything we can do for you?" There was no reply.

It is believed that D. B. parachuted over a wilderness area north of Portland, which includes the tiny village of Ariel, Washington. A snowstorm was raging outside, while the temperature was 7 below zero. The crew of the 727 continued on to Reno, landing hours later without coming out of the cockpit.

Back in Seattle, passengers and stewardess Florence Shaffner were questioned extensively. They were able to provide surprisingly little in the way of helpful information regarding D. B.'s appearance. Most had not really seen the skyjacker and had no reason to pay particular attention to him since they were not aware a skyjacking was taking place until they had landed. Miss Shaffner did her best. D. B. had been wearing a brown business suit and sunglasses. That was pretty well it. He wasn't noteworthy in any way. The 727 was searched for clues, but D. B. left nothing behind except unanswered questions.

Did he parachute out of the aircraft at 8:10 p.m. into a driving snowstorm or did he parachute out later, extending the ramp as a subterfuge to throw police off his track? Did he survive? Above all, who in tarnation was D. B. Cooper?

For over eight years nothing was heard of D. B. Cooper. Many admired the idea of an individual planning and executing the daring skyjacking without hurting anyone. To police, he is the criminal responsible for hatching a diabolical plot which placed 42 lives in jeopardy.

Whatever your feelings, D. B. Cooper caught on. First came the t-shirts, then the movie, then the songs. You can even sip a D. B. Cooper cocktail in many western U.S. bars. No question about it, D. B. became an American folk hero.

On Feb. 12, 1980 the man without an identity again made his way into the headlines. Children on a family picnic about 32 kilometers outside of Portland found a bundle of decomposed twenty dollar bills. The FBI verified that the serial numbers of the bills, which totalled $6000, matched those of the bills handed over to D. B. eight long years before. They also verified that all the bills were from one bundle.

Did the recovered money provide any answers or did it lead to more unanswered questions? Was that rascal D. B. clever enough to toss away $6000 so that searchers would believe he died in the lonely woods upon landing, or did he really perish and was his body ravished by wild animals?

The mystery continues to intrigue Laurel and Dave Fisher, the owners of the Ariel Store and Tavern in Ariel, Washington. Each year, on the Saturday following the U.S. Thanksgiving, they celebrate D. B.'s dramatic jump on D. B. Cooper Day. Laurel tells me that there generally isn't that much excitement in Ariel, whose population is about 100, with another hundred or so "within shouting distance".

However, on D. B. Cooper Day all that changes. Over 450 patrons sign the guest book on the big day. Dave stocks up with 100 cases of beer and barrels of chili for the guests, some of whom come from as far away as England. You can purchase D. B. Cooper t-shirts and an engraved certificate attesting that you are a member of the D. B. Cooper fan club. The party starts at ten in the morning and ends at two the next morning.

Did finding some of the ransom loot in 1980 put a damper on the fun in Ariel? "Not on your life," replies Laurel Fisher. "It added to the speculation. Among our customers it's about 50-50 whether old D. B. is dead or alive. We all hope he shows up for a bowl of chili and a beer on D. B. Cooper Day."

So does the FBI, Laurel, so does the FBI.

THE
BANNISTER BROOD
A New Brunswick family affair

In 1936, the population of Pacific Junction, New Brunswick, located about 10 miles outside of Moncton, was an even dozen. Among those who called Pacific Junction home was the Lake family, which consisted of Phil, 30, his wife Bertha, 28, son Jackie, 20 months, and the baby of the family, four-month-old Betty. Big Phil Lake and his family lived in a 26 by 10 ft. home in a little clearing in the woods near the CNR railway tracks.

Eight miles away in Berry Mills lived May Bannister and her four children, Daniel, 20, Arthur, 18, Frances, 14 and Marie, 13. May Bannister had been deserted by her husband shortly after Marie's birth. The family had lived in abject poverty ever since.

They sold blueberries, cut firewood, and snared rabbits to eke out a meagre existence. Often, they wandered the streets of Moncton looking for day-old bread. None could read or write. Both boys were of below average intelligence.

Strangely enough, the members of these two families would become the main characters in a murder case which would make New Brunswick history and capture the imagination of the entire nation.

On Monday, Jan. 6, 1936, Otto Blakeney was cutting firewood near the Lakes' home. Normally, he ate his mid-day meal with the Lakes. Otto was shocked to find nothing but a smouldering burnt-out ruin where once the Lake home had stood. Upon closer examination, Otto made out the horribly burned body of Phil Lake.

He scurried down the railway track toward the CNR office. Tiny droplets of blood were clearly visible in the fresh snow. Every hundred yards or so there were larger blood smears, as if someone had fallen and risen, only to fall again. Further on Otto came across a baby's bottle.

Exactly 471 yards from the Lake's home he sighted the frozen body of 20-month-old Jackie Lake. A few yards further on was Bertha Lake's almost nude body. The snow beside the body was thrashed, giving mute evidence that, after dropping her son and falling herself, Bertha had made vain attempts to rise before dying alone in the snow.

Otto raised the alarm and soon the RCMP was on the scene. An entire family had been wiped out in one night. Although four-month-old Betty's body was not recovered from the blackened ruins, it was assumed that it had been totally consumed by the flames. Phil's body, minus his burned off arms and legs, was readily identified by two conspicuous gold teeth. Why had someone annihilated the Lake family? The answer was soon forthcoming.

Police noted what appeared to be two sets of tracks beginning in the snow where Bertha had died in agony and leading into deep woods. Utilizing snowshoes, the police followed the tracks. They observed small holes in the deep snow beside the tracks, as if someone had used some sort of cane while trudging along.

RCMP Sgt. Bedford Peters, following closely along the trail, found a mitten. It would become the most important piece of evidence in one of the weirdest murder cases in Canadian history.

Meanwhile, CNR employee David Barron volunteered that around nightfall the day before he had seen one of the Bannister boys walking the tracks. Mounties called on the Bannister home and were greeted by Daniel. Shown the mitten found along the trail, Daniel exclaimed, "Hey, that's mine, where'd you guys get that?"

Questioned further, Daniel stated that he had loaned his mittens to his brother Arthur on the previous day. David Barron identified Arthur as the man he had seen walking along the tracks. Arthur was arrested and charged with murder.

Arthur confessed, admitting that he had visited the Lakes' home. Daniel and Frances showed up to take him home. Phil Lake made an improper advance to Frances. A brawl had ensued, in which Bertha was accidentally struck on the head by a piece of firewood thrown by her husband. Daniel then hit Phil on the head with another piece of firewood, at the same time overturning an oil lamp.

According to Arthur, the three Bannisters took off and never looked back. No doubt Bertha Lake ran from the fire and collapsed, dropping her baby, who froze to death while she died from the wound to her head. In a general way, Frances and Daniel backed up their brother's story. Daniel was taken into custody and charged with murder. Frances was held as a material witness.

The murder victims were duly buried. It was then that the Bannister-Lake case took a bizarre twist. While questioning a neighbor of the Bannisters', one Milton Trites, the police learned that there was a baby at the Bannister home. RCMP officers faced May Bannister with this information. Reluctantly, she turned the baby over to the officers. When asked who the mother of the child was, she curtly replied, "It's mine." In reality, the baby was four-month-old Betty Lake, who for a week was believed to be dead.

May had concocted a diabolic plot. In order to give the appearance of having given birth to a baby, she had sometime before purchased a doll at the Metropolitan Store in Moncton. She was seen by several people carrying a bundle, which everyone assumed was a baby. When questioned, all admitted that they had not actually seen the child. Why did May Bannister pose as the mother of a doll, and later somehow come into possession of the Lake baby?

Milton Trites had befriended the Bannisters for years. He

often loaned May small amounts of money. During the previous year she had worked for him as a housekeeper. When she left his employ in November, 1935, she told him she was leaving to have his baby. She did in fact go away for some time. When she returned she told Trites she had left their child in Moncton. On the day after the Lake murders she invited Trites to her home to see his baby.

It was also learned that Albert Powell, a CNR freight clerk and part-time Sunday school teacher, had conducted Sunday school classes at the Bannister home for about two years. He was often alone in the company of Marie Bannister. May had accused Powell of being responsible for Marie's fictional pregnancy.

It was obvious May Bannister was planning to blackmail two men into supporting two nonexistent babies. There was one tricky detail. At some point May had to produce a real live baby.

Evidence given by Frances Bannister further incriminated her brothers. She stated that, together with Arthur and Daniel, she arrived at the Lake house around 7 p.m. on the night of the murders. Arthur went in the house. When he came out, he passed her the baby and she started home alone. She heard a scream. Shortly after, her two brothers caught up with her.

During their investigation, the RCMP heard persistent rumors that big, tough Phil Lake could not have been overpowered by a boy with a piece of wood. Phil's body was exhumed. Doctors removed a .22 calibre bullet from his brain.

Now, the cane-like marks in the snow beside the tracks took on a new significance. Maybe they were made by a rifle. Volunteers shovelled tons of snow from the area along the trail. The tedious task paid off. The rifle was recovered and proved to be the murder weapon.

Daniel and Arthur Bannister were tried for the murder of Philip Lake. Both were found guilty and sentenced to death. On Sept. 23, 1936, the two brothers were hanged in the County Jail at Dorchester, N.B. No one claimed their bodies.

May Bannister, who no doubt hatched the plot, and ordered

her dull, obedient sons to carry out her evil scheme, was found guilty of harboring a stolen child. She received the maximum sentence of three and a half years imprisonment. May served her time and returned to Berry Mills, where she was a rather feared curiosity, until 1971, when she died of natural causes.

SCREEN STAR JEAN HARLOW
Sex symbol's short life surrounded by mystery

T here are many similarities between Marilyn Monroe
and Jean Harlow. Both were blonde sex symbols who achieved
fame and fortune in the movies. Both had several husbands.
Above all, the deaths of both ladies were surrounded by
mystery and intrigue. The details of Miss Monroe's life and
untimely death are well documented in some 40 books, in
itself a tribute to her charismatic personality and lingering
popularity. Jean Harlow's life is not as well known.

Jean was born Harlean Carpentier in Kansas City on March
3, 1911. When she was only 16, she ran away and married
wealthy bond broker Charles McGrew. The young bride
returned to her parents and received their blessing.

The McGrews settled down in California, where they lived
off the income from a fortune inherited by McGrew. Two
years later they were divorced.

Still only 18, with an outstanding figure, good looks, and
almost white, flowing hair, Jean entered the entertainment
world by accident. One day she drove a friend to a
movie studio. A motion picture executive noticed her and sent
her to the Central Casting Office. She immediately received
work as an extra and was noticed by famed movie maker Hal
Roach, who signed her to a five year contract.

She worked for months in small walk-on parts until 1930,

when millionaire Howard Hughes chose her to play the lead in the movie *Hell's Angels*. The ensuing publicity and the movie itself made Jean Harlow a star. Overnight, young girls were copying her sultry walk. Women across the country were dying their hair platinum blonde.

Jean met Paul Bern, assistant to the head of production of M.G.M. Studios. Bern was 22 years Jean's senior. He had come up the hard way, starting off working for $3.50 per week for the Produce Exchange Co. in New York. Later he entered the Academy of Dramatic Arts and was bitten by the entertainment bug. Bern travelled to Hollywood, worked as a film cutter, became a script editor, then director, until finally at age 37 he achieved the status of supervisor at M.G.M. Soon after he was promoted to assistant of production.

Bern was well liked and respected in Hollywood. An extremely intelligent, introspective man, there were many who thought there never was a more unlikely pair than Jean Harlow and Paul Bern.

The Hollywood crowd was surprised when Harlow and Bern married. It was a sudden affair. Jean and Paul both had unbreakable schedules on July 2, 1932, the day they were wed. They didn't take a honeymoon. They waited the few months until both were free of their obligations.

In the weeks following their marriage, Paul and Jean appeared to be extremely happy. Individually they told acquaintances how thrilled they were with their married life. Paul presented Jean with a beautiful new home in Benedict Canyon in Beverly Hills.

Toward the end of August, Paul changed. He no longer appeared happy. Instead, he went into long periods of depression when he hardly spoke. Acquaintances and colleagues noticed the abrupt change in his personality.

On Sept. 5, 1932, two months after his marriage, Paul Bern put a .38 calibre pistol to his head and killed himself. The bullet entered the right temple, plowed through the brain, ending up imbedded in a wall. Paul left a note which read, *"Dearest Dear; Unfortunately, this is the only way to make good the frightening wrong I have done you and wipe*

34

out my abject humility. I love you. Paul. P.S. You understand that last night was only a comedy."

Hollywood was aghast at the untimely death. What had caused such a successful man, married to one of the most glamorous women in the world, to kill himself? Rumors flew throughout the movie capitol.

An inquest into the suicide was held. The only point of contention was motive. The most widely accepted reason for Bern taking his own life proved to be an embarrassment for all concerned. Evidently, Bern had suffered from a physical deficiency which made the consummation of his marriage an impossibility. His reference to "last night being a comedy" was held to mean that a desperate Bern had attempted to consummate the marriage by artificial means. If this was true, one wonders why Bern ever married Jean Harlow.

Shortly after Bern's suicide, it was revealed that he had previously lived with movie actress Dorothy Millette. Miss Millette became mentally ill and was confined to an institution. Paul Bern paid all expenses during her illness and provided her with a living allowance after her release. Miss Millette resided in the Algonquin Hotel in New York.

The day after Bern's suicide, Dorothy was staying at the Plaza Hotel in San Francisco. She boarded the Delta King, a Sacramento River steamer sailing from San Francisco to Sacramento. A pair of shoes and a ladies' coat were found beside the steamer's railing. Two weeks later fishermen found Dorothy Millette's body. The official verdict was suicide, possibly over the loss of a great love or possibly over the loss of her only means of support.

Meanwhile, back in Hollywood, Jean Harlow was so distraught she was placed under a doctor's care. She recovered rapidly, and remained one of Hollywood's leading actresses. In 1933, she married cameraman Harold Rosson. A little over a year later she divorced Rosson, charging cruelty. Seems Harold kept the light on late at night reading. Harlow couldn't get the sleep required to enable her to go before the cameras the next day.

Jean Harlow continued to star on the screen. Beloved by

all, the dynamic blonde actress had the world by the tail. Her public was shocked when, in June, 1937, her mother announced that Jean was seriously ill. Four days later Jean Harlow was dead. Apparently she had influenza which caused inflammation of the gall bladder. She died of uremic poisoning. Jean Harlow was 26.

Like Marilyn Monroe years later, the suddenness of her death gave rise to rumors of foul play, but nothing was ever uncovered to lend credence to these reports.

NEW ENGLAND
SERIAL KILLER
A Connecticut Yankee gone wrong

As I drove down the main street of Jewett City, Connecticut, Al Schumanski was busy at his Amoco Gas station pumping air into the rear tire of a little boy's bicycle. Hendel's Furniture Store didn't have a single customer despite the big mattress sale signs in their front window. Claire LaPointe sold gas and cigarettes at Chucky's Country Store.

"Visited Toronto years ago," Al Schumanski told me. "Is the Spaghetti Factory still there? Great place. Haven't been back for years." The little boy pedalled away toward the town square where East Main and North Main intersect. It's dry and hot in the David Hale Fanning Park where three large stones list the names of every soldier in the vicinity who served in World Wars I and II and the Korean War. There is no memorial for those who served in Vietnam.

This is small town New England, the heart and soul of the U.S. The tiny Connecticut towns are reminiscent of Norman Rockwell paintings: Danielson, Brooklyn, Canterbury, Plainfield, Jewett City, Lisbon, Griswold, Preston. They run into each other, similar, neat, sun drenched, off the beaten path. No real need to lock a door at night. Most neighbors have known each other for a lifetime. Violence and its ugly ramifications belong in Boston and New York, not in these pleasant, quaint towns.

Police Chief Thurston Fields knows pretty well every one of Jewett City's 4000 inhabitants. His five man police force keeps the peace with the aid of two patrol cars. Chief Fields assures me, "There has never been a murder in Jewett City in the 11 years I've been chief and I can't remember one before that."

On Jan. 5, 1982, the small community of Brooklyn, Conn. was shocked when Tammy Williams, 17, disappeared. Hundreds of acres of brush and swamp in the area along Route 6 were searched. Tracking dogs were used. Five hundred volunteers searched the rough terrain. No trace of Tammy was found.

On June 15, 1982, Debbie Taylor and her husband James of Jewett City ran out of gas near Danielson. Debbie walked down the highway looking for a service station, while James walked in the opposite direction. Debbie never returned. Next day she was reported missing. Four and a half months later, Debbie's body was found in a Canterbury cornfield. Her skull had been crushed.

No doubt a sex-crazed stranger had lured Debbie into his car. It was horrible. It was shocking. But after all, it was an isolated incident.

Over a year passed. Most people forgot about Debbie Taylor's fate. Most forgot about the missing Tammy Williams, but not Tammy's father. He frequented flea markets, bazaars and other public gatherings, inquiring about his missing daughter. He never turned up a clue.

On Nov. 16, 1983, Robin Stavinsky disappeared off the streets of Norwich. The attractive high school student and state discus champion had a date that day, but never kept it. A week later a jogger found her body in a wooded area on the outskirts of Norwich on Thames Hospital property. Robin had been strangled to death.

Two girls murdered and one missing in two years. Were they unrelated or were the murders the work of one deranged individual? Rumors spread throughout the Connecticut towns.

Leslie Shelley, 14, and April Brunais, 15, were last seen walking on the streets of Jewett City. When they failed to return to their respective homes on April 22, 1984, they were thought to be runaways. The two friends had run away once before for one day. This time they apparently left for good.

Seven weeks later Wendy Baribeault, 17, left her Lisbon home on Round Hill Court to make a purchase at Chucky's Country Store. She left a message for her parents telling them where she was going.

Police Chief Fields and I measured off the distance between Wendy's home and the Country Store. It is exactly 1.6 miles. Somewhere in that short distance Wendy Baribeault disappeared. Wendy was immediately reported missing. A massive search of the area uncovered her body two days later. She had been sexually attacked.

The killer's luck had run out when he murdered Wendy Baribeault. This time an alert citizen informed police that she had seen Wendy walking along the road. A man in a blue 1983 Toyota seemed to be following her. Police checked over 2000 vehicles with the State Department of Motor Vehicles. By elimination they came up with Michael Ross, 24, a man who had attacked a woman in Ohio years before.

At that time Ross pretended to run out of gas in front of a house he had picked at random. He asked to use the telephone. Once inside, he attacked the lone woman occupant. Ross had picked the wrong woman. She was an off-duty police officer who was an expert in ju jitsu. He managed to get away, but was arrested a short time later.

Michael Ross was arraigned in Ohio, but allowed to return to his Brooklyn, Conn. home when his parents posted a $1000 bond. He received psychological evaluation for two months before being brought back to Ohio, where he served four and half months in jail. He was released on Dec. 22, 1982 to spend Christmas with his parents in Connecticut.

Michael Ross was arrested and charged with the murder of Wendy Baribeault. Connecticut detectives are reluctant to discuss details, but the fact remains that almost immediately after Ross' arrest, they recovered the bodies of Tammy Williams, Leslie Shelley and April Brunais in woods beside local roads. Ross has been charged with felony murder in the deaths of all six girls. Felony murder carries the death sentence in Connecticut.

Born in Brooklyn, Michael Ross lived most of his life in eastern Connecticut. In 1977 he graduated as an honors student from nearby Killingly High School. His teachers remember him as a keen student, who was quiet and well-behaved. In 1981 he graduated from Cornell University with a major in agricultural economics.

He lived in Jewett City in a large green and white house at 158 North Main St. His girlfriend, Debbie Wallace, divorced mother of three children, lived there with him. She refuses to believe that Michael could be responsible for the brutal murders of six women. Neighbors also find it difficult to believe that the polite, well-dressed, friendly young man could be a killer.

While living in Jewett City, Ross was employed with the Prudential Insurance Co. of America as a district agent and registered representative. An official of the insurance company has stated that of the 26,000 agents employed across the U.S. by the company, nothing like Michael Ross has ever happened before.

The hamlet of Brooklyn, Conn., population 900, was incorporated in 1796. A large statue of Major General Israel Putnam, a hero of the War of Independence, adorns its main thoroughfare. A little further up the road Michael Ross' family owns and operates one of the largest businesses in town, a poultry and egg factory.

It is here that Michael grew up, an unobtrusive boy who worked hard at his father's business. His parents refuse to discuss their son since his arrest. Some of the townspeople can't believe that their town may have spawned a serial killer.

Carol Kovacs, an employee of the New England Centre for Contemporary Art, remembers well hearing the devastating news that an acquaintance had been arrested for the alleged murder of six girls. Carol knew Tammy Williams, one of the victims. She intersperses her emotions with such words as "unbelievable", "dumbfounded", "shocked" when discussing the arrest of Michael Ross.

40

Connecticut police are inquiring as to Michael Ross' activities in other locations. While he was attending Cornell University in Ithaca, New York, 25-year-old Vietnamese student Drung Ngoc Tu was murdered. Her body was found at the bottom of a gorge. Miss Tu was majoring in agricultural economics and lived one block from the Alpha Zeta fraternity house. Michael Ross lived at the fraternity house at the time of her murder.

Epilogue: Ross' connection with Miss Tu was dropped when he was found guilty of murdering Tammy Williams and Debbie Taylor. For these murders he was sentenced to life imprisonment.

On July 6, 1987 Michael Ross was found guilty of the murders of Robin Stavinsky, Leslie Shelley, April Brunais and Wendy Baribeault. He has been sentenced to death in Connecticut's electric chair.

THE BEAST OF JERSEY
A monster loose in paradise

Jersey has been described as a little bit of rustic paradise which accidentally dropped into the English Channel. The lush British island lies only 15 miles from the coast of France. It is a strange place for a man to turn into a monster.

Around 1:30 a.m. on Sunday, March 27, 1960, a woman living in a rather isolated cottage in the parish of St. Martin was awakened by the family's black Labrador. Normally, the Lab spent the night downstairs by the stove, but on this night the dog refused to leave his mistress' bedroom. Cautiously the woman went downstairs to investigate.

Once there, she was attacked by a man wearing some kind of mask. The intruder tied the helpless woman's hands behind her back. At that precise moment, her 14-year-old daughter woke up. Distracted by the young girl, the attacker relaxed his grip. The frantic woman raced out of the house across a field to a neighbor's cottage. No one was home. Unable to procure assistance and fearing for the safety of her daughter, she returned to her own cottage.

By the time she got back, her daughter had been taken to a nearby field where she was beaten about the head and brutally raped. The young girl later told police that the man had tightened a rope around her neck and seemed to derive pleasure from tightening it until she almost choked to death.

At the last moment, he would loosen the rope, allowing her to breathe. She described her assailant as being between 30 and 40 years old and about 5 ft. 7 inches tall.

Police investigating the vicious attack found a partially eaten box of raw chicken on the kitchen floor, obviously placed there to distract the family dog.

A month later, another girl was attacked while asleep in her room. This time the girl screamed and frightened off her assailant. Not all victims were as fortunate. Again and again the mad rapist found his way into bedrooms in the middle of the night and led his victims out of their homes to nearby fields, where they were beaten and ravished.

In the wee hours of a Sunday morning in St. Martin, the rapist was successful in gaining entrance to the bedroom of an 11-year-old girl. He whispered in the child's ear, "Be quiet or I'll kill your mother and father." Terrified for her parents, who were asleep in the next room, the child allowed herself to be led out of the house, where she was brutally assaulted.

Nothing remotely resembling a sadistic crime wave had ever occurred on Jersey before. Realizing their limited experience in such matters, local authorities called in Scotland Yard.

The English police quickly ascertained that the attacker knew the area well. The houses he entered were in isolated areas which had good escape routes. They believed they were looking for a local man who behaved normally during the day, but turned into a monster at night. He wore a cloth mask, dressed in rough oversized clothing and entered houses he had reconnoitred some time previously.

Because of the intense police inquiries, or maybe because the madman was able to control the Mr. Hyde within him, the attacks ceased for two years.

The calm was broken at 1 a.m. on April 19, 1963. That's when a man crawled through a window and abducted a nine-year-old Chateau Clairvale boy. He led the frightened boy into some nearby fields and sexually assaulted him. The lad was then led back to his bed at knifepoint, while his younger brother slept peacefully in the same room. The boy's father heard the child's moans and soon the police were at the scene. They found footprints in the soft earth outside the boy's window. They were size nine.

Through 1964, several more attacks took place on the island of Jersey. Little by little police learned more about the man they were seeking. He had type O blood. He wore gloves without fingers and constantly talked about smoking cigarettes. These bits of information did not aid in apprehending the attacker. After an assault on a 16-year-old mentally retarded boy, the deviate left a palm print on a bedroom windowsill.

Scotland Yard and the Jersey police came under intense pressure to bring in the mad rapist. In desperation they decided to take the palm print of every male between the ages of 19 and 60 living on the eastern end of the island where the attacks had taken place. In the months to follow a six man identification team took over 10,000 palm prints. None matched the one left on the victim's windowsill.

Thirteen men stubbornly refused to voluntarily give their palm prints. This was not to infer that one of the 13 was necessarily the mad attacker. Some of the men had airtight alibis for the times of some of the attacks. Some claimed it was against their right to privacy. However, when the killer was unveiled, he proved to be one of the men who had refused to be printed.

The mad attacker, or Beast of Jersey, as he was now called by the press, was apprehended because he went through a red light. It was July 10, 1971 when police took off after a Morris 1100 through the narrow streets along the seafront. The vehicle ended up stuck in a tomato field. The occupant ran away. P.C. John Riseborough, a former rugby player, gave chase and brought down his man with a flying tackle. Riseborough knew that he had more than a traffic violator on his hands. No man drives through fences and fields to avoid being ticketed for a minor traffic violation.

Besides, there was the driver's appearance. Ted Paisnel, 46, was wearing slippers. Despite the hot July evening he had on fingerless gloves. He also wore a home-made leather sheath. Paisnel's large blue coat held a stiff black wig and a face

44

mask. He claimed he was travelling to some kind of weird meeting but police felt sure they had captured the Beast of Jersey.

Paisnel, a building contractor, was married and was the devoted stepfather of a little boy. A search of his home, which he had built himself, uncovered a secret room. In it he had built an altar. On the altar police found glass bowls, cloves, a chalice and a china toad. He also kept a wooden dagger on the altar, along with several books on witchcraft. Ted Paisnel was a Satan worshipper.

His wife was unaware of the existence of her husband's secret room. Joan Paisnel could only volunteer that sexual relations between herself and her husband had ceased some years before.

Inside Ted's secret room, police found photographs of the homes he had terrorized. Some were taken years before the attacks, indicating that Paisnel's rapes had been planned well in advance. They also found homemade bracelets made of spikes. Several of his victims had parallel scratches on their bodies, which were identified as marks left by the bracelets. Paisnel's reference to cigarette smoking was a ruse to throw police off the trail. Ted didn't smoke.

On Nov. 24, 1971, Paisnel stood trial for his crimes. Despite defense attorneys attempts to prove him insane, he was judged by the court to be sane. Ted Paisnel was found guilty of 13 charges connected with his vicious attacks. He was sentenced to a total of 30 years in prison.

The 11-year reign of the Beast of Jersey had come to an end.

FRANCE'S WAYWARD PRIEST
He did more than save their souls

As a general rule, gentlemen of the cloth have enough to do saving souls without going around killing people. But, as we all know, it is the exception to the rule that makes life so very interesting.

The 400 citizens of the tiny French village of Uruffe, France, were delighted when Cure Guy Desnoyers was assigned to their village to assist their aged abbé in his divine tasks. At 31, Father Desnoyers was somewhat older than the average novice priest, having spent the first two years of his education pursuing a medical degree. Father Desnoyers' parents could not afford to financially assist their son. As a result, he had to leave the field of medicine, eventually to arrive at ecclesiastical pursuits. He brought to the village a smattering of medical knowledge and a flair for the theatre.

Father Desnoyers was soon dispensing quasi-medical advice for minor ailments. He also organized a teenage theatre group. When the abbé went to that great parish in the sky, Father Desnoyers became the village's chief spiritual leader, a position he was to retain for six years.

In August, 1956, an incident took place in Uruffe which would have far-reaching effects on Father Desnoyers' religious career. Nineteen-year-old Regine Fays checked her lunar calculations one more time. There was no doubt about it. She was pregnant. Before too long her condition would be evident to anyone with average eyesight. Regine had to tell someone. After much soul searching, she chose her mother. Her mother cried. Uruffe girls didn't do such things. In Paris, yes, but not in their own little village. There would be a scandal. Worse, a disgrace on the Fays' good family name.

When Madame Fays had spent her wrath, she faced her fallen daughter and gingerly inquired, "Who's the father?" Regine refused to tell. She would never give away the identity of the father of her child. When Papa Fays heard that he would soon be a grandpere, he too begged for the name of the impregnator. Regine declared that she would go to the grave with her secret.

That night as they were lying side by side in bed, Mama and Papa Fays discussed the mystery and came up with a solution. Their daughter had made love to a stranger. Maybe someone who was merely passing through the village. Who knows, she might not even be aware of her lover's name. Mon Dieu, what is the world coming to!

Months passed. Regine could no longer conceal her delicate condition. Tongues wagged. The word spread. It was a juicy scandal. Truth to tell, Mama and Papa Fays wouldn't have made it through that fall if it hadn't been for Father Desnoyers. The kindly priest spent many an evening comforting the parents of the disgraced girl.

On Saturday, Dec. 1, Father Desnoyers had dinner at the Fays' home. He told Monsieur Fays that he would be travelling to Applemont to visit his parents on Monday. M. Fays remarked that he too would be away from the village that day. He was travelling to Commercy to purchase a carriage for his expected grandchild.

On Sunday, Father Desnoyers conducted services and showed a movie at the village hall. At the movie's conclusion he announced that on the next day he would be visiting his parents for a few days.

Bright and early the next morning, Father Desnoyers raced away in his Citroen. M. Fays left for Commercy by bus. That evening at 6 p.m., Regine told her mother that she was going for a walk. Some villagers saw her strolling through town. While she was out, her father came home with the new baby carriage.

A few hours passed. Regine failed to return home. Monsieur and Madame Fays became worried. They took to the streets, inquiring about their daughter. Some people had seen her walking, but that was all. In desperation, they called Father Desnoyers in Applemont. He told them not to worry, but was himself disturbed enough to return to Uruffe immediately. By 10 p.m. that night he was in the Fays home.

A search party was organized. Over a hundred volunteers trampled across roads and frozen fields throughout the wee hours of that cold December morning. Searchers didn't find Regine. Father Desnoyers, accompanied by three men in his Citroen, came across a crumpled heap about three kilometers from the village. Regine lay partially nude under her overcoat. She had been shot in the back of the neck. Her abdomen had been slashed open. Beside her on the road was a 6 mm. cartridge case. Not far from her body lay the body of her newborn child. The baby had been stabbed several times. Both mother and child were dead.

Father Desnoyers took charge. He advised the villagers to guard the bodies while he returned to Uruffe for the police. Police from Nancy had been assisting in the search, and it was these officers who returned with Father Desnoyers to the scene of the macabre murders. Before they could begin their investigation, the good father dropped to his knees and prayed at the top of his voice for the fallen girl.

The bodies were removed and examined by medical experts. Unbelievably, Regine had been subjected to a Caesarian operation performed by someone with some medical knowledge but no skill. Her unborn child had been taken from her body after she was dead. Doctors stated that the child was alive when delivered and subsequently stabbed to death. Rarely had such a repulsive, heartless act taken place in the annals of crime.

Commissaire Jean Chapuis from Nancy headed the investigation. He found out immediately that there was only one registered automatic pistol in Uruffe. It was owned by none other than Father Guy Desnoyers.

Chapuis received a strange visitor at his makeshift office. She was a young girl of the village who would only divulge her information with the understanding that Chapuis would never reveal her identity. He agreed, and the young girl told how she had been a virgin until Father Desnoyers had his way with her in the presbytery. She believed that other girls of the village had been shorn of their virginity by the priest. She also believed that Father Desnoyers was the father of Regine Fays' baby.

Chapuis called on Father Desnoyers and asked him to produce his pistol. Ballistic evidence proved that the automatic was the murder weapon. Father Desnoyers maintained his innocence for some time before suddenly exclaiming, "It was I." He then went on to dictate a formal statement revealing that he had been intimate with Regine on 31 occasions. He admitted killing the helpless girl and using his pocket knife to perform the Caesarian operation.

At the movies held on Sunday night at Uruffe, he had arranged a clandestine rendezvous with Regine for Monday night at 7 p.m. Regine kept the appointment. She got into his car and they drove away, stopping three kilometers from the village. Regine was puzzled as to why he wanted to meet with her. Father Desnoyers told his astonished interrogators that he informed the girl he wished to give her absolution.

Regine ridiculed him and ran from the car. Father Desnoyers ran after the fleeing girl, firing two shots into the back of her neck. He conveniently claimed that he had no memory of what transpired after the shooting, stating that he came to his senses wiping blood from his pocket knife. He then raced to his parents' home in Applemont in plenty of time to receive M. Fays' phone call. Later, Father Desnoyers revealed that on that cold winter night he had baptized his baby daughter before killing her.

When his confession became public knowledge, Guy Desnoyers was defrocked as a priest of the Roman Catholic

Church and excommunicated. His murder trial was nothing more than a formal stage for one of the most horrendous crimes ever committed. Father Desnoyers was found guilty of murder and sentenced to life imprisonment at hard labor.

After being confined for 22 years, Guy Desnoyers was freed in August, 1978, due to an amnesty granted by the French government.

THE
BUGSY SIEGEL
STORY
From Hell's Kitchen to Las Vegas

Jennie Siegel's second child, Benjamin, was the prettiest baby that Jennie or any of her friends had ever seen. Eight days after his birth on Feb. 28, 1906, at his ritual circumcision, close friends of the Siegels had no way of knowing that little Benjamin would one day grow up and leave his home in New York's Hell's Kitchen to become a leader of organized crime in the U.S. and the leading force in the development of one of its cities, Las Vegas, Nevada. You see, little Benjamin became better known to the world as Bugsy Siegel.

One of Benjamin's close friends during his formative years was Georgie Ranft. The two youngsters were to take different paths to success but would remain friends all their lives. Georgie became Hollywood movie star George Raft, who made it big in the movie industry portraying gangsters. Young Raft didn't have to do much acting. His training ground, Hell's Kitchen, was one of the toughest slums in the world.

As a schoolboy, Benjamin pulled off many illegal criminal capers. Rolling drunks brought in a few dollars spending money. Shaking down young messengers could be lucrative in a small way.

Just short of his twenty-first birthday, while employed as a cab driver, Ben took a side trip to an isolated section of

Central Park with a female passenger. He forced the girl out of the car and raped her. After the rape, Ben drove the girl to her destination. Next morning he was picked up. His fare had given police Ben's cab registration number, as well as his licence plate number. When the complainant didn't show up on the trial date, the charges were dropped. Rumor had it that several of Ben's unsavory acquaintances had convinced the girl not to testify.

With the advent of prohibition in the roaring twenties, Bugsy gravitated to the enormously profitable traffic in illegal liquor. While not a household name yet, he knew men who were. His acquaintances, later to become partners, included Charles "Lucky" Luciano, then heavily involved in narcotics, Joe Adonis, Vito Genovese, Albert Anastasia, Louis "Lepke" Buchalter and Meyer Lansky.

Bugsy, a name which was never uttered in his presence, was in and out of a series of scrapes with the law without being convicted. The young hood, who looked good, acted cool and could take care of himself, soon came to the attention of Meyer Lansky. At that time, Lansky was a young man himself, only a few rungs up the ladder.

Back in the twenties, Siegel and Lansky formed the Bugs-Meyer gang. They began modestly enough, providing a vital service to big time gangsters, guaranteeing delivery of illegal booze from the New York docks to the gangsters' warehouses. One of their customers was Arthur Flegenheimer, better known as Dutch Schultz. Another was Lucky Luciano.

The Dutchman was the dominant New York gangster of the roaring twenties. Besides his illegal trade in booze and prostitution, Schultz could arrange to have a man disappear for a price. The Bugs-Meyer gang specialized in transportation and protection, with the odd contract killing thrown in. Life was cheap. A broken leg could be arranged for $50. For $100 a body could be dispatched into the East River attached to a block of cement.

Small time gunsel Whitey Krakower introduced Bugsy to his sister Estelle. Bugsy was smitten. He and Estelle were married in 1927. In the next five years the Siegels had two daughters,

Millicent and Barbara. Bugsy moved his family into a stucco Tudor style home in the fashionable community of Scarsdale. Neighbors thought quiet Mr. Siegel was the head of a national corporation which required a good deal of travel. In a way this was true.

As the twenties gave way to the thirties, the Bugs-Meyer partnership grew in power. Lucky Luciano's organization also became prominent. Dutch Schultz remained king.

When it became known to Luciano that Tony Fabrizzo, the killer of "Mad Dog" Coll, was planning on retiring from the mob, it was time for a meeting. When Luciano heard that Fabrizzo was planning to sell his memoirs to a publishing company, it was time for a killing. Lucky talked it over with Dutch. They decided that the Bugs-Meyer boys would do the hit.

A few days before the date of the execution, Bugsy's headquarters was bombed. Fabrizzo was strongly suspected. Bugsy was fortunate to escape with a severe gash to the forehead. While recuperating in Governeur Hospital, Bugsy hatched his great plan.

One night, with the help of henchmen, he sneaked out of his private room in the hospital and drove to Fabrizzo's home. His henchmen knocked on the door. Tony answered. His mouth opened wide and his eyes popped in horror as he looked into the muzzle of a .45 calibre submachine gun held by Bugsy Siegel. Three bullets found their mark in Fabrizzo's forehead, the exact location where Bugsy was bandaged. Bugsy made his way back to his hospital bed unseen. Next morning he was awakened to the news that Tony Fabrizzo had been shot to death on his front steps.

In 1934, the Mafia, under the executive genius of Lucky Luciano, had gained full power over organized crime in the United States. Its enforcement arm, Murder Inc., had as its president Louis "Lepke" Buchalter, sometimes called the Lord High Executioner. Lepke left the running of day to day affairs to Abe "Kid Twist" Reles.

When prohibition came to an end, the Mafia had no difficulty adjusting their closely knit organization to other profitable activities. Their biggest threat came from aggressive district attorney Thomas E. Dewey. Dutch Schultz felt that Dewey had to be killed. Wiser heads, including Luciano, believed Dewey's death would bring intolerable heat on organized crime. Luciano gave the word. To prevent Dewey's death, Dutch Schultz had to go.

The job was done efficiently at the Palace Chop House in Newark, N.J. on the night of Oct. 23, 1935. Three of the Dutchman's henchmen, Lulu Rosenkrantz, Abe Landau, and Abbadabba Berman, were killed in a fusillade of gunfire. Dutch lived long enough to make it to the hospital. When asked to identify his assassins, he gave the classic gangland reply, "I didn't see nobody." Then he died.

With Dewey continuing to aggressively prosecute gangsters in the east, the mob looked for greener untapped pastures in which to make a dishonest buck. California, in particular Hollywood, beckoned. Who else but Bugsy Siegel, with his good looks and fine family, would make a lasting impression on the glitter capital of the world? Bugsy's assignment was to ingratiate himself in the movie industry with an eye towards setting up any rackets which would prove profitable to the boys back east.

For starters, Bugsy settled his family into a mansion on McCarthy Drive, formerly owned by opera star Lawrence Tibbett. His old buddy George Raft introduced him to all the right people, passing him off as a big time businessman from the east. Respectable Mr. Siegel soon had a system set up whereby narcotics were shipped from Mexico to California to New York. He also dabbled in white slavery and the labor rackets.

Virginia Hill went from a cotton patch in Bessemer, Georgia, through three husbands to the Cotton Club in Harlem, where she met Bugsy. Bugsy fell hard. Seldom was he seen in public without his Ginny. Back at the mansion, Mrs. Siegel had enough. She filed for divorce. Ginny and Bugsy returned to Hollywood, where Ginny leased the Falcon's Lair, a mansion once owned by Rudolph Valentino.

Nosy law enforcement agencies began investigating reputable

Mr. Siegel's affairs in California. Bugsy got the message. He looked for new worlds to conquer. While in Las Vegas, he got the brilliant idea of building the grandest gambling palace in the world. He would call it the Flamingo.

Bugsy travelled back east to confer with the mob. Meyer Lansky, Frank Costello and Joe Adonis agreed to the idea. Bugsy returned to Vegas with the mob's blessing. Dell Webb, who would one day own the New York Yankees, was hired on as the general contractor for the job of building the Flamingo. Construction costs went way over the proposed budget of $5.6 million.

The club was a success right from opening night. Everyone who was anyone in Hollywood attended. Despite its success, profits did not cover the vast sums Bugsy had borrowed to complete the Flamingo. To meet obligations, he held out on the share allotted to the boys back east. That was a cardinal sin in the eyes of the mob. Now it was Bugsy's turn to go.

Some say Virginia Hill had prior knowledge of the hit. She left for France after giving Bugsy the keys to her leased Moorish castle on North Linden Drive in Beverly Hills. A few days later Bugsy was in L.A. with friends Allan Smiley, Charles Hill and Jerri Mason. They decided to stay over at Ginny's home.

At 11 p.m. on June 20, 1947, Charles and Jerri retired for the night. Bugsy and Smiley sat down on opposite ends of a divan beside the fireplace. A gun roared seven times from the terrace window. Smiley, unhurt, hit the floor. Three of the seven bullets entered Bugsy's head. The man who put Las Vegas on the map was very dead.

Bugsy's old Flamingo has changed hands many times since he built it. Today it is called The Flamingo Hilton. You can still catch a flight from almost anywhere in the world to try your luck at the gambling tables just as Bugsy Siegel had predicted so many years ago.

. . .

How the others fared:

* Joe Adonis was deported to Italy where he died of a heart

attack in 1971 at age 69.

* Albert Anastasia was shot to death in 1957 while having his hair cut in the barber shop of the Park Sheraton Hotel in New York City.

* Louis "Lepke" Buchalter was executed in Sing Sing Prison's electric chair on March 5, 1944 for the murder of Brooklyn storekeeper Joseph Rosen.

* Thomas E. Dewey served three terms as governor of New York State and twice ran unsuccessfully for the presidency of the U.S. He died in Miami of natural causes on March 16, 1971. He was 68.

* Vito Genovese died on Feb. 13, 1967 in prison at Springfield, Missouri.

* Virginia Hill married for the fourth time after Bugsy's untimely demise. She took her own life with an overdose of barbituates near Salzburg, Austria. Ginny was 50.

* George Raft, retired from a successful acting career that included 105 movies. He died in 1980 of lung cancer at age 85.

* Abe "Kid Twist" Reles became a key witness against his former buddies. He was given police protection and placed in the Half Moon Hotel on Coney Island. Despite being heavily guarded, his body was found on the ground below his open window.

PROSTITUTE KILLER
Computer expert by day, killer by night

Richard Cottingham was employed for over a decade with the Blue Cross and Blue Shield of Greater New York. He was a valued and highly regarded member of the company's large computer staff.

Richard and his wife Janet lived in a pleasant three bedroom home in Lodi, New Jersey. They had three children, two boys, Blair and Scott, and a daughter Jenny. Richard commuted to New York each day. Because of the nature of his employment, he had the option of reporting to work at any hour convenient to him. He normally worked from 4 p.m. to 11 p.m.

Among his colleagues, Richard Cottingham was a regular guy. Janet was the first to become aware that her husband was not what he appeared to be to the outside world.

In 1976, after Jenny's birth, 28-year-old Richard refused to have sexual intercourse with his wife. As a result, she gravitated to spending more and more time with her own friends. Richard, in turn, spent most of his time at home in his own private room. After work, he rarely drove directly home. Indeed, it was common for Richard to arrive home at dawn with the smell of alcohol on his breath. Sometimes he stayed away for several days.

One day, Richard inadvertently left his private room

unlocked. Janet walked in. She was amazed to find an assortment of ladies' used underclothing and cheap jewellery scattered about the room.

No, Richard Cottingham was not normal. He was clever and cunning, but far from normal. For years he had led a double life, committing abnormal criminal acts which had not been attributed to one man.

On Dec. 16, 1977, the body of 26-year-old nurse Maryann Carr was found in the parking lot of the Quality Inn in Hackensack, N.J. Maryann, who had been married only 15 months, had been handcuffed hand and foot before being strangled to death. Despite an intensive investigation, her murder went unsolved.

Two years later, in December, 1979, New York firemen were called to the Travel Inn Motor Lodge on West 42nd St. The blaze was localized in Room 417. Firemen had no trouble extinguishing the flames which originated from a double bed. When the smoke cleared, even the hard-nosed New York firemen recoiled in horror. There, on the bed, were the bodies of two nude, partially burned females. They were headless and their hands had been removed.

The investigation into the gruesome murders revealed that both girls had been prostitutes. Lighter fluid had been sprinkled over their bodies and ignited. New York detectives surmised that the strange mutilations had a purpose. With no heads, there were no teeth to check against dental records. With no hands, there were no fingerprints to compare. It would be six weeks before one of the girls would be identified. The identity of the other girl has never been established.

The man who had checked into Room 417 at the Travel Inn had given his name as Carl Wilson of Merlin, N.J. Both his name and the name of the town were fictitious. The room was clean. No fingerprints, no cigarette butts, nothing that would lead to the identity of the killer. He had checked in on Wednesday evening, Nov. 29, and for four days was rarely seen by hotel staff. The "Do not disturb" sign hung from the doorknob of 417 for almost all of those four days.

After weeks of tedious legwork, detectives identified one of the victims as Deedeh Goodarzi. Jackie, as she was known, plied her trade in Atlantic City and New York City. The beautiful five-foot six-inch Kuwait native had left Atlantic City to attend a meeting with her pimp in New York during the last week of November. She never kept the appointment. Instead, she ended up in Room 417. It has never been ascertained whether a headless corpse greeted her when she entered the room or whether she was the first of the two to die. For the time being, the Times Square Torso Murders, as they came to be known, remained unsolved.

Valorie Street found Miami too hot for comfort. She had been arrested for prostitution several times. Once more on the street, she decided to try the Big Apple. Valorie arrived in New York City on May 1, 1980. Four days later, using the name Shelly Dudley, she signed herself into the Quality Inn Motel in New Jersey. Valorie was assigned Room 132. Her nude body was found under the bed. She had been handcuffed, bitten, beaten and raped.

Twenty-five-year-old prostitute Jean Mary Ann Reyner's body was found in the Hotel Seville on May 15, 1980. She had been stabbed to death and her breasts had been removed. The police had only a composite drawing of the fictional Carl Wilson to work on, provided by employees of the Travel Inn Hotel off Times Square.

Three days later, on May 18, 1980, Leslie Ann O'Dell, 18, arrived in New York by bus from Washington, D.C. Alone in the big city, without money or friends, Leslie was approached by a friendly man who bought her breakfast. The man explained that he could put her in touch with another man who would see to it that she made plenty of money. Within 24 hours Leslie was walking the New York streets under the protection of a pimp.

Leslie, on her fourth night as a New York streetwalker, was motioned over to a blue and silver Chevy Caprice. The man, who called himself Tommy, suggested a drink at a bar in New Jersey. Leslie was happy to comply. Tommy proved to be a pleasant companion. He even seemed interested in her problems.

They left the bar and dropped into a restaurant for a bite to eat. Over coffee they negotiated, finally agreeing to the fee of $100 for a half hour of Leslie's time. Dawn was breaking when they pulled up to the Quality Inn Motel in Hasbrouck Heights, the very same motel where Valorie Street had been murdered. Tommy paid $27.77 in advance for the keys to Room 117.

Soon they were in bed. Without warning, the now wild-eyed Tommy pulled a knife from his attache case. He quickly fastened handcuffs about the helpless girl's wrists. Gruffly Tommy ordered, "You have to take it. The other girls did. You're a whore and you have to be punished."

For the next three hours, Leslie endured sexual perversions and torture rarely equalled in the annals of crime. Her attacker threatened her with a pistol if she screamed. Leslie bit her lips until blood ran down her chin as she muffled her cries of pain.

At one point, while being whipped, she fell to the floor beside Tommy's gun, which he had put down so that he could wield his whip to better advantage. Leslie picked up the gun. Tommy advanced towards her with his knife. Leslie, who had never before held a firearm, pulled the trigger again and again. Nothing happened. The gun jammed. Figuring she was about to die, she screamed at the top of her lungs.

It was 9 a.m. A maid doing her rounds heard Leslie scream and called the front desk. Todd Radner, the assistant manager, called police. Together with head housekeeper Paula De Matthews, Radner headed for Room 117. Inside, the man known as Tommy, had clamped a hand over Leslie's mouth. Radner knocked on the door.

Under instructions Leslie, leaving the chain intact, opened the door. Her eyes were black and blue, her cheeks swollen. "Everything is okay. I have no clothes on. I can't open the door." As she talked, Leslie attempted to signal that she was in trouble. Radner and De Matthews walked away.

Just then a police car arrived. Tommy saw the car pull up.

He frantically dressed and gathered up his implements of torture. As he ran down the hall, Leslie hollered, "Stop him, stop him! He tried to kill me."

Tommy, carrying a small calibre weapon, unknowingly ran directly toward Patrolman Stan Melowic. The police officer raised his shotgun and commanded, "Hold it right there and don't move."

The hunt for the madman who had raped, mutilated and murdered prostitutes for several years had come to an end. Tommy was identified as computer expert Richard Cottingham. Costume jewellery and bits of clothing found in his home enabled detectives to link him with the previous killings, as well as several vicious rapes that they had thought were perpetrated by several different men.

After a series of trials in New Jersey and New York, Cottingham was convicted of assault, kidnapping, rape and murder. His accumulated sentences total 250 years in Trenton State Prison, where he is currently incarcerated.

A NIGHT OF HORROR
Patrolman's hobby catches killers

The evening started out pleasantly enough, but fate would decree that it end in a hideous web of kidnapping, rape and murder.

Mrs. Eleanor Ewell, 50, her son James, 23, a Columbia University student, together with family friends Robert and Eleanor Tyson, 50, drove to Herm's Restaurant in Plainfield, N.J. in the Ewell's Cadillac. Mrs. Ewell's husband Elliot was not a member of the dinner party that balmy May evening in 1961. As executive vice president and a director of the Mack Truck Company, he had been called out of town on business. Robert Tyson, a Wall Street broker, had previously been an executive of the Mack Truck Co.

As if pre-ordained, a series of strange unconnected events took place, which would turn the harmless dinner party into a night of horror. During dinner, Robert Tyson, who had complained of a bad head cold earlier in the day, now felt so poorly that James drove him home. James then returned to the restaurant and rejoined his mother and Mrs. Tyson.

Shortly after midnight, they left the restaurant. Mrs. Ewell complained about her son's driving. An argument broke out in the car. Enraged, James slammed on the brakes, causing the Caddy to stall. When he attempted to restart the car, the motor wouldn't turn over.

James walked the short distance to the Plainview Union Water Co. and called the Mack Truck Co. for assistance. He stayed in the company's office for some time and then left the area on foot. He assumed that an employee of his father's firm would show up to assist his mother and Mrs. Tyson.

Instead of sending someone over, the employee who had received the call at Mack Truck Co. called the Dora Cab Co. The dispatcher radioed one of his cars to drive to where the women were stalled. He was instructed to drive the stranded women home.

Cab driver Wilbur Morris was sent to pick up the two ladies. He arrived just outside the water company's property where the Caddy was parked. Morris had often driven Mrs. Ewell and recognized her sitting alone in the front seat. Mrs. Tyson, whom Morris didn't know, was sitting in the back seat. The cabbie chatted for a moment with the women and then suggested that he attempt to start the car. Try as he might, he couldn't get the engine to turn over.

Just as he was about to give up and drive the women to the Ewell residence, a black Chevy pulled up. The two male occupants offered to help. One opened the hood and fiddled around for a minute. Sure enough, when Morris turned the key the engine caught. Morris then told the women he would drive them home in their own car as soon as he parked his cab. He left the Caddy in order to park his cab, when suddenly one of the strangers jumped in the Caddy, shouting, "Come on," to his companion, and drove away in the Caddy. The second man raced after the Caddy in the black Chevy.

Wilbur Morris hopped in his cab, radioed his dispatcher advising him of the bizarre turn of events and gave chase. He soon lost both the Chevy and the Caddy. The dispatcher at the Dora Cab Co. notified police that a kidnapping had taken place. Police were waiting for Wilbur Morris when he returned to the original kidnap site.

At 4 a.m. one of the scores of patrol cars searching for the missing Cadillac, found the vehicle about a mile from the site of the kidnapping. Under the left front wheel of the cream colored hard top convertible was the raped and broken body of Eleanor Ewell. Someone had driven back and forth over her body. In the back seat was the body of Mrs. Tyson. She too had been raped before being strangled with what appeared to be a string of her own pearls.

The prime clue to the identity of the killers was the description of their car, a black 1950 or 1951 Chevy with New Jersey licence plates. It would take months to check out the registered owners, if ever such a task could be completed. This avenue of investigation became unnecessary because of one man, Patrolman John Trembicki, an 11-year veteran of the Scotch Plains, N.J., police department.

You see, John Trembicki had, over the years, developed the habit of jotting down the licence plate numbers of vehicles he didn't feel right about. Earlier on the night of May 26, before any crime had been committed, Trembicki had spotted two black men purchasing gas for their black 1950 Chevy. He picked up his notebook and jotted down the licence number — FLC-492 — Blue Star Esso gas station.

This practise had become automatic for Trembicki over the years. Once, he was instrumental in recovering a stolen vehicle, but he had always had hopes of one day taking down the licence number of a vehicle involved in a major crime. The night of May 26, 1961 was to be Patrolman Trembicki's night.

Patrolman Trembicki's radio hummed. A black 1950 or 1951 Chevy driven by two black men was involved in a kidnapping. Trembicki was sure it was the one he had seen at the gas station. He radioed the licence number to his police station.

The vehicle was registered to 23-year-old Joey Maxey of Dunellen, N.J. Maxey was immediately picked up. He had been employed as a washer of new and used cars at a dealership for the previous two years. Maxey readily admitted that he and a friend, Lorelle Parks, had helped start the stranded Ewell Caddy, but swore he had no guilty knowledge of the murders.

Parks, 22, was taken into custody. He stated that he knew

nothing of the killings, until forced to view the victims' bodies at the morgue. He then broke down shouting, "I'll talk, I'll talk! I know they're going to burn me, so it doesn't make any difference. I killed Tyson and Maxey killed the other one."

The two men had been cruising around looking for women when they came across cabbie Morris attempting to start the Cadillac. They kidnapped the two women on the spur of the moment. Mrs. Ewell and Mrs. Tyson pleaded for mercy, but were raped and killed. Maxey throttled Mrs. Ewell and drove the Cadillac over her nude body again and again. He urged Parks, "We have to kill them; make sure you kill her."

Parks tightened the string of pearls around Mrs. Tyson's neck. When he detected that she was still breathing, he looped his belt around her neck and "pulled as tight as I could. She stopped breathing, there was no doubt about it, she was dead all right. I saw Mrs. Ewell lying on the ground beneath the front wheels. She was a real mess."

After submitting to a lie detector test, Maxey grudgingly admitted involvement in the double murder.

Joseph Maxey was tried and convicted of kidnapping and murder. He received two life sentences. Today he is still incarcerated in Trenton State Penitentiary. Lorelle Parks was sentenced to life in prison for murder. He was paroled on Nov. 18, 1975, after serving 14 years behind bars.

THE BODY COLLECTOR
Fantasies graduate to murder

J erry Brudos didn't smoke or drink. His I.Q. was well above average. He was a skilled electronics technician, as well as a qualified electrician. Jerry was a big man, standing an even six feet and weighing a solid 180 pounds. When he was 23, an acquaintance introduced him to his first real girlfriend, 17-year-old Ralphine Leone.

In 1962, Jerry and Ralphine wed. That same year Ralphine gave birth to a daughter, Therese. In 1967 their second child, Brian, was born. The Brudos family lived in a pleasant little house on Center St. in Salem, Oregon.

To the outside world, Jerry appeared to be a quiet, happy family man. To Ralphine he was a considerate, sensitive husband. Unknown to Ralphine, there were two incidents in her husband's past which may have served as warning signals had she been aware of their existence.

When Jerry was 17, he became frustrated when a date repulsed his sexual advances. Enraged, he beat the girl badly with his fists. As a result, Jerry was committed to the Oregon State Mental Hospital in Salem. The terms of his committment allowed him to attend high school during the day. Nine months later he was released to his parents.

The other incident occurred after Jerry graduated from high school and joined the U.S. Army. Stationed at Fort Gordon,

Georgia, Jerry fantasized that a woman entered his barracks each night and went to bed with him. Each night he beat her unmercifully. The dreams were so real that Jerry sought out Army psychiatrists. When they heard his story, they recommended that he be discharged as not being fit for military service.

What no one knew, not his high school teachers, not the mental health people in Salem, not the Army psychiatrists, and certainly not his wife, was that Jerry Brudos had been stealing ladies' underwear and high heeled shoes for years. Initially, underclothing was taken from clotheslines, but Jerry was not above entering houses while the occupants slept, in order to steal items to satisfy his fetish.

Behind his home in Salem, Jerry had a garage. He outfitted the garage with an intercom connected to the house. When Ralphine wanted him for meals, she called on the intercom. There was a hard and fast rule, Ralphine was never to enter the garage. Jerry told her he developed pictures there, and didn't want sunlight pouring in unexpectedly. Men do have hobbies. Even when her husband moved the family freezer into the garage, Ralphine put up with the inconvenience.

Jerry Brudos was a time bomb ready to explode. He paraded around in women's underclothing and high heels in the privacy of his own garage. Sometimes he took pictures of himself in the stolen clothing, but the games had become less stimulating. True, he had talked Ralphine into posing in the nude, but she did so reluctantly. No, there was no other way. He had to have his very own woman in order to act out his fantasies.

An encyclopedia saleslady knocked on Jerry Brudos' door on Jan. 26, 1968. Faking interest in purchasing books, Jerry had no trouble enticing her into the basement of his home. Once there, he hit her over the head with a plank. Then he choked her to death.

Jerry was happier than he had ever been in his life. He had his very own model. For hours he dressed and undressed the body in his collection of women's underwear. Slowly the realization came to him. His new friend would have to leave. But surely there was something he could keep.

Jerry took a saw and cut off the left foot of his victim. It would serve him well in the weeks to follow as a form for his high heeled shoe collection. He placed the foot in the freezer for safekeeping. Jerry tied an engine block to the body. At 2 a.m., displaying unusual strength, he tossed his macabre cargo into the Willamette River. Days later, he weighed down the foot and threw it into the river as well.

Jerry loved the game and could hardly wait for his next victim. Jan Susan Whitney was a 23-year-old University of Oregon student. On Nov. 26, 1968, Jan disappeared while driving her old Rambler from Eugene to McMinnville. It had been Jan's misfortune to have car trouble. It had been her fatal misfortune to encounter a monster posing as a good Samaritan. Jerry told her he could repair her car, but first he had to go into Salem to get his tools.

Jan jumped in Jerry's car and ended up in his garage in Salem. He throttled her with a leather strap. Jerry had outfitted his garage for just such an occasion. He now had the proper photographic equipment. A pulley system had been installed and a hook inserted in the ceiling. The body could be raised to a standing position. Jerry dressed and undressed his victim. To add to his many perversions, he had now become a necrophiliac.

Jerry left the body hanging there in the garage when he and his wife took a trip to Portland. While they were away, a stranger drove into the side of the garage. When Jerry came home he found a card from the police department in his mailbox. It had been a close call. Police inspected the damage. Jerry repaired the garage. The body inside had not been detected. Later, Jerry weighed it down with scrap iron and threw it in the river.

Pre-med honor student Karen Sprinker, 19, was plucked off the streets of Salem four months after Jan Whitney met her terrible fate. Her car was recovered, but gave no clue as to the owner's whereabouts.

Jerry had forced the hapless girl to his garage with a toy gun. Once there, he took pictures before strangling his victim.

He then indulged in his fantasies, weighed down the body with a cylinder head and tossed it into the Long Tom River.

A month later, on April 23, 1969, Linda Dawn Salee, 22, became Jerry's fourth victim. After work, Linda had driven her Volks to a shopping centre, where she purchased a birthday gift for her boyfriend. Jerry pointed his gun at Linda's head just as she was about to enter her parked car. She ended up in Jerry's garage. She too was subjected to the madness that was Jerry Brudos. That night he threw her body into the Long Tom River.

Eighteen days later, a fisherman discovered Linda Salee's body. Her killer had been careless and had thrown her into a shallow section of the river. A car's transmission had been tied to the body with nylon cord and a copper wire.

While diving for other clues, police discovered another body, that of Karen Sprinker. The macabre details made the front pages of the nation's newspapers. No one was more interested than Jerry Brudos.

Despite his madness, Jerry was an intelligent, cunning adversary. He read about the bodies, but was sure he had covered his tracks and would not be apprehended. He had no intention of curtailing his bizarre activities.

In fact, Jerry had hit upon a new scheme. He discovered that by phoning the university and asking for a common female name, he could get a girl to the phone. In this way he sometimes enticed girls to meet him for coffee. So far none had appealed to him. By interviewing Oregon State co-eds, detectives learned of the man who attempted to get blind dates.

Finally, they found one girl who had met him for coffee in her dormitory's cafeteria. When interviewed, this young girl stated that the man had kept talking about the two murder victims taken from the river. Police instructed the girl to stall her caller if he ever phoned again. Sure enough, she heard from him again. She told him it would take her some time to dry her hair. In the meantime, she called police. Detectives greeted Jerry Brudos.

A search of Jerry's garage turned up his vast array of

women's underclothing and high heeled shoes. Police also discovered photos of the dead girls, as well as one shot which revealed Jerry's image in a mirror. In the same photo was a picture of one of his victims.

Once in custody, Jerry made a full confession. Seven psychiatrists conducted extensive tests. Their conclusions were unanimous. Jerry Brudos had killed in a planned and premeditated manner. He was judged to be sane.

Jerry Brudos pleaded guilty to three counts of first degree murder and was sentenced to three consecutive life sentences in Oregon State Penitentiary.

Ralphine Brudos obtained a court order forbidding her children to visit their father in prison. In 1970, she obtained a divorce.

Officials of the Oregon State Prison in Salem advise me that Brudos has made a "good institutional adjustment". Initially, as a high profile inmate whose crimes were committed against women, he was the subject of abuse by other prisoners. One inmate made an unsuccessful attempt to stab him. The Oregon State Parole Board has decreed that he will never be paroled.

DELAYED JUSTICE
Crime solved after twenty years

The murders which shocked the tiny New England town of Fort Fairfield, Maine, 20 years ago may never be solved to anyone's satisfaction. The scenario reads like a tangled plot of an Agatha Christie whodunnit.

There were two murders within two months. A wayward citizen of the town was a suspect. So was an Air Force lieutenant. A prominent citizen of the county also came under suspicion. Throw in the attractive teenage daughter of a convict, mix well with a poem sent to a newspaper and you begin to get some idea of the intrigue which enveloped this otherwise peaceful rural community.

Fort Fairfield is in potato country. The rich soil which gives sustenance to New Brunswick's potato processing industry stretches across the international boundary into Aroostook County, Maine. The Interstate Food Processing Corp. is the largest employer in Fort Fairfield. The town's population hovers around 4000.

On the day after Christmas, 1964, 14-year-old Cyrus Everett, a newspaper delivery boy for the Bangor *Daily News*, started out from his home on Presque Isle St. at 5:15 p.m. to make collections. Within hours, Cyrus Everett would be dead.

As the evening wore on, Cyrus' mother began to worry. Cyrus had never been late before. By 9 o'clock Mrs. Everett was frantic. She had called all her son's friends. Finally, she called her pastor, Rev. John Goodhart. Together they drove along Cyrus' paper route. An hour later they called police.

Investigating officers ascertained that Cyrus was carrying a Northern National Bank purse containing between $12 and $20 in coins and bills when he was last seen along his route. Naturally they were interested in the last homes where Cyrus had been seen alive and well. One of the occupants of these homes was Philip Adams, who had a lengthy police record. Adams was questioned but not detained.

On the day following the disappearance, Adams reported that he had been attacked by a man in Jerry's Gym, a ramshackle building located close to Adams' home. Red marks on Adams' throat gave credence to his story. A truck, which had been seen near the gym, was later located. There were bloodstains on the front seat. These seemingly unrelated events were to take on more sinister connotations much later. At the time police were looking for a missing teenager.

Local authorities were baffled. No youngster had ever run away from Fort Fairfield. Cyrus Everett was a conscientious, well-behaved teenager, who had acted normally in every way right up to the time of his disappearance. Weeks passed. Cyrus was listed as a missing person with Maine authorities.

During the time that Cyrus was missing, Shirley Harrison, a Portland housewife with a wide reputation for extra-sensory perception, gave a lecture to a group of funeral directors at the Holiday Inn in Portland. She brought up the missing Cyrus Everett case, stating emphatically that the boy was dead and had been murdered. She said that he would be found under a log in a swampy area near the Chaney Place. Her prediction would prove to be eerily correct.

Two months after Cyrus Everett went missing, the town of Fort Fairfield experienced its second shock. Donna Mauch, 24, a pretty brunette cocktail waitress employed at the Plymouth Hotel in Fort Fairfield, rented the very same apartment which Philip Adams had lived in at the time of Cyrus Everett's disappearance.

Donna moved in on Feb. 15, 1965. Nine days later, when

she failed to show up for work at the hotel, her brother called at the apartment. He found his sister's body in the living room behind the sofa. Donna was fully clothed. Her head, wrapped in a towel, was lying in a pool of blood.

An autopsy indicated that Donna died of a "fractured skull and brain lacerations". She had been beaten to death with an instrument which has never been recovered.

The town buzzed with rumors. Cyrus Everett was last seen calling on a certain apartment. Donna Mauch moved into that very apartment and was murdered nine days later. Was it a mere coincidence or was there a more sinister connection?

Events were soon to unfold which would pose more questions than answers. On May 3, 1965, three youngsters playing in a swampy area known as Chaney's Grove found Cyrus Everett's body. It was partially held down under an 800 pound tree trunk. The body was found lying on its back, arms extended above the head. Cyrus' jacket and shirt were bunched up over the upper portion of his torso, indicating that he might have been dragged by the legs to the huge stump.

Then began a series of blunders which contributed to a classic case of a bungled investigation. An autopsy, performed the day after the body was found, incorrectly indicated that the body was too decomposed to determine "anatomical evidence of the cause of death". This statement converted what had obviously been a murder into an accidental death. It was pointed out that the boy might have been playing on the tree trunk, tipping it over and may accidentally have been pinned underneath.

Few believed the accidental death theory. All that summer, rumors spread throughout Aroostook County. One vicious rumor making the rounds was that a prominent politician, known to have a drinking problem, had been out driving with Donna Mauch on the night of Cyrus Everett's disappearance. Driving while drunk, the politician hit Cyrus. He then dragged the boy's body into the nearby swamp. Two months later he killed Donna to insure her silence. The theory held no matter. At the time of Cyrus' death, the politician was in an institution "drying out".

To quell the rumors once and for all, Attorney General Richard Dubord issued an official statement: "A complete autopsy and State laboratory examination disclosed there were no fractures, or any other indications of violence or foul play on the body." This statement effectively brought the investigation into the boy's death to a close.

Incensed at the lackadaisical attitude of certain officials, Fort Fairfield Town Manager Leonard Kyle elicited the aid of an experienced investigator, Otis LaBree. In a matter of days LaBree established that Everett had been a murder victim. He concluded that the position of the body was not consistent with accidental death. The clothing of the dead boy indicated that he had been dragged to the location where he was found.

As a result of LaBree's findings, Cyrus Everett's body was exhumed. Dr. Michael Luongo, one of the top pathologists in the U.S., performed the autopsy. Dr. Luongo detected a skull fracture. He believed the victim had been beaten to death.

Meanwhile, the investigation into the murder of Donna Mauch was being actively pursued. Twice divorced Donna had had many boyfriends. At the time of her death her beau was First Lieutenant Kenneth Fore, a member of the U.S.A.F. attached to nearby Loring Air Force Base. Fore was a young bachelor. He had loaned Donna his sportscar while he was on temporary duty in Texas. When he returned, he learned that Donna had dated other air force men, using his car.

He and Donna had argued. On the morning before her death, he had removed his T.V. and other personal belongings from her apartment. Fore had also made assorted threats to other personnel on the base who had dated Donna. When questioned, he could provide no airtight alibi for the night of Donna's murder. True enough, he was officially on duty at the air force base that night, but he was unobserved for long periods of time, and could have made his way to Fort Fairfield, killed Donna and returned without being seen.

Fore was taken into custody and tried for Donna's murder. The evidence pointing to his guilt was woefully thin. On the night of the murder it was 25 degrees below zero. Fore's car was inoperable. He was acquitted after going through the ordeal of a murder trial, knowing full well that he was innocent.

Why did a private investigator have to be brought into Fort Fairfield to prove that murder had taken place in the case of Cyrus Everett? The answer lies with a newspaperman named Kingdon Harvey, who until 1979 was owner and editor of the Fort Fairfield *Review*. Kingdon Harvey has been described as stubborn, obstinate, totally fair and, above all, a great old time newspaperman. His beloved Fort Fairfield *Review*, published weekly, has never had a circulation of more than 2000.

In 1965, when the official report stated that Cyrus Everett's death was an accident, Harvey was furious. He ran a picture of the boy and his tombstone on the front page of the *Review*. Many believe it was this pressure that was instrumental in bringing Otis LaBree into the case. After LaBree proved that murder had been done, Harvey ran the names of Donna Mauch and Cyrus Everett on the front page of his little newspaper for two years.

When Lt. Fore was arrested, Miss Mauch's name was deleted. When the lieutenant was acquitted, crusty King Harvey placed Donna Mauch's name back on the front page. In 1968, even King Harvey ceased in his efforts to urge officialdom to take action to solve the murder cases. In 1980 Harvey suffered a series of strokes and today lives in a convalescent home. His son, Tom Harvey, a former school-teacher, has taken over the family newspaper.

Years passed. In fact, 20 years. Fort Fairfield's population has not increased. Potatoes remain the chief crop. In recent years there has been talk of bringing in broccoli to give the area some economic flexibility. The old Everett-Mauch murders were forgotten.

One day in 1984 Tom Harvey, editor of the Fort Fairfield *Review*, received a poem in the mail alluding to the old murders. It had been sent anonymously from the Somers Correctional Institution in Somers, Conn. Philip Adams, one of the men who had been questioned regarding the disappearance of Cyrus Everett, was an inmate of the institution. Subsequent investigation by Harvey indicated that Adams had written the poem.

Adams, 42, had a long criminal record, dating back to 1957 when he was only 15. His current incarceration was the result of attacking a ten-year-old boy in Wallingford, Conn. To prevent the youngster from revealing the details of a sexual attack, he had punched the boy in the face and choked him, leaving him unconscious. The boy spent nine days in the hospital. On another occasion Adams had been convicted of sodomizing a nine-year-old boy in Fort Fairfield. Adams, a native of Fort Fairfield, had been in and out of reform schools and training centres throughout his formative years.

In 1965, exactly 46 days after Cyrus Everett was murdered, Adams voluntarily committed himself to the Bangor Mental Hospital. He was released on Feb. 18, six days before Donna Mauch was found murdered in her apartment.

Twenty years later he was writing poems about the old murder cases. Tom Harvey informed police of the poem, which was immediately brought to the attention of District Attorney John McAlwee. McAlwee asked Harvey to sit on his potentially explosive story for six weeks. Harvey agreed. Meanwhile, McAlwee was pursuing the old case from another angle.

Karen Sprague, Philip Adams' former wife, had remarried. Her daughter, Jodie, now an attractive 18-year-old student at Fort Fairfield High School, expressed an interest in contacting her biological father, from whom she had been separated since she was a child. Initially they corresponded. Eventually a meeting was set up.

Jodie visited the correctional institution accompanied by her stepfather. Phil Adams let his daughter know that he would soon be coming up for parole. He suggested that when he was released they could live together, maybe start life anew in Alaska. Other visits took place. Jodie wanted to know more about her father, specifically if he was responsible for the murders in Fort Fairfield. Adams reply was ambiguous but startling, "I'm not saying I did do it and I'm not saying I didn't." Subsequent visits brought forth intimate knowledge of the old crimes. Jodie and her stepfather consulted a lawyer, who advised them to pass along the information to D.A. John McAlwee.

McAlwee felt sure his man was ready to talk. He faced the mammoth task of piecing together two separate investigations which had taken place twenty years apart into a cohesive case for the State of Maine.

Phil Adams waived extradition and was brought back to Maine in January 1985 to stand trial for the murder of Donna Mauch. The Cyrus Everett case was not mentioned during the trial.

The State slowly but surely presented its circumstantial case. The most startling evidence was that of Wayne Adams, brother of the accused. He revealed that Phil phoned him on April 16, 1984, stating, "There's something you've been waiting to hear for 20 years." Phil went on to reveal that on the night of the Mauch murder he had attempted to borrow money from his parents. When they refused he went to Donna's apartment looking for money. She was asleep on the sofa. As he searched the apartment she woke and he killed her. Phil said he covered her face with the towel because she looked at him.

Adams' 18-year-old daughter Jodie told of getting to know her father while he served time. He never actually confessed the killing to her, but he told her he had spent the night in Mauch's apartment and had found her body when he awoke.

Jodie's mother testified that she was a high school student at the time of the Mauch murder. Phil Adams gave her a watch as a gift the day after Donna Mauch was killed. He told her he had purchased the watch at a pawnshop weeks earlier. Later he asked her to return the watch. When she gave it to him, he threw it away, telling her he would get her another one.

Donna Mauch's watch was missing when her body was found. Her mother now testified that Donna was wearing a watch the last time she saw her daughter alive. Did

Adams rip the watch off Donna's wrist and present it to his girlfriend as a gift? Did he later think better of it and dispose of the damning evidence?

Jodie's sister Kelly testified that her father confessed to her that he had killed Donna, but afterwards claimed he was only kidding.

Evidently the jury believed he wasn't kidding. Phil Adams was found guilty of the murder of Donna Mauch. He has been sentenced to life imprisonment.

In an anteroom in the courtroom during the Adams murder trial sat a man who was not called to give evidence. Col. Kenneth Fore of the U.S. Air Force, now in charge of security at a U.S. missile installation at Cosimo, Sicily, had been flown over from Italy by District Attorney McAlwee in case his evidence was required. Col. Fore never expressed his feelings when he watched a man convicted of the murder he had been accused of committing twenty years before.

CANNIBALISM
Survival at sea

When wealthy Australian Harry J. Want purchased the yacht *Mignonette*, he had no idea he was about to precipitate a sensational murder trial and at the same time alter the culinary habits of three true blue English sailors.

Harry bought the 52-foot yacht in England. He was desirous of having his new possession brought back to his home in Syndey, Australia. He let it be known in that spring of 1884 that he was looking for a capable sailor to take charge of the journey. Thirty-one-year-old Thomas Dudley applied for, and was successful in obtaining, the position of captain. From other applicants Dudley picked his crew, experienced sailors Edwin Stephens, 36, and Edmund Brooks, 33. The cabin boy was Richard Parker, 17.

The *Mignonette* was overhauled and supplies taken aboard at Southampton. On May 17, she sailed for Madeira and from there, on June 2, she set sail on the long journey to Australia. The first weeks of the small yacht's voyage were uneventful, but on July 5 the weather worsened. Gales and heavy seas battered the *Mignonette* until her starboard side caved in.

The four men scampered aboard a 13-foot long lifeboat. They were able to grab a few navigational instruments and two tins of turnips before abandoning the yacht. Within five minutes the *Mignonette* disappeared in the heavy seas.

Thomas Dudley took stock of the desperate situation. They were in the middle of the South Atlantic, well off travelled shipping routes. Two tins of turnips stood between the men in the lifeboat and starvation. They had no water. South America lay some 2000 miles away. Their situation appeared hopeless.

The four men made a crude sail from their shirts and attempted to head toward South America. Four days later, half-starved from their rations of tinned turnips, which can be trying at the best of times, they captured a turtle. The turtle, with the exception of the skin and shell, was devoured in the next few days. By July 18, the few drops of water they had managed to catch in their oilskins were gone. So were those dreadful turnips and the turtle.

For the next five days, the men had absolutely nothing to eat or drink. Dudley approached Stephens and Brooks. He suggested that they draw lots to see which man would be killed so that the remaining men could survive by drinking human blood and eating human flesh. The captain's suggestion was not received favorably. Young Parker, being a lowly cabin boy, was not consulted.

On the same day that this rather horrid idea met with rejection, Dudley wrote to his wife. He told her how very sorry he was to have undertaken such a perilous journey. He had signed on strictly for the remuneration. He went on to tell her that their plight was desperate and that all four would soon be dead. He closed by expressing his love.

Soon after Dudley wrote what he thought would be his last act of consequence, Richard Parker took ill. Parker couldn't stand his thirst. He commenced to drink sea water and as a result rapidly grew weaker. He lay outstretched on the bottom of the boat with his arms over his eyes.

Three torturous days passed. Once more Dudley approached the two older men about drawing lots. Brooks expressed the opinion that they should all die together. Stephens didn't agree with Dudley but didn't object strenuously to the idea. Dudley went a bit further. Maybe lots wasn't the only solution. After all, the boy Parker was obviously about to die anyway.

By killing him the rest might survive. Dudley felt that if they weren't rescued by the next morning, the only thing to do would be to kill Parker.

Next morning, Dudley gave the high sign to his two companions. Brooks would have none of it. He went forward and placed an oilskin over his head. Stephens positioned himself so that Parker couldn't move his legs. He had agreed to hold the boy's legs should there be a struggle. Dudley said a short prayer. Then he opened his penknife and bent over the cabin boy. "Now, Dick, my boy, your time has come." Barely conscious, Parker inquired, "What me, sir?" Dudley responded "Yes, my boy." Then he plunged the two inch blade into the side of Parker's neck, killing him painlessly and instantly.

Any type of utensil within reach was used to capture the blood from Parker's neck. Brooks, while not taking part in the killing, wasn't above quenching his thirst with Parker's blood. Parker's liver and heart were then extracted and ravenously consumed. For four more days the survivors subsisted on the flesh of Richard Parker.

On July 29, the small lifeboat was sighted by the German barque *Montezuma*. The three men were so weak that they had to be raised aboard the barque by means of ropes. Only Brooks could walk. No effort had been made to dispose of what was left of Richard Parker. Two German sailors threw the remains overboard. With the little lifeboat in tow, the *Montezuma* made her way to Falmouth, England.

During the voyage home, the three men, while still in terrible condition, regained some strength. They readily told their German rescuers of their adventures, including the killing and eating of Richard Parker.

Once in port, Captain Dudley and his crew of two went directly to the authorities reporting their lost yacht, as well as their ordeal at sea, including the consumption of the cabin boy. It was obvious that the men didn't feel they had committed any crime.

That very night they were arrested and taken into custody. Within days, their adventures on the high seas were being retold throughout England and wherever men go down to the sea in ships. Dudley had the unexpected thrill of personally presenting his wife with the hastily written letter he firmly believed would be his last meaningful act on earth. The three men told similar stories, all verifying the details as outlined here. The court unanimously ruled that Brooks had not taken part in the killing. Charges against him were dropped.

Dudley and Stephens were charged with the murder of Richard Parker. Throughout the land there was much sympathy for the accused pair. During their trial both men testified, as did Brooks. Defense attorneys pointed out that, while in the lifeboat, the two accussed discussed the fact that they had wives and children back home in England, while Parker had no dependents. Parker was surely at death's door when he was killed. So weak was he that although he knew he was about to die, he did not have the strength to struggle. It was stressed that had the two accussed not killed Parker, they would surely have perished during the four days that elapsed before they were rescued. Parker, by far the weakest, would have died first.

In essence, the Defense pleaded that under these particular unique circumstances, the accused had the right to kill. The Crown argued that the accused had no right under any circumstances to measure the value of life. They chose to eliminate the youngest and most unresisting and had in fact committed murder.

Thomas Dudley and Edwin Stephens were found guilty and sentenced to death. That same afternoon the Home Secretary advised Queen Victoria to "respite the prisoners until further significance of her pleasure". Within four weeks, their sentences were commuted to six months imprisonment. So ended the strange adventure of the sailors of the good yacht *Mignonette*.

It is seldom that we delve into the area of cannibalism, but alas, when this reprehensible practice is coupled with trailblazing points of law, we feel we must. The following tale is not highly recommended before breakfast reading.

During the trial of Dudley and Stephens in 1884, Edgar

Allen Poe's novelette, *The Narrative of Arthur Gordon Pym*, published in 1838, was passed around in court. Poe's story vividly described castaways in a similar position to the accused men standing trial. In Poe's story the men drew lots. The unlucky man who lost the draw consented to being stabbed in the back. By an astounding coincidence, his name was Richard Parker.

MASSACRE AT HI-FI SHOP
Innocent victims of madmen

Dale Pierre and William Andrews never adjusted to air force life. Both had been in and out of scrapes and both had applied for early discharge from the U.S. Air Force. In April, 1974, they were assigned to janitorial duty at Hill Field Air Force Base near Ogden, Utah as punishment for minor infractions.

Pierre, a native of Trinidad, was a short, powerful man with delusions of grandeur. The air force wasn't for him. He would get out, make a lot of money any way he could and live in luxury. Andrews was a follower rather than a leader. Much taller than Pierre, he was the type of individual who went along with the tide. He and Pierre spent a great deal of time together performing their janitorial duties at the base.

The two men planned a robbery. Andrews owned a van. They would rob the Hi Fi Shop in Ogden and stash their loot in a storage warehouse. It should be easy. They would tie up the owner, drive the van up to the back door and be gone before anyone was the wiser.

There was some talk about what to do should there be any eyewitnesses who could later identify them. Pierre felt they should kill any such witnesses. Andrews agreed. A third airman, Keith Roberts, was brought into the scheme to help drive the van and load the equipment.

On April 23, 1974, just before 6 p.m. closing time, the three airmen drove up to the Hi Fi Shop in Ogden. They pulled into the alley behind the store. Stan Walker, 20, was in charge of the store that day. The owner was in San Francisco attending an electronics show. Stan and clerk Michelle Ansley were about to close when they looked up to see two black men armed with hand-guns.

As Stan and Michelle stood there transfixed, the door to the shop opened. In walked a mutual friend, 18-year-old Cortney Naisbitt. He was told to keep his hands high. Cortney obeyed without question. All three young people were pushed downstairs into a sound studio. Their hands were tied behind their backs and their feet secured with electric wire. Two hours passed while the robbers loaded turntables, amplifiers and speakers into Andrews' van. The three captives lay in mortal fear for their lives. It was 8 p.m.

Meanwhile, at the Naisbitt residence, Cortney's mother Carol was concerned. At around 8:30 p.m., she mentioned to her husband, Dr. Byron Naisbitt, that it wasn't like Cortney to be late for dinner. Dr. Naisbitt, an obstetrician, thought his wife was making a mountain out of a molehill. Carol didn't see it that way. She jumped in her car and did the rounds, looking for her son.

Stan Walker's father dropped by the Hi Fi Shop to see what was keeping his son. Tentatively, he walked through the shop only to be confronted by the intruders. He too was tied hand and foot and placed in the downstairs sound studio.

Carol Naisbitt was the next to arrive at the Hi Fi Shop in her search for Cortney. She opened the back door and peered directly into the barrel of a revolver. Mrs. Naisbitt was tied and placed on the floor beside her son and the other captives. In all, there were now five helpless victims lying on the floor in the small basement room.

Dale Pierre produced a cup of foul smelling liquid. He propped Carol Naisbitt into a sitting position and put the cup to her lips. Carol was told the liquid would put her to sleep. She was forced to take a gulp and immediately commenced to spit, cough and vomit. Soon her mouth and lips started to burn. The liquid in the cup was Drano.

Each of the five captives were made to drink the Drano. The last, Mr. Walker, recognized the smell of the caustic. He allowed his captor to pour the liquid in his mouth but only pretended to swallow. Once his head was placed back on the floor, he silently let the liquid pour out of his mouth.

Systematically the five captives were stripped of wallets, purses and jewellery. William Andrews left the shop. Dale Pierre then stepped over the sprawled forms on the floor. He felt for Mrs. Naisbitt's head, placed his gun to the back of her head and pulled the trigger. She was killed instantly. Her son Cortney was next. Then Stan Walker was shot in the same way. His father was shot in the back of the head as well. Michelle Ansley begged for her life. Pierre untied her feet and forced her into an adjoining room. There he raped the helpless girl before returning her to the floor beside the other four victims.

One individual remained conscious throughout the nightmarish incidents in the Hi Fi Shop. Mr. Walker, despite being shot in the back of the head, never lost consciousness. Pierre sensed that he was not dead. He strung a cord around Walker's neck and tied it three times, as tight as he could. Walker tensed his neck muscles. After Pierre had finished knotting the rope, Walker found he could still breathe. Walker was playing dead. Pierre then leaned over Michelle and fired a shot into the back of her head. She died immediately.

Orren Walker believed that he was the lone survivor. Lying helpless, his mouth and lips burning from the Drano, a bullet in his head, he fought to retain consciousness and yet appear not to be breathing. His tormentor wasn't through. Pierre pushed a ball point pen into Walker's ear. He stomped on the pen once, twice, but the pen didn't enter Walker's head. He felt the pen point angle down into his throat. Then the assailant was gone.

Mrs. Walker was waiting at home, beside herself with worry. Her son Stan hadn't come home from work at the Hi

Fi Shop. Her husband had gone to the shop looking for Stan and had also failed to return. Together with her strapping 16-year-old son Lynn, she decided to visit the shop. When they got there they heard Orren screaming for help. Young Lynn kicked down the door and summoned police. His father embraced him. Orren Walker had a ballpoint pen sticking out of his ear.

One other victim of the Hi Fi Shop massacre lived through the ordeal. Cortney Naisbitt was barely breathing when rushed to hospital. Doctors were undecided whether to put him on life support systems or not. The decision was made to undertake heroic measures. After numerous operations and years in hospital and convalescent homes, Cortney recovered.

Within 24 hours, the perpetrators of the heinous, senseless torture and murder were themselves apprehended. An informant at the air force base revealed that he had heard three men plan the robbery. He named Dale Pierre and William Andrews. Orren Walker identified Pierre from a photograph.

At the same time two youngsters, 12-year-old Charlie Marshall and 11-year-old Walter Grisson were hunting for empty bottles in a trash dumpster at the Hill Field Air Force Base. They found wallets, credit cards and other documents, all taken from the five victims before they were shot. The dumpster was located 30 feet from Pierre's barracks.

Pierre and Andrews were taken into custody. Pierre's room was searched. Detectives found a white envelope under a carpet. It contained a rental agreement between Dale Pierre and Wasatch Storage, located only a few blocks from the Hi Fi Shop. Pierre had rented space on April 23, the day of the murder. Inside Pierre's storage facility, detectives found the equipment carted away from the Hi Fi Shop. They also found a large bottle of Drano.

Pierre, Andrews and Roberts were charged with three counts of first degree murder and two of aggravated robbery. Pierre and Andrews were found guilty on all charges. The jury couldn't agree on the murder charges concerning Roberts. He was found guilty on the two counts of aggravated robbery.

Epilogue: Orren Walker — Despite his ordeal, he was not as badly injured as Cortney Naisbitt. He survived to testify against Pierre and Andrews. Mr. Walker still resides and works in the Ogden, Utah area.

Cortney Naisbitt — Near death when taken from the Hi Fi Shop basement, he miraculously survived months in a coma to graduate from high school. He is presently employed at the Hill Field Air Force Base, the same base where his assailants were stationed.

Keith Roberts received a lengthy prison sentence for aggravated assault. Still in prison he is due for release on Nov. 10, 1987.

Dale Pierre and William Andrews — Both received three death sentences. Now 13 years after the murders, they remain in the maximum security section of the Utah State Prison. They have had five dates with Utah's firing squad, but each time have won last minute reprieves. Both men have achieved the highest privilege level obtainable in maximum security. This allows them to be out of their cells for two hours per day, as well as a further two hours a week for recreation.

* On August 27, 1987, Dale Pierre was executed by lethal injection.

POISONING IN JAPAN
Phony bank inspector was a poisoner

Sadimacha Hirasawa is an embarrassment to an entire nation. He is living far too long and his country, Japan, is reluctant to execute him.

There is little doubt that the murders which took place at precisely 3:20 p.m. on Jan. 26, 1948, were the strangest and most infamous in Japan's criminal history. On that day, Manager Takejiro Yoshida beckoned to an employee to secure the doors of Tokyo's Teikoku Imperial Bank. The last customer left the bank, but just before the doors were locked one individual gained entrance. He wore a white cotton smock. An armband indicated that he was a Welfare Department health officer.

In those long ago days of 1948, Japan was governed by U.S. Occupational Forces under the command of General Douglas MacArthur. The Japanese were forced to follow scores of rules and regulations, many of which pertained to preventive medicine in an attempt to avoid epidemics.

The Welfare Department official approached manager Yoshida. He introduced himself as Dr. Jiro Yamaguchi. He explained that the U.S. authorities were concerned about an outbreak of dysentery in the area. They also feared a typhoid epidemic. He went on to state that his mission was to have all 15 bank employees take medicine to prevent a typhoid outbreak. He assured the manager that he was making the rounds of all business establishments in the area. Yoshida listened. The doctor made a certain degree of sense. He summoned his 14 employees and explained the reason for the doctor's visit.

Dr. Yamaguchi then took over. He reviewed his assignment, advising that each employee would be required to take two doses of medicine. He suggested they procure their personal teacups. Everyone did. Then the doctor demonstrated the method of taking the rather disagreeable medicine in one gulp. He extracted a large bottle from his official looking case and poured the liquid into each of the 15 cups. At the command, "Dozo," everyone gulped down the liquid.

Many gasped. Some complained of a burning sensation. The doctor quickly explained as he filled the cups for the second time that this cup would neutralize any bad effects. Once again, the employees drank from their personal cups. Several dashed to a water fountain in an outer office, but it was no use. Like rag dolls, they crumpled and fell in agony. All the while, the man known as Dr. Yamaguchi calmly stood by watching his victims die. He then scooped up 164,400 yen in cash and a cheque for 17,400 yen, at the time the equivalent of about $800 American. Dr. Yamaguchi strolled out of the bank and disappeared.

Inside the bank, lying in grotesque heaps, were the bodies of the madman's victims. Of the 15 employees in the bank that day, 12 were dead. Only the bank manager, Takejiro Yoshida, Mrs. Masako Takauchi, and one other employee, survived. Mrs. Takauchi crawled over her dead comrades toward the door and raised the alarm.

Within hours, the liquid left in the teacups was analysed. It contained potassium cyanide. The following day, news of the weird robbery and murders was given wide publicity. Soon the case became the most widely publicized and discussed crime ever committed in Japan. Despite the publicity, on the day following the murders, a careless teller cashed the 17,400 yen cheque stolen from the bank.

Investigating officers were amazed to discover that two

previous attempts had been made to rob banks using the same method as at the Taikoku Bank. Three months before, a bogus doctor, introducing himself as Dr. Shigeru Matsui, entered the Yasuda Bank. He presented his personal card to the manager and convinced the 18 member staff to take medicine. The employees became ill, but there were no fatalities. The phony doctor left the bank without being apprehended. Later, the liquid was found to contain potassium cyanide, but the mixture was too weak to cause death.

Just nine days before the murders, a second attempt to rob a bank failed. This time a man posing as Dr. Jiro Yamaguchi presented his card to the manager of the bank. When the manager became suspicious, the man fled.

Detectives knew they were after one man. Eyewitnesses identified him as middle-aged, with a mole on the left cheek and a scar under his chin. The killer had left his personal card at each bank.

The card bearing the name of Dr. Matsui was traced to the real Dr. Matsui, a respected physician, who had absolutely nothing to do with any crime. Dr. Matsui informed police that he had ordered 100 personal cards, and had only four left in his possession. Each time the doctor gave out his card, he received one in return, as is the custom in Japan. Someone had used one of his 96 cards in the robbery attempt.

Police undertook the arduous task of tracing the 96 cards in Dr. Matsui's possession. The job took weeks. Finally, 95 suspects were cleared, leaving only one name to be checked. The card belonged to a well-known artist, Sadimacha Hirasawa. Hirasawa belonged to several prestigious art societies and was indeed an unlikely mass murder suspect. Dr. Matsui remembered exchanging cards with the renowned artist while travelling on a ferry to Hokkaido.

When questioned, Hirasawa readily admitted meeting Dr. Matsui on the ferry and exchanging personal cards. In fact, Hirasawa recalled that the doctor had written an address on his card with a fountain pen before giving it to him. When asked to produce the card, Hirasawa claimed that it had been stolen by a pickpocket. Dr. Matsui told police that the artist must have been mistaken. He never carried a fountain pen.

There was other strong evidence against Hirasawa. Samples of his handwriting matched the signature on the cheque cashed the day after the murders. Shortly after the robbery, he displayed large amounts of money, but could give no explanation as to how it came into his possession. Hirasawa also had a mole on his left cheek and a scar under his chin. A search of his home uncovered a brown suit and white smock identical to those worn by the killer.

Pleading innocence, Hirasawa was arrested and taken into custody. His arrest caused a sensation throughout Japan. Could this mild mannered artist, who had a clean record all his life, be the diabolical killer who calmly watched his victims die? Many believed that there had to be some kind of mistake.

Two survivors of the mass murder positively identified Hirasawa, but the third victim wasn't sure. The employees of the first two banks could not identify him positively.

Police claimed that Hirasawa, faced with the seemingly insurmountable evidence against him, admitted, "I am the man." Five months later he recanted his confession, stating that it had been forced out of him by the police.

Hirasawa was tried in 1950, found guilty of murder, and sentenced to death. His case has never ceased to fascinate the Japanese. Many feel that Hirasawa did not confess, or that if he did, his confession was obtained by force. They believe that he was made a scapegoat because police were under intense pressure to apprehend the killer. His supporters continue to press for a new trial for the condemned man. There is even a Save Hirasawa club in Japan today.

In all, Hirasawa has appealed his conviction five times. Each appeal has been turned down. Under Japanese law, only the Minister of Justice can trigger an execution by sealing the death warrant. Not one of Japan's Ministers of Justice has been willing to take this unpopular step since Hirasawa's original conviction.

Today, 93-year-old Sadimacha Hirasawa languishes in a Sandai prison, located about 200 miles north of Tokyo. He has been under sentence of death for 35 years.

THE DEMETER FILE
He thought he was above the law

On Dec. 4, 1974, intelligent, wealthy real estate developer Peter Demeter was sentenced to life imprisonment for procuring the murder of his wife, Christine.

Christine's body was found on the garage floor of the Demeter home in Mississauga. She had been bludgeoned to death.

The gates of Millhaven Penitentiary closed behind the tall, debonair builder as they have closed behind hundreds of convicted murderers who preceded him.

Most are never heard of again.

But Peter Demeter was different. He was not an average man, or more precisely, he was not an average prisoner. European born, university educated, he was poles apart from the three-time losers and impulsive killers with whom he came in contact.

After Demeter was classified and commenced serving his sentence, word drifted back to the law enforcement community that he harbored a grudge against the Peel Regional Police, who had gathered the evidence which had convicted him of his wife's murder. In particular, he had a passionate hatred for Deputy Chief William Teggart.

In Millhaven, Demeter made a friend. Some say a friend who received payment for his services, for Demeter had entered Millhaven with a net worth in excess of $1 million.

Mike Hodgson, better known as "The Butcher", was Demeter's bodyguard. To harm Demeter was to cross the Butcher's path. Hodgson, serving time for manslaughter, cast a long shadow. Few dared mess with Peter Demeter at Millhaven.

After Demeter had served four and a half years at Millhaven, Hodgson was transferred to the medium security facility at Warkworth. Three days later, Peter Demeter, now without his bodyguard, was attacked by a fellow inmate in his cell. Demeter let it be known that without protection he was a dead man. As if by magic, within 72 hours, he was transferred to Warkworth.

During the intervening years and, in fact, from the day of Christine Demeter's murder in 1973, the couple's daughter, three-year-old Andrea, lived with Peter's cousin, Dr. Steven Demeter and his family. Peter readily gave Dr. Demeter power of attorney, enabling him to act on Peter's behalf in financial matters.

By 1981, the over $1 million insurance on Christine's life had accumulated to over $3 million, including interest. Peter initiated legal action against the three insurance companies in order to lay his hands on the money. He also instructed Dr. Steven Demeter to initiate an action on Andrea's behalf against the same companies. The Demeters lost the lawsuits. Both appeals were dismissed.

Dr. Demeter approached Peter with $30,000 in legal fees which the insurance fight had cost him. Peter refused to pay, and the two former friends had a falling out. Dr. Steven Demeter was secretly placed on Peter Demeter's hate list, along with the Peel Regional Police and Deputy Chief Teggart.

Dr. Demeter didn't have long to wait to hear from his cousin. In April, 1982, he received a threatening letter from Peter. He travelled to the prison and informed Peter that the letter would be turned over to the authorities should anything happen to him. Dr. Demeter also expressed his concern to parole authorities, as well as Dep. Chief Teggart. From that day to this, there has been no communication between the two cousins.

Andrea Demeter had initially been told that her father was on a prolonged business trip in Europe. As the years passed, this pretense was dropped and the little girl was told the truth about her father. In 1979, at the age of nine, Andrea was visiting her father at Warkworth. She had difficulty coping with the visits. At times, her father was rude and abusive. Finally, she stopped visiting.

Meanwhile, Mike Hodgson was paroled from prison, and had become involved in a fraud-related matter in Hamilton. He skipped to England, where he stayed a short time before returning. Once back in Hamilton, he lived with Anthony Preston, 48, a former prison inmate, who had spent eight years behind bars.

By the summer of 1983, Peter Demeter had himself spent over eight years in prison. His status had greatly changed since his Millhaven days. He was domiciled at Edmison House, a halfway house in Peterborough. He was required to spend from 12 a.m. to 7 a.m. each day at the house. He also had to return to Warkworth each weekend.

Demeter, with an I.Q. of 146, considered to be in the genius category, had no difficulty ingratiating himself with prison officials who controlled his destiny. He had the key to the parole officer's home and often attended family barbecues there. Demeter spent many pleasant evenings at his parole officer's home. Occasionally, he took the official's two children swimming.

Demeter visited his living unit officer's cottage in the Muskokas, and has admitted giving gifts such as liquor, to the families of other correctional facility officials. His classification officer's son received a gift of designer jeans. On one occasion, charming Peter took the boy to Toronto and lined him up with a prostitute.

Correctional authorities maintain a Life Skills office at 331 Rubige St. in Peterborough, where six inmates counsel institutionalized inmates on how to cope with life on the outside. Peter Demeter ran the office.

That summer of 1983, Demeter arranged a meeting with Anthony Preston and Mike Hodgson at the Holiday Inn in Peterborough. Shortly after the meeting, Hodgson returned to Hamilton and turned himself in to the police. Two months later, Demeter set up another meeting with Preston at the House of Chan on Eglinton Ave. in Toronto. For the first time, Peter Demeter told someone in an ambiguous manner that he had a job he needed done. Preston listened and was interested. He returned to Hamilton, but was once more summoned by Demeter, this time to Peterborough. Coincidentally, they met a mutual friend, Mike Lane, an ex-convict on parole from a life sentence for manslaughter. Lane left the meeting. Demeter and Preston sat around a picnic table in the park.

According to Preston's later testimony, Demeter said, "My cousin's been cheating me out of my money." Demeter went on to accuse his cousin of stripping his house in Mississauga of valuable paintings and of turning his daughter against him. At this time, Demeter was well aware that Dr. Demeter had applied to the public trustee to be appointed Andrea's legal guardian.

The meeting continued. Preston claims Peter said, "While in jail I have worked out a three part plan. I spent an awful lot of time working it out."

In essence, Peter wanted his home in Mississauga burned to the ground in order to collect the insurance of $138,000 to finance the rest of his scheme. The second phase involved the kidnapping of his cousin's son, Stuart Demeter, 19, a computer science student. He was to be lured to a parked van on the pretext of obtaining summer employment. Preston would want a van for this purpose.

When the unsuspecting boy opened the door of the van, Peter Demeter would be secreted inside and shoot him dead. Preston later testified, "Demeter said Stuart was going to have to be sacrificed, because Dr. and Mrs. Demeter had to pay for what they had done to him." After the murder, the boy's teeth were to be removed and his fingers amputated to deter identification. The body was to be placed in a body bag and burned.

The third phase of the overall scheme was the kidnapping of a Progressive Conservative fundraiser living in Rosedale. The kidnappers were to appoint Peter Demeter as mediator. The goodwill generated by Demeter in returning the politician to his family, would go a long way with the parole board.

Preston agreed to the razing of Demeter's house, but was leery of Demeter and his talk of murder and mutilation. The sum of $8,000 was agreed upon for the torch job. Demeter passed over a down payment of $500 to Preston. Preston returned to Hamilton, and made up his mind to go through with the arson job, but to have nothing to do with the murder and kidnapping.

In subsequent meetings between the two men at Hy's Restaurant on Richmond Ave., Hemingway's on Cumberland and the Long Bar in the Sheraton Centre, Preston received a further $3500 in cash and a ransom note to be read over the phone to Dr. Demeter after the job was done.

On Aug. 15, 1983, the Mississauga Fire Dept. extinguished a blaze at Demeter's vacant house at 1437 Dundas Cres. in Mississauga. Seven days later, on Aug. 22, the house again mysteriously caught fire, but burned itself out. The very next night, the luxurious home burned to the ground.

Anthony Preston had done his job well, but wanted nothing more to do with Demeter, who made several attempts to contact him. Preston feared for his life. He gave a copy of the ransom note to his girlfriend, instructing her to go to the police with it if anything ever happened to him.

On Sept. 3, 1983, Police Chief D. K. Burrows and Dep. Chief William Teggert of the Peel Regional Police met with Insp. Noel Catney, a veteran of 18 years police work and 46 murder investigations. They advised him that they felt that Peter Demeter was behind the suspected arson of his home. Insp. Catney was given the green light to consider the arson a major project. He hand-picked his team of investigators.

Five days later, Catney was advised that Peter Demeter would be at the site of his burned out home. Catney made a point of being there. The two men met. The master manipulator gazed at the ruins of the home which he hadn't seen for nine years. Catney, the professional cop, asked Demeter if he had any idea how the house had burned down. Demeter replied that he didn't know. Catney promised Demeter he would find out who set the fire. At the time he had no idea that he would live and breathe the Peter Demeter saga for the next two years.

Three weeks later, the arson was to take a back seat when Insp. Catney received a phone call from Insp. Bob Lewis of the Peterborough Police Dept. Lewis had a strange story to tell. The night before, Mike Lane, 32, a parolee who had somewhat of a reputation as a strongman, had flagged down a police cruiser. Lane reported that Peter Demeter had approached him with a proposition to lure a 19-year-old boy to a van in a parking lot, where Demeter would shoot the boy. He went on to relate many of the same details that Preston would later reveal to the police. Mike Lane wanted no part of Demeter's murderous scheme.

Insp. Catney had questioned the Demeter family during the arson investigation and knew that the intended victim was Stuart Demeter. Catney travelled to Peterborough and received Mike Lane's promise of co-operation. Meetings were set up between Demeter and Lane at the Holiday Inn in Peterborough. Unknown to Demeter, video and audio tapes were made of these conversations.

Demeter went through his entire plan to kidnap and murder Stuart Demeter. He had purchased a home at 426 Donegal St. in Peterborough. The old home had a crawl space with a dirt floor. Part of Lane's job, for which he would receive $10,000, was to dig a hole in this crawl space. Demeter wanted the hole to be six feet four inches long. Stuart Demeter's exact height. The hole was to be Stuart Demeter's grave.

On Oct. 19, 1983, Insp. Catney arrested Peter Demeter. He was charged with two counts of counselling to commit murder, three counts of arson, and one count of conspiring to commit arson. At the same time, Anthony Preston was taken into custody and charged with arson. He would later be found guilty, and sentenced to nine months imprisonment. He also told police of Demeter's plan to murder Stuart Demeter. He even turned over a ransom note complete with Peter Demeter's fingerprints.

Noel Catney's two year odyssey was over. Today, Catney says, "Peter Demeter is probably the most dangerous individual I have ever been involved with during my police career. He should never be considered for parole."

On July 8, 1985, Peter Demeter, 54, was found guilty of two counts of counselling to commit murder.

THE LADIES
AND THE TRAMP
Chaplin's love life was often a trial

Charlie Chaplin — The Little Tramp.

The name means little to the Michael Jackson generation, but to the millions throughout the world whose memories go back more than 30 years, Charlie Chaplin is synonymous with comedic genius. Charlie's movies, both silent and talkies, which he wrote, produced and starred in, stand as classics of the film art.

The Little Tramp was born to poverty, in London, England's Kensington district in 1889. His parents, unsuccessful vaudeville entertainers, lived from hand to mouth. When Charlie was three and his older brother, Sydney, was seven, his father died of alcoholism.

Mrs. Chaplin left the theatre in an attempt to support herself and her sons, but found that the periodic sewing jobs which came her way were not enough. Desperate and alone, Hannah Chaplin had a nervous breakdown and was institutionalized. The two boys were placed in an orphanage.

Fortunately, Hannah recovered, and her two sons were returned to her. Their life of poverty continued. Charlie sold newspapers and did odd jobs around pubs. Often, he wore nothing more than rags and roamed the streets barefoot.

In desperation, Charlie sometimes made faces, sang ditties and danced. He soon discovered that he had the ability to make people laugh or cry as he chose. Charlie developed his talent and was successful in obtaining a few small parts in English music halls.

Charlie's big break came when he joined Karno's Comedians, a well-known act which had several bookings in the U.S. While performing in New York, he was noticed by Mack Sennett of Keystone Cop fame and was lured away from the Karno troupe to make a movie. Charlie was paid $150 per week to act in a film. He was a hit and was recognized as such from the very beginning. Charlie went from $150 to $1250 a week with one raise in pay.

With stardom came the spotlight. Some resented the fact that Charlie never became a U.S. citizen. Others never cared for the Little Tramp because of his sympathy toward the Communist Party. But it was not politics that catapulted Charlie into hot water. It was, in a word, women — *young* women.

In 1918, when Charlie was approaching 30, he was seen regularly with cute little blonde Mildred Harris. No one would have blinked an eye were it not for one thing. Mildred was an overdeveloped 16. It became a mild scandal. But Charlie had an answer for the rumormongers. He married Mildred. The fun didn't last. The odd couple divorced in 1920.

Sixteen seems to have been Charlie's favorite number. In 1924, at the mature age of 35, he took up with Lita Gray. You guessed it. Lita was 16. After Charlie and Lita were an item, as they used to say in Hollywood, Charlie was visited by Lita's uncle who, surprise, happened to be a lawyer. Unc pointed out rather forcefully that intimacy with an underaged girl was, in legalese, statutory rape. On Nov. 24, 1924, in dreary downtown Empalme, Mexico, Lita and Charlie became husband and wife. That same afternoon, Charlie went fishing.

Charlie's indifference was a forerunner of things to come. The newlyweds simply didn't hit it off. They tolerated each other for three years until Jan. 10, 1927. That was the day Lita filed a 42-page complaint against Charlie. Let's see now, there was the little matter of intimacy before they were married, when she was underage. Then there was Charlie's abnormal sexual demands. Throw in mental cruelty and running around with other women, and you get the general idea.

Charlie caught everyone by surprise when he announced to the press that he loved his wife and was deeply hurt that she didn't care for him anymore. Eventually, the charges concerning events which had occurred before the marriage were dropped. Charlie settled out of court on the other charges and managed somehow to weather the storm.

Charlie's star shone brightly. Unlike some silent movie actors, he made the transition to talkies without any difficulty. Soon he owned a large estate and was considered one of the wealthiest men in Hollywood.

At the height of his fame, Charlie never wavered in his leanings toward the Soviet Union. Perhaps it was his impoverished youth that influenced his pro-Communist tendencies. Whatever the reason, he raised the ire of anti-Communist groups in the film industry.

In 1936, Charlie married movie star Paulette Goddard on a ship off Canton, China. They stayed together for five years before Paulette obtained a Mexican divorce.

Shortly after his divorce from Goddard, Charlie was introduced to Joan Barry, 20. Within a year, Joan contacted powerful Hollywood gossip columnist Hedda Hopper with the rather startling news that she was pregnant. Hedda, who didn't trust her own mother, took Joan to a doctor, who confirmed that Joan was indeed expecting a child. Joan claimed that Charlie Chaplin was the father, and what's more, he would not even allow her into his mansion where she had once been so very welcome.

It was all too much for Joan. She took an overdose of sleeping pills and was only saved by an alert police officer, who rushed her to hospital, where doctors pumped out her stomach. Joan was booked as a vagrant. The charges were dropped in exchange for a promise to leave town. She hopped a train for New York, but got off in Omaha and headed back to Hollywood, where she broke into Charlie's home. Police were summoned and Joan was sentenced to 90 days in jail. Charlie interceded. He had Joan transferred from the jail to a hospital in Santa Monica. In return for the favor, Joan slapped Charlie with a paternity suit.

Charlie was also charged with violation of the Mann Act (the interstate transportation of women for immoral purposes) and having denied Joan her civil rights.

Joan claimed that earlier that year Charlie had travelled to New York, where she was staying at the time. True enough, he lived at the Waldorf Towers, while she roomed elsewhere. One night she joined Charlie at the Waldorf, where sexual intercourse had taken place.

In regard to the civil rights action, Joan claimed that her rights were denied her when she was forced to leave Hollywood. She also brought the same action against the judge, lawyer and the police officers involved in the incident. The civil rights indictment was eventually dropped, but Charlie stood trial on the Mann Act violation.

Charlie hired famed Hollywood lawyer Jerry Geisler. He proved without a doubt that there was little need for Charlie to follow Joan to New York. She was constantly attempting to throw herself at him, to the point of breaking into his home in Hollywood. On the night Joan claimed they were intimate, Charlie admitted escorting her to the Waldorf, but vehemently denied that intercourse had taken place.

Joan took the witness stand. Geisler had her admit that, on one occasion when she broke into Charlie's home, she had held a pistol on the comedian for an hour and a half, after which she jumped into bed and had intercourse with Charlie.

Joan also admitted that many of her travels were financed by the richest man in the world at that time, Jean Paul Getty. She usually stayed at the fashionable Hotel Pierre while in New York. This was particularly convenient, since Getty owned the Pierre.

Charlie beat the rap. He was acquitted of the charge, which could have brought him a 25 year prison sentence.

Joan gave birth to her baby, Carol Ann. Blood tests performed on Joan, Charlie and Carol Ann proved conclusively that Charlie could not have been the father of the child. Despite this scientific proof, Charlie was brought to trial.

Strangely, the jury could not reach a verdict. Even stranger, at a second trial, Charlie was judged to be the father of little Carol Ann. The baby was awarded $75 a week and was entitled to use the Chaplin name.

The sentimental verdict passed down by the Chaplin jury can never happen again. In 1955, California passed a law prohibiting paternity trials after blood tests have proven the impossibility of the defendant being the father.

While still on trial, Charlie, now 54, married 18-year-old Oona O'Neill, daughter of playwright Eugene O'Neill. Charlie's fourth marriage proved to be his most successful. Over the years he and Oona had seven children. But Charlie Chaplin was to have still more problems from another direction.

At the conclusion of World War II, the U.S. became enmeshed in the Cold War. Everything Communist was a lurking danger. Charlie openly supported Communist causes. In 1952, Charlie and Oona sailed for Europe on vacation. While at sea, they were informed that U.S. Attorney General James F. McGranery had announced that he was rescinding Chaplin's re-entry permit. Charlie decided not to fight. He and his family settled in Vevey, Switzerland.

Charlie was not to return to the U.S. until 20 years later. In 1972, in one of the most emotional ceremonies ever witnessed on television, Hollywood presented Charlie with an honorary Oscar "in recognition of the incalculable effect he has had in making motion pictures the art form of this century." Three years later, confined to a wheelchair, Charlie was knighted by the Queen of England.

In 1977, Sir Charles Chaplin, the Little Tramp, father of 10 children, married four times, innovative genius who had made millions laugh and cry, died peacefully at his home in Switzerland with his wife and seven of his children by his side. He was 88.

The Little Tramp from Kensington had lived a full life.

THE
SCOTTISH KILLER
Peter Manuel was a bad seed

Scotland has nurtured its share of evil men. Maybe Peter Manuel was the nastiest of all. During his criminal career he was responsible for snuffing out the lives of nine innocent individuals. Manuel, a muscular, dark complected youth, lived in Glasgow. His family, decent, hard-working people, stuck by their wayward son to the bitter end.

By the time he was 12, Manuel was breaking into houses and stealing anything of value. For some strange reason, he never rushed his work, but took his time, usually opening canned fruit and other food he found in the house and eating heartily before departing. By the age of 19, he had spent time in ten different correctional facilities.

On the nights of March 3, 4, and 8, 1946, three women were attacked on the outskirts of Glasgow. In two cases, Manuel viciously beat the women, but was interrupted before he could ravish them. On the third occasion, the unfortunate victim was raped. As a known criminal in the area, Manuel was placed in an identification lineup. The two women who were not raped positively identified him. The third woman had not seen her attacker. However, while Manuel was in custody, police were able to gather enough scientific evidence from the scene of the rape to bring their suspect to trial. Manuel was found guilty and sentenced to eight years imprisonment. With time off for good behaviour, he was released after serving six years.

Upon his release from prison, Manuel met Anna O'Hara, a bus conductress, to whom he soon became engaged. He obtained employment and, to all outward appearances, seemed to be going straight. Manuel and Anna were scheduled to wed on July 30, 1955, but the wedding never took place. Anna and her family discovered Manuel's unsavory past. The wedding was cancelled. Anna refused to marry a jailbird.

On the night he was to be married, Manuel attacked a woman in the suburb of Birkenshaw. This time he carried a knife. The woman talked Manuel into releasing her and went to the police. She was able to identify her attacker. Manuel was taken into custody and charged with assault.

Acting as his own defence counsel, Manuel made an extremely good impression on the jury. Taking the witness stand in his own defense, he put forward the view that the lady in question was really his girlfriend. She was taking this vindictive action to gain revenge for his trying to break off their relationship. The jury brought in the unique Scottish verdict of "Not Proven". Manuel walked out of court a free man.

At this point in his criminal career, Peter Manuel had stolen, lied, asaulted, injured and raped. His status was soon to change. It was time to kill.

On Jan. 2, 1956, Anne Knielands, 18, of East Kilbride had a date to meet Andrew Murnin, a young Scottish soldier, in nearby Capelrig. It was Scotland's rather rowdy New Year's holidays, Hogmanay. The young soldier was partying with some friends and simply forgot his date with Anne. Somewhat disappointed, Anne decided to visit old family friends in Capelrig, the Simpsons.

The Simpsons were no ordinary family and deserve mention. Pat Simpson, 47, had lost his arm when he fell under a train at the age of eight. The Simpsons had 17 children, but there was an explanation. Both had been married before. Between them, they had brought ten children to their union. A further seven were the product of their own marriage.

At 8:40 p.m., after passing the time of day, Anne Knielands left the Simpson household. Two days later, George Gribton was taking his daily walk along the East Kilbride golf course when he discovered Anne's body near the fifth fairway. From the physical evidence at the scene, police were able to ascertain that she had been attacked, but had managed to break free of her attacker and run in the darkness down an embankment, over a barbed wire fence and across a field before being overtaken by her pursuer. Her underclothing had been ripped from her body, but she had not been sexually attacked. Several articles of her clothing had been spread over a wide area.

As a previously convicted rapist, Manuel was questioned about the Anne Knielands murder. He told a simple story. On Jan. 2, he had been home all night. There was nothing to connect him with the killing. Months passed.

To keep his hand in, Manuel pulled a few robberies. On one occasion, he was interrupted during the commission of a robbery. While running away from the scene, he ripped his pants on a barbed wire fence. When the police caught up with him, the piece of cloth found on the fence perfectly matched the tear in his pants. Manuel was arrested but was released on bail.

Mr. and Mrs. William Watt and their 16-year-old daughter Vivienne lived at 5 Fennsbank Ave., Burnside. On Sept. 9, Bill, who owned his own bakery, went on vacation with his black Labrador, Queenie. He loved to go fishing at Lochgilphead, near Argyll, where he often stayed at the Cairnbaan Hotel. It was some 90 miles of twists and curves around Loch Lomand.

While Bill was away, Mrs. Watt's sister, Mrs. George Brown, came to spend a night or two at the Watts' home. Eight days after Bill left on his vacation, his wife, sister-in-law and daughter were shot to death with a .38 calibre pistol as they lay sleeping in bed. There was some evidence that Vivienne had awakened when her aunt and mother had been shot. She had put up a struggle before being killed.

Unfortunately for Bill Watt, two eyewitnesses swore that on the night of the killing, they had seen him and Queenie driving the 30 miles between his hotel and his home. Poor Mr. Watt. Devastated at losing everyone near and dear to him, he was arrested and taken into custody.

Most researchers of the Manuel case believe that there was someone in a vehicle similar to Mr. Watt's maroon Vauxhall driving toward Burnside that night. No doubt there was a dog in the car. However, it definitely was not Bill Watt and his dog Queenie. The man has never come forward, nor has he been found, but the strange coincidence was to haunt Bill Watt for weeks before he was exonerated and released. Peter Manuel must have enjoyed the lark.

Once again, Manuel was questioned. In fact, his father Samuel claimed police were harassing his son. He threatened to take the matter to his member of parliament. While Peter enjoyed Mr. Watt's predicament, he did not appreciate all the attention which had been directed to that unfortunate man. Manuel attemped to remedy the situation. He contacted Bill Watt's lawyer, Lawrence Dowdall, and told him that he had been approached by a man who wanted him to get rid of a .38 calibre pistol. Manuel claimed that this man had described the interior of the Watts' home to him. He, in turn, described it to the lawyer. This information was turned over to the police, but of course the suspect named by Manuel had nothing whatever to do with the crime.

Meanwhile, Manuel, who had been out on bail on the breaking and entering charge, was found guilty and sentenced to a year in jail. On Nov. 30, 1957, he was released from prison.

Three days later, Manuel travelled to Newcastle looking for employment. On Dec. 7, he hailed a cab. Cab driver Sydney Dunn, 36, didn't know his fare was a mass murderer. He would never know. Peter Manuel shot him in the head, slashed his throat, and for some reason known only to himself, smashed in every window in the cab. Dunn's body and cab were found next day on the lonely moors near Edmundbyers.

Peter Manuel was now a killing machine. Isabelle Cooke of Glasgow became his sixth victim only 20 days after Sydney Dunn's murder. When Isabelle failed to return home, Mr.

Cooke notified police. Pieces of her clothing were found near a footpath, but police were unable to ascertain the fate of the missing girl. Peter Manuel had buried her body in a nearby plowed field.

Nothing could stop the killing machine. It was New Year's Eve. Mr. and Mrs. Peter Smart and their ten-year-old son were anticipating the 70 mile drive to Ancrum to visit Mr. Smart's parents. The family never showed up. They were all dead. Peter Manuel had claimed his seventh, eighth and ninth victims.

On Jan. 6, Mr. Smart's employers called police, who broke into the Smarts' home and found the bodies. Neighbors stated that they hadn't become suspicious because the house had appeared to be occupied. Blinds were up one day, down the next. Newspapers were taken in each day. Inside the house, police found evidence that the Smarts' killer had remained for days after the murders. He had eaten heartily.

Once again, Manuel was suspected and questioned, but this time it was different. Mr. Smart's employers had paid his expense account in new pound notes. They had a record of the serial numbers of these bills. The money was traced to pound notes which Peter Manual had spent in a pub the day after the triple murder.

Manuel was arrested. The jig was up. He gave a detailed account of all of his crimes and led police to the plowed field, where Isabelle Cooke's body was recovered.

Peter Manuel was hanged at Glasgow's Barlinnie Prison on July 11, 1958.

REVENGE OF
THE TONGS
Murder triggered hatchet killings

H er name was Bow Kum (Sweet Flower) and her murder would ignite New York's Chinatown as nothing has before or since.

At the turn of the century, New York's Chinatown was not the tourist attraction it is today. The dark narrow streets, mainly Mott, Doyers and Fell, were dotted with opium dens where, for a price, you could share a pipe guaranteed to dream your troubles away. If you tired of the pipe, you could pass the wee hours of the morning at the fan tan tables.

The Chinese of New York had long since discovered that they could best take care of their own disputes and problems by forming secret clubs or societies. These clubs, known as Tongs, sprung up throughout Chinatown. The two most powerful were the On Leong Tong or Protection Society and the Hip Sing Tong or Help Each Other Society. Initially, these Tongs served useful purposes in arbitrating domestic and legal disputes. However, it wasn't long before the Tongs themselves were selling protection, as well as being deeply involved in the illicit opium trade.

Of the two powerful Tongs in New York, the On Leong emerged as the most powerful. Under its leader, Tom Lee, it controlled most of the profitable opium dens in Chinatown. Lee saw to it that the New York police were paid off.

What did a little girl born in the Canton district of China have to do with the affairs of her countrymen in America's largest city? Bow Kum's parents were dirt poor. Another girl child to feed was considered a curse rather than a blessing. They sold their beautiful five-year-old daughter for $300, a great deal of money to the struggling family.

The little girl's owner was a slave dealer. To him, the purchase was strictly business. He would raise Bow Kum for five or six years and, if she grew to be a beauty, would sell her at a substantial profit. In China, there was a great demand for beautiful young girls who could be bought and owned without the legal encumbrances of marriage.

Bow Kum developed into a lovely young woman. Shy, but very bright, she moved with grace and poise. Her unblemished skin was like pale yellow satin. Altogether, Bow Kum was a rare beauty.

When Bow Kum was 15, her owner made a deal with a wealthy Chinese merchant from San Francisco named Low Hee Tong. Bow Kum was purchased for $3000 and sent on her way to a new life. The elderly merchant was good to her. She had more to eat and better clothing to wear than she had ever had in Canton. She spent four happy years in San Francisco's Chinatown until one day Low Hee Tong's shop was raided by the police. They found Bow Kum living above the shop. When she confessed that she was neither the wife nor daughter of the shopkeeper, they questioned her further. No matter how she tried to explain, they didn't understand that she simply belonged to Low Hee Tong. When Low Hee Tong produced a receipt for $3000, they still didn't understand.

As a result of the raid, Bow Kum was taken away from her home and placed in a mission. The good ladies of the mission attempted to explain to Bow Kum that it wasn't exactly proper to live with an elderly gentleman without benefit of marriage.

Bow Kum had an idea. If marriage was the big problem, she knew someone who might be interested. She once had met a farmer named Tchin Len in Low Hee Tong's shop. He had expressed an interest in marriage. The ladies of the mission allowed Tchin Len to visit. He was deeply moved that such a beautiful woman wanted to be his bride. In due course, the pair became engaged, and Bow Kum travelled to Tchin Len's farm to await the happy day.

Word of Bow Kum's betrothal drifted into Chinatown. Low Hee Tong was fit to be tied. He was out $3000 and wanted either Bow Kum or his money back. He approached Tchin Len, who listened to his argument and told him he would discuss it with the head lady at the mission. When that stalwart representative of all that is good and holy heard the problem, she was aghast. Women were not to be bought and sold like cattle. Tchin Len owed nothing.

Tchin Len passed the word back to Low Hee Tong. He didn't take it well. He swore he would get his money or Bow Kum. If he failed, he would kill her.

Tchin Len took the threat seriously. He sold his farm for $50,000 and moved with Bow Kum to New York's Chinatown, secure in the belief that his adversary would not follow him. Upon arrival in New York, Tchin Len became a member of the On Leong Tong. Low Hee Tong didn't follow, but he wrote influential friends in New York's Chinatown, informing them of his situation. These friends approached the On Leong Tong, demanding that their friend back in San Francisco be paid $3000 for Bow Kum.

The On Leongs agreed to sit in judgement, hear both sides of the case and render a decision. The arguments were duly presented to the tribunal. They passed down their decision. Tchin Lee was not obliged to pay anything for his bride. The laws of the new homeland had been instrumental in removing Bow Kum from Low Hee Tong's guardianship. Tchin Len had been free to marry her without payment.

That very night, in August, 1903, when the decision was reached, Tchin Len celebrated by playing fan tan. Then he made his way to his home on Mott St. He reeled back in horror when he opened the door. Beautiful Bow Kum lay sprawled on the floor. Her throat had been slit from ear to ear with a hatchet. She had also been stabbed directly in the heart with a dagger, which was stuck upright in the floor beside her body.

New York's finest investigated the ritual murder. They received little co-operation from the closed-mouthed Chinese. Finally, they dropped the case.

The On Leong Tong did not take Bow Kum's death lightly. After all, she was the wife of a Tong member. Besides, her murder was a direct result of their decision. Someone had defied the Tong's authority. They made it their business to learn the identity of the culprit. Low Hee Tong's friends, who had represented him at the tribunal, were members of an ancient fraternal society known as the Four Brothers. It was this group which had murdered Bow Kum.

The On Leongs decided that members of the Four Brothers had to be punished. On the day war was declared by the On Leongs, one of the Four Brothers was found dead in a Chinatown alleyway. His throat had been cut with a hatchet. Within two days, five more victims met the same fate, all by means of the deadly sharpened hatchet.

For retaliatory purposes, the Four Brothers recruited the Hip Sing Tong. Within weeks, the most devastating Tong war New York's Chinatown had ever known was in progress. In all, it is estimated that 100 Chinese died, the vast majority by having their throats slit by a hatchet.

Often, in darkened movie houses, when the customers left, a couple of theatre goers would be left sitting in an upright position. Their throats had been clearly slit with a hatchet. One night, five members of the On Leong Tong were found sitting like grotesque statues, all in a row, all dead.

Eventually, the Chinese themselves realized that things had gone too far. Influential Chinese scholars and wealthy merchants arranged a meeting. It wasn't easy to organize such a meeting, for the hatchet killings had bred deep hatred between the two groups. But the killings couldn't go on. In due course, the Tongs signed a treaty, bringing peace to New York's Chinatown.

The Sweet Flower, who was sold in Canton for $300 at the age of five, has long since been forgotten. But not by all. A few years ago, a man was arrested for murder in Chinatown.

He had killed a man with a hatchet. When questioned he would only mumble, "Bow Kum, Bow Kum."

ALL-AMERICAN MONSTER
Star athlete was a killer

Where do the monsters lurking in our society come from? Are they the products of abusive parents? Is there insanity in the family tree? Truth is, in many cases disruptive family backgrounds have contributed to those personalities who are responsible for the most horrific of crimes.

Randall Brant Woodfield was an exception. He was a member of an extremely stable family. His father, Jack Woodfield, held a responsible position with Pacific Northwest Bell Telephone Co. Jack and his wife, Donna Jean, were thrilled when Randy was born on Dec. 26, 1950 in Salem, Oregon. They already had two daughters, Susan and Nancy. The Woodfields really wanted a boy.

And a fine boy Randy grew up to be. He was extremely handsome and it was soon obvious that he was a natural athlete. Jack Woodfield was transferred to the small town of Otter Rock, Ore., and it was here that Randy grew up, attending school in nearby Newport.

Randy excelled in track and field, baseball, basketball and football. During his teenage years, he had the reputation of being the best all-round athlete in the area. Many believed that his future lay in professional sport. Randy basked in his popularity. He dated only the prettiest and most popular girls in his high school. They considered themselves fortunate to get a date with the football team's star wide receiver. The world appeared to be the oyster of the handsome, 6 foot 2 athlete.

Other honors came Randy's way. At Newport High School, he excelled in mathematics and was accelerated into an advanced class. The Rotary Club once selected him as their Boy of the Month.

In his senior year at high school, Randy was recruited by several colleges in the northwest. He chose Treasure Valley Community College in Ontario, Ore. Randy stayed a year, did well scholastically, but it was in athletics that he excelled. He was co-captain of the football team and a star member of the Varsity basketball team. He also broke the school's record for the long jump.

At the age of 20, Randy transferred to Portland State University, feeling that at a larger school he had a better opportunity to be noticed by big league football scouts. In his new surroundings, Randy again proved to be a good student and an exceptional athlete. However, it was while attending Portland State that the image of the all-American boy began to tarnish.

On Aug. 7, 1972, Randy Woodfield was apprehended in the act of exposing himself to a young girl. Charged with indecent exposure, he was convicted but received a suspended sentence. University officials were never notified of Randy's arrest and so his reputation on campus was unaffected. During the next summer's vacation, it happened again. On June 22, 1973, he was captured by a police officer after exposing himself to a woman in Portland. Randy received a sentence of one year's probation. That winter he was arrested for public indecency and was sentenced to five years probation.

Perhaps if Randy Woodfield had received professional help with his sexual problems at this juncture, his life might have taken a far different turn. After all, this star athlete, whom most girls would consider a "catch", was receiving sexual gratification out of lurking in bushes around darkened park paths, exposing himself to unwary women. Something was definitely wrong.

But professional help was not in the offing. A far more thrilling experience was to take place in Randy's life. He was drafted by the Green Bay Packers football team.

On Feb. 20, 1974, Randy signed a professional football contract. He was to receive $16,000 for the season no matter what happened. There were bonus clauses as well. He received $3000 for signing, and would receive a further $3000 if he made the team. Of course, room, board and airline tickets to pre-season practices would all be handled by the Packers organization. The whole thing was a dream come true. Randy headed for Green Bay.

Then the bottom fell out of the dream. Randy was cut by the team. He caught on with the Packers' farm team, the Manitowac Chiefs, and played out the season in the hope of being called back up to the Packers. It never happened.

Randy returned to Portland, but never went back to university. Instead, he obtained a job tending bar. Now 25, Randy may have realized that his chance to become a professional athlete had passed. He was at a crossroads.

During that winter of 1975, Portland police were investigating a rash of strange crimes. A tall, good-looking young man was sexually assaulting and robbing young women at knifepoint in Duniway Park.

A lady police officer, acting as a decoy, was used to apprehend the attacker. He turned out to be Randy Woodfield. When searched, Randy was carrying a gun and a knife. On June 10, 1975, he was sentenced to 10 years in the Oregon State Penitentiary for armed robbery. After serving less than four years, he was released as "not being a violence risk".

Randy borrowed his mother's Volkswagen, obtained jobs tending bar in several lounges, and dated pretty girls. Randy was 30, but looked 25. Sometimes he would live with a girl for a few months, but generally he lived alone. An ex-con had told him that a good way to effect a disguise was to use bandaids on his face. Randy expanded the disguise to include a crude beard. Brandishing a tiny revolver, he held up scores of fast food operations. More often than not, he struck late at night, sexually attacking the young girls who worked at such outlets.

On Jan. 18, 1981, at around 9 o'clock, Randy was out

prowling the suburbs of Salem, Oregon. It didn't matter much to him any more — women working at a fast food store, women strolling on the street, any woman would do. Four days earlier, he had attacked two children, ages eight and ten. Now the man with the physique and looks of a movie actor and the mind of a monster, was stalking the streets.

Two girls, Beth Wilmot and Shari Hull, worked for Shari's father, who owned a janitorial service. They were best friends. On this particular night they were cleaning the Trans America Title Building. Suddenly they were confronted by a man waving a revolver. He herded them into the lunch room.

For 20 minutes the intruder sexually attacked the two girls. He then forced them to lie on the floor, face down. Beth Wilmot would later relate that the next thing she remembered was a shot being fired. The attacker shot Beth in the head. The crazed gunman alternately shot the girls five times. Three bullets entered Shari's body and two were fired at Beth's head. He left, sure that his victims were dead.

Unbelievably, Beth Wilmot, with two bullet wounds in her head, got up from the floor, walked to the telephone and called an emergency hot line. An ambulance arrived in minutes. Next morning, Shari Hull died in hospital. Miraculously, Beth Wilmot survived.

Doctors found one .32 calibre flattened bullet in her hair. They surmised that the ammunition used may not have been the correct calibre for the gunman's weapon. At any rate, the bullet had not penetrated her skull. The second bullet had dug a furrow under the skin, coming to rest under her right ear. Beth had beaten the odds. As she recovered from her wounds, she gave detectives a detailed description of the killer.

Randy Woodfield was on the move. Robbing as he went, he made his way 400 miles to Mountain Gate, California, where he walked into a home and sexually attacked the occupants before shooting them to death. Donna Lee Eckard, 37, and her 14-year-old stepdaughter, Janell Jarvis, lay dead in the madman's wake. Authorities connected the California murders to the crime wave in Oregon.

Strangely enough, Randy Woodfield's name first came to

the attention of investigators in a case thought unrelated to the wanton attacks on women up and down the west coast of the U.S. On Valentine's Day, 1981, Julie Reitz, 18, was found dead in her Beaverton, Ore. home. Someone had shot the girl in the back of the head as she fled nude down her front stairs in an effort to elude her killer.

Subsequent investigation indicated that Julie knew her killer. Because of this, her murder was not connected to the rash of crimes then being investigated. However, one of her slight acquaintances, Randy Woodfield, was questioned and subsequently released. He was known to drive a gold-colored Volkswagen. Several fast food holdup victims reported that their attacker had driven a gold Volkswagen.

Investigators checked out Randy's record and discovered he had been in prison on a sex-related charge. Witnesses were contacted, all of whom picked Randy Woodfield out of police lineups. Beth Wilmot had no hesitation in identifying the attacker and the killer of her best friend.

On June 3, 1981, Randy stood trial in Salem, Ore. on charges of murder, attempted murder and sodomy. Prosecuted by District Attorney Chris Van Dyke, (son of comedian Dick Van Dyke), Randy Woodfield was found guilty of all charges. Randy was sentenced to life plus 90 years, with a recommendation that he not be eligible for parole until he has served 50 years.

Another trial followed on Dec. 18, 1981. Randy was found guilty of sodomy and being an ex-convict in possession of a weapon. He was sentenced to a further 35 years in prison. The judge stipulated that the 35 year sentence was to run consecutive to the sentence handed down on the murder charge. Randy Woodfield in total faces life plus 125 years in prison. The star athlete from a good family will never be a free man again.

WHO CAN YOU TRUST?
He led the search
for his daughter's killer

What has happened to the standards by which normal folks live? Where has decency gone? Is anyone to be trusted? These are some of the questions the 332 citizens of Underwood, Minnesota, are asking themselves.

Chances are you never heard of Underwood. The tiny community is located in dairy country southwest of Duluth. Because the rich pastureland is sprinkled with lakes, the area is a popular tourist attraction. Names such as Turtle, Bass, and Otter Tail dot the map in that section of western Minnesota.

Underwood was virtually free of violent crime. In Duluth, maybe, but never in Underwood, where neighbors relied on each other through good times and bad, where doors were often left unlocked. That is, until between 6 and 7 p.m. on May 29, 1985, when 13-year-old Sara Ann Rairdon disappeared while walking the four and a half miles from school to her home just east of the town.

Sara was a popular youngster. She was an honors student attending the seventh grade. She was also a valued member of her school's track team. On the evening of her disappearance, she had stayed late at school to do extra work on a home economics project.

The Rairdon family was distraught. Sara's father, mechanic John Rairdon, 38, made impassioned pleas over television, urging his daughter's abductor to return Sara safely to her family. Everyone in town knew how John felt about his family. Nine years earlier, when he and his first wife, Linda, were divorced, he obtained custody of their five children, including Sara, their only daughter. In 1975 John married his present wife, Marilyn, who brought four childen from a previous marriage to the union. Together John and Marilyn had two more children.

The community of Underwood gathered around one of its own. A massive search was conducted throughout the area along county road 122, where the child was last seen. No trace of Sara was uncovered. The community dug deep. Eight thousand dollars was raised. John Rairdon worked elbow to elbow with other members of the community late into the night, stuffing Sara's photograph into envelopes, which were sent to all 50 states and neighboring Manitoba.

Despite the search parties, despite the flyers, no trace of Sara was uncovered until July 6, over six weeks from the day of her disappearance.

About 25 miles from Underwood, a farmer noticed that his cattle were shunning a small section of his pasture. Initially, the farmer paid no attention, but when the grass grew tall in the neglected patch, he figured there was something there which discouraged the cattle from eating. He walked over and discovered the body of Sara Rairdon. Sara had died as the result of a puncture wound to the left side of her abdomen.

The community of Underwood was stunned; the Rairdons were devastated. What maniac had committed such a horrific crime? Surely the madman was an outsider. Yet there were those who pointed out that the tourist season had hardly begun when Sara went missing. Others pointed out that the back road leading from the school to her home was rarely utilized by strangers. It was beyond belief that a local resident could be the perpetrator of such a crime.

Some members of the community had difficulty coping with the tragedy which had taken place in their midst. Volunteers organized a meeting of parents and children in an attempt to better comprehend Sara's disappearance and death. John and Marilyn Rairdon attended the meeting.

Sara's funeral took place on July 9. The citizens of Underwood, along with the Rairdon family, gathered in the town's gymnasium to mourn the loss of Sara Ann. Some citizens will never forget the heart-rending scene of one of the younger Rairdon children sitting on their father's knee at the funeral service. Tears streamed down John Rairdon's face.

Shortly after the funeral, John joined a group known as Search and Find Missing Persons Inc. The aim of the group was to assist in the search of missing children. As one who had been personally touched by the death of a daughter, it was only natural that John Rairdon acted as chairman of the board of directors of the organization.

Then, in mid August, a rumor spread through the town of Underwood. It couldn't be. Had the entire community been deceived or was it all a terrible mistake? As the hours passed that Aug. 14, it became apparent that no mistake had been made. Under question by police, John Rairdon had confessed to his daughter Sara's murder.

According to court records, John revealed that he had been sexually abusing his daughter for the past five years, since she was eight. In recent months, Sara had resisted his advances. Rairdon related that on the day of her death, he had picked Sara up in his truck as she walked home from school. He drove the youngster to an abandoned farmhouse, where he attempted to have sexual relations with the child. When she resisted he became angry. He took an awl from his truck and stabbed Sara in the abdomen. John then hid Sara's body in the farmhouse, returning later that night to transfer the body to the farmer's pasture some miles away.

John Rairdon's family is understandably numb with shock. Marilyn Rairdon was completely unaware of what was taking place in her own home. Married to a man who sexually abused his own child for five years, she could only say, "He was a caring parent and husband." Later, she said, "He's going to pay for it. He'll never see his family grow up."

Social workers questioned the other Rairdon children, and have satisfied themselves that none were abused by their father. Sara's school friends have also been questioned. The little girl had told no one of the ordeal she was living through.

Underwood had been deceived by one of its own. The citizens felt betrayed. The hours of work, the thousands of dollars raised and spent, the strained emotions, all for naught. John Rairdon had known who had killed his daughter for the three months during which he had accepted their concern, love and assistance.

A scholarship fund has been set up in Underwood in memory of Sara Ann Rairdon. Her father's confession has complicated matters for the volunteers who raised $2500 as a reward for the capture of Sara's killer. They are considering donating the $2500 reward money to the scholarship fund. John Rairdon was to be on the committee to decide who should receive the scholarship.

Meanwhile, Rairdon has had his day in court. He has been found guilty of intrafamilial sexual abuse and guilty of murder in the first degree. John Rairdon was sentenced to 13 years imprisonment for the murder of his own daughter. The sentences are to run consecutively. The outside world has heard the last of John Rairdon for a long, long time.

CATCH ME
IF YOU CAN
Erler was a good police officer

When Robert Erler moved from Phoenix, Arizona to Dania, Florida, it was only natural that a police officer acquaintance in Dania talked Bob into carving out a career for himself as a law enforcement officer. After all, Bob had served as a Green Beret in Vietnam from 1963 to 1966.

True enough, he and his wife Pat were having marital difficulties. That's why the Erlers decided to start life anew in southern Florida in the first place. A month after they settled in Dania, Pat gave birth to a baby boy. Little Bobby was his father's pride and joy.

Bob joined the Dania police force and proved to be an efficient, capable officer. However, his marital difficulties went from bad to worse. Pat simply wasn't the type to stay home day after day with her young son. Besides, she spent far more money than the young police officer earned. Gradually, the Erlers fell deeper and deeper into debt, which led to constant bickering. Despite this, the young couple continued to live beyond their means. Bob rented a new three bedroom mobile home, purchased a new Dodge Dart and an extensive wardrobe for his wife. Nothing satisfied Pat. One day, after a particularly nasty argument, she simply walked out.

In the course of his police work, Bob had become friends with Jim Walsh, a colleague on the nearby Hollywood, Fla., police force. Jim convinced Bob to join the larger, more modern Hollywood force.

While serving with the Hollywood police, Bob gained a degree of notoriety for his uncanny ability to smell out trouble. On more than one occasion, while on patrol, he merely looked at a speeding vehicle and declared that it was stolen. When licence numbers were checked, he proved to be correct far more often than he was wrong. Soon his fellow officers were callling him "Super Cop". No question about it, Robert Erler had a bright future as a law enforcement officer.

During the early morning hours of Aug. 12, 1968, Bob was on patrol. Later, in his police report, he described how he pulled up at a Shell service station at the corner of I-95 and Sheridan St. As he was leaving his patrol car, a blue 1968 Ford Falcon drove up. The occupants, a man and woman, told Bob that they had seen someone lying on the road a short distance away.

Bob radioed headquarters. As he was doing so, the blue Falcon drove away. Unable to see the licence number as the car sped away, Bob decided to proceed up the road, where he sighted the body of a young white female lying in the ditch. Bob radioed the exact location of the body to headquarters. In a matter of minutes, investigating officers were on the scene and had cordoned off the area. Bob typed out his report of discovery of the body and the investigation was turned over to the detective bureau.

During that early Monday morning, further developments took place. At precisely 8:18 a.m., the Hollywood police department received a phone call. The call was taped.

"I'd like to report a murder."

"A what?"

"Murder."

"A murder?"

"I just killed three people."

"Are you serious?" asked the officer.

"I'm serious. Please catch me. Please."

"Where are you, son?"

"I'm going to kill 'em tonight, too. Please."

"Where are you?" the officer persisted.

The caller hung up. Twelve minutes later, at precisely 8:30 a.m., the phone rang again.

"If you want to find those bodies, go down to the airport."

"Lauderdale Airport?" the officer asked.

"There's one in the water and one on a sidestreet."

"Route 1?" the officer asked.

"The Shell gas station. Hurry up, please."

"Okay."

The caller hung up. The strange phone calls were taken seriously. Before they could be acted upon, Bob Erler had found one victim, a young girl, who was obviously the one referred to as the victim beside the ditch.

The Fort Lauderdale police soon located a 1960 green Falcon near the Fort Lauderdale airport. Slumped over the steering wheel was a woman, who had been shot several times in the head. Miraculously, she was still alive.

From documents found in the vehicle, it was ascertained that the victim was 42-year-old Dorothy Clark, who had arrived in Florida from Clarkston, Georgia. Further investigation indicated that the dead girl found beside the road was Merylin Eileen Clark, her 12-year-old daughter.

Three weeks earlier, Dorothy and her daughter had left Georgia and were touring Florida while Dorothy sought employment.

The emotional calls received from the killer had mentioned three victims. He had also stated that he would kill that night. Investigating officers decided to inform the public of the danger through the media. Because of the phone calls, the press dubbed the murderer the "Catch Me Killer". Despite the madman's threats, there would be no third victim.

On the afternoon of the murder, an autopsy was performed on Merylin Clark. She had been shot five times directly in the head with a .22 calibre weapon. Meanwhile, her mother, Dorothy, lay in hospital near death. With each passing day, it became evident that this remarkable woman would survive.

A month after the attack, Mrs. Clark was strong enough to be interviewed by Hollywood detectives. She told them that she and her daughter had attempted to sleep on the beach at Dania. A police officer had approached and told her that sleeping on the beach was prohibited. On that particular night, swarms of mosquitoes were in the area. When the officer suggested that she and her daughter were welcome to spend the night in his air conditioned trailer, they jumped at the opportunity.

Mrs. Clark followed her benefactor in her car. They drove into a trailer park. The police officer's trailer was large and well appointed. She and her daughter flopped down on two separate couches. Suddenly, the officer stripped naked, made lewd suggestions, waved a .22 calibre pistol at the startled pair and demanded their money.

Dorothy and her daughter ran from the trailer and jumped into their car. Before they could start up, the police officer jumped in beside them. As they drove, Merylin Clark was shot five times in the head and thrown from the car. Near the airport, Dorothy was ordered to stop. She, too, was shot five times in the head. The killer never for a moment believed that Mrs. Clark could possibly survive the shooting.

Investigating officers were stunned. Had one of their own been involved in one of the most senseless, cruel crimes they had ever investigated?

With Mrs. Clark's eyewitness report, the investigation swung into full gear. Hollywood detectives consulted with Dania Police Chief Parton. These discussions revealed that a Dania police officer had left that force and joined the Hollywood Police some months before the assault on the Clarks. What's more, the same police officer had been the one to find Merylin Clark's body — Super Cop Bob Erler.

Hollywood detectives learned that Erler had resigned from the Hollywood force three weeks after the murders. Strangely enough, the trailer he had rented at the Bell Trailer Court had been taken over by the Dania Police Chief for the use of his son.

The trailer had been refurnished by the Chief's son, but he told authorities that when he took possession of the trailer, he had thrown away several .22 calibre shells. Police, standing in front of Erler's trailer, had a clear view of the highway leading to the International Airport. They could also see a revolving Shell gasoline sign. Nearby was a public telephone booth. The evidence against Erler mounted. Personal friends now listened to the Catch Me tapes. Without being told of the status of the investigation, they identified the voice as that of Bob Erler. When Mrs. Clark identified Erler from a photograph as her attacker, police felt they had more than enough to act.

Erler was located in Phoenix and returned to Florida, where he was charged with the murder of Merylin Clark. Despite maintaining his innocence, Bob Erler was tried, found guilty of second degree murder and sentenced to 99 years and six months at hard labor at the Florida State Prison.

The existence of an ex-police officer in prison can be a living hell. Erler was no exception. He was beaten unmercifully on several occasions. However, his life still had many strange turns to take. After serving three years in the maximum security prison, Erler was transferred to the medium security institution at Belle Glade. A few months later, he escaped by climbing a wall and, in the dark, swimming an alligator-infested moat to gain his freedom.

Seven months later Erler was apprehended by the Mississippi Highway Patrol. After a six mile chase, Erler's car careened off the road. As he fled by foot, he was shot in the left hip. At the time of his apprehension, he was armed with a .357 Magnum revolver.

Back in prison, Bob Erler became deeply involved in religion. In 1977, under terms of an interstate agreement, Erler was transferred to an Arizona prison, where he could be close to his immediate family. While confined, he openly confessed to the murder of 12-year-old Merylin Clark and the attempted murder of Dorothy Clark. He has since been paroled, remarried and is presently an ordained minister in Arizona.

BASEBALL'S
DENNY McLAIN
Decline and fall of a baseball great

Ron Taylor toiled for years as a relief pitcher in the major leagues. In four appearances in two World Series, he held his opponents scoreless. Today, Ron Taylor is a medical doctor with a flourishing private practice and is team physician to the Toronto Blue Jays.

Don Getty starred as quarterback for the Edmonton Eskimos in the fifties and sixties. After football, he successfully embarked on a political career. Today, he is the premier of Alberta.

Syl Apps starred at center ice for the Toronto Maple Leafs during their glory days of the thirties and forties. After hockey, the Leafs old captain became a member of the Ontario Legislature for 12 years, and served in the cabinet as Minister of Correctional Services before retiring to his home in Kingston.

These men were achievers in sport and in the game of life. They epitomize how we want our sports heroes to turn out after they complete their athletic careers.

Unfortunately, some athletes step off the playing field and find the game of life far different from their athletic endeavours.

Maybe the handwriting was on the wall for Denny McLain while he was still basking in the limelight as a true sports hero. One of his old Detroit Tiger teammates, Mickey Lolich, explains, "We used to say he was either going to wind up in concrete shoes or in prison. I guess he got the latter."

Denny was first noticed by the baseball world while still a youngster, pitching at Mt. Carmel High School in Chicago. No wonder. He had a 38-7 won-lost record. That same season of 1962, the Chicago White Sox gave Denny a $17,000 signing bonus and assigned him to their Harlan, Kentucky farm club.

In the minors, Denny didn't impress. His record in the minors was 5 wins and 8 losses. At the ripe old age of 18, Denny was just another gifted kid, one of thousands who played baseball with one dream in mind — to make the big leagues.

In 1963, Denny received what appeared to be a setback. At spring training, the White Sox had three rookie pitchers vying for a place on the team. One of the boys had signed for a larger bonus. The other had a better minor league record than McLain. Denny became expendable. He was exposed to the rookie draft which, in effect, meant that any other major league club could pick him up for $8000. Denny was drafted by the Detroit Tigers, who shipped him to Duluth.

In Duluth, Denny displayed the magic which was to become his trademark. He chalked up a 13 win, 2 loss record. At the end of the season, he was brought up to the Tigers.

Tiger pitching instructors taught fastballer McLain how to throw a change-up curve. Denny became a bonafide major leaguer, compiling records of 16-6 in 1965, 20-14 in 1966 and 17-18 in 1967.

His 1967 season ended on a sour note. Denny didn't win a game after Aug. 29, and the Tigers lost the pennant by one game to the Boston Red Sox. During that time, Denny was sidelined with an injured foot, which was to raise ugly questions in the not too distant future.

But all that was forgotten during the 1968 baseball season. That was Denny McLain's year. Victory after victory was savored by Denny and the delirious Detroit fans. When it was over, Denny had compiled the unbelievable record of 31 wins against 6 losses and the Tigers rolled to the American League pennant.

No pitcher had won 30 games in over three decades, since Dizzy Dean accomplished the feat in 1934. Denny's achievement was one of the great sports stories of modern times. No one has won over 30 games since. That season, baseball heaped honors on Denny. He was voted the American League's Most Valuable Player and won the Cy Young Award as Pitcher of the Year.

In 1969, he was almost as invincible. He racked up a 24-9 record with a 2.80 earned run average. Once again, he received the Cy Young Award. Denny McLain had won 108 ball games. He was 25, the toast of baseball and the world of sport.

Along the line, Denny had become an airplane pilot, a better than average organ player, and had married Sharyn Boudreau, daughter of baseball immortal, Lou Boudreau.

In 1970, Denny's salary was $90,000. His income from other sources, including television appearances, organ concerts and the banquet circuit, added up to another $100,000. Remember, this was back when the average U.S. salary was well under $9,000. The talented, all-American hero was riding high.

The rumors began in magazine articles. They were made official by Bowie Kuhn, then Commissioner of baseball. Denny McLain's off field activities dating back to 1967 were being investigated. It was alleged that Denny had invested in a bookmaking establishment in Flint, Mich. in 1967. It was further alleged that the celebrated injury to his foot had been incurred by a Mafia enforcer while collecting a $46,000 gambling debt owed by McLain. While the rumors flew, it was revealed that Denny owed $2,450 in back rent on his Lakeland, Fla. home, $779 to Consumer Power Co. in unpaid bills and several months rent on his $75,000 airplane.

After a hearing before Commissioner Kuhn, baseball's brightest star was suspended from the opening day of the 1970 season to July 1, a period of two months and 24 days.

On July 1, Denny returned to the Tigers. Over 50,000 fans,

the largest crowd to fill the Detroit stadium in nine years, cheered his appearance. The bad boy of baseball was back. He wasn't his old, sharp self, but the Tigers won the game and the multitude had paid homage to their talented hero.

Denny couldn't stay out of trouble. In August, he poured a bucket of ice water over the heads of two Detroit sports writers. This time, his own organization suspended him for "conduct unbecoming a professional baseball player". A week later, after apologizing to the two writers, Denny was back in the Tigers' starting rotation. To gain relief from the hords of creditors hounding him, he declared bankruptcy.

It was a rough season for McLain. In September, he was suspended for the balance of the 1970 season by Commissioner Kuhn for carrying a gun.

At the conclusion of the season, Denny was reinstated, but the Detroit organization had had enough of their bad boy star. The same day he was reinstated, he was traded to the Washington Senators. The end was in sight. That season in Washington, Denny suffered the most losses by a pitcher in the big leagues with 22 defeats. He was later traded to the Oakland A's, and from Oakland to the Atlanta Braves. Then began the lonely trip to the minors.

In May, 1974, 30-year-old Denny McLain was out of shape and vastly overweight. He was signed to pitch a game for the London, Ont. Majors against Kitchener. In typical McLain fashion, he showed up an hour before game time. Nine hundred and four fans attended the game. The majority were there to see with their own eyes the major league's last 30 game winner. Denny received $30 for his appearance. He had slid a long way down the ladder.

Denny spent the next few years doing sports announcing for minor league teams. He even managed to catch on as manager of an American Association team. Nothing worked. Outside businesses failed. In 1977, Denny filed a personal bankruptcy petition for the second time. He listed debts of over one million dollars and assets of $900.

Throughout Denny's glory days and bad times, his wife,

Sharyn, remained at his side. They have four children. She has watched her husband deteriorate from a handsome, flamboyant sports hero to a bloated 270 pound failure. During the seventies, the sports world had had enough of Denny McLain. New heroes had taken his place, but McLain's unsuccessful battle to cope with life off the baseall diamond didn't stop.

In 1984, Denny made the headlines once more. He was indicted for racketeering, conspiracy, extortion, possession and distribution of cocaine and conspiracy to import cocaine. It was alleged that he had been involved in these activities since June, 1978. In 1985, Denny was found guilty of racketeering, conspiracy, extortion, and cocaine possession. He was sentenced to 23 years in prison. As the sentence was passed, Sharyn McLain and her two daughters wept openly in court.

Today, Denny McLain, 41, one of baseball's greatest heroes, languishes in a cell at the Federal Penitentiary in Atlanta, Georgia.

Epilogue: In August 1987, the Eleventh Circuit Court of Appeals in Atlanta threw out all of McLain's convictions, citing improper conduct by both judge and prosecutor. McLain was released.

BEST FRIENDS
Self-defence or brutal axe murder?

T he peaceful little town of Wylie, Texas is a good place to live. Located about 25 miles northeast of Dallas, many of its 3500 residents are employed in the booming computer industry that has blossomed in recent years throughout the area.

Typical of the prosperous young families living in the neat middle class homes were the Montgomerys: Pat, 35, and Candy, 30, had been married for 10 years. They had two children; Jenny, seven, and Ian, five. Pat was an electronics engineer with a Ph.D. degree.

On the evening of June 12, 1980, Jenny Montgomery's best friend, seven-year-old Alisa Gore, slept over at the Montgomery home. Next day, Alisa wanted to stay over an extra night. Everyone agreed it was a good idea. Alisa's father, Allan, who was also employed in the electronics industry, was out of town on business, leaving his wife Betty and their 11-month-old baby daughter, Bethany, alone in their home at 410 Dogwood St. in Wylie.

There was one minor detail which popped up that morning. Alisa had to attend her swimming lessons. Candy decided to drive over to the Gore home to pick up the youngster's bathing suit.

It was hot that summer in Texas, one of the hottest on

record. The picture of domestic tranquility presented by the Montgomery and Gore families camouflaged the turbulent emotional lives being led by the four adults. You see, Candy Montgomery and Allan Gore had carried on a torrid love affair for 10 months. The affair had been terminated seven months earlier.

The Gores and Montgomerys attended the same church — the United Methodist Church of nearby Lucas. It was here that bored, restless Candy Montgomery became infatuated with Allan Gore. Her own husband, Pat, deeply involved in a budding career, was preoccupied with his job and children. Candy's sex life with an attentive, but passive husband left a lot to be desired.

Candy picked Allan Gore. It wasn't just sex. She wanted someone she could talk to, who would understand and sympathize with her predicament. One suspects Candy also sought the adventure and thrills the clandestine affair would afford. Allan was vulnerable to her offer. His wife, Betty, was high strung and prone to minor ailments. The idea of an affair appealed to him. Theirs was no impetuous, damn the world affair, but rather a well thought out plan of action, where both parties would receive mental stimulation as well as sexual gratification. The two lovers met each week in a motel for ten months.

It was Allan who broke off the affair. Their church had instituted a program to assist troubled marriages. The counselling seemed to bring Betty and him closer together. He no longer required Candy's solace. There were no tears, no recriminations. Candy wasn't pleased, but she and Allan had entered the relationship with the understanding that they would harm no one and would break off the relationship whenever either one desired it.

Candy Montgomery drove her own children and Alisa Gore to Bible school that Friday morning in June. Ironically, it was Friday the thirteenth. Candy taught the first class and then took the opportunity to hop over to the Gores' to pick up Alisa's bathing suit. From the moment Candy drove her white station wagon into the Gore driveway, we have only her word as to what transpired. A few hours later, the Montgomery and Gore families would never be the same again. Indeed, most of the U.S. would soon learn of the dreadful deed which took place in the utility room at 410 Dogwood St.

Later, under the glare of a much publicized murder trial, Candy testified that she had chatted briefly with Betty that fateful morning. Bethany was asleep in her crib. After several minutes of small talk, Candy asked for Alisa's bathing suit. Without warning, Betty looked in her friend's eyes and said, "Candy, are you having an affair with Allan?"

Candy replied, "No, of course not."

"But you did, didn't you?"

"Yes," Candy replied.

It was out in the open now. Somehow, Betty had found out. The tense moment was broken when Betty abruptly left the room. She returned in an instant, carrying a three foot long axe. According to Candy's testimony, Betty did not threaten her with the axe, but vehemently ordered her never to see Allan again.

During a calm in the storm, Betty suggested that Candy pick up Alisa's bathing suit from the utility room, while she fetched a towel from the bathroom. The two women met at the entrance to the utility room. Betty passed the towel to Candy. They looked at each other. Candy blurted out, "Oh, Betty, I'm so sorry."

As if a trigger had been pulled, Betty's repressed fury erupted. She suddenly pushed Candy into the utility room. Both women held the axe handle. Betty jerked the handle. The flat side of the blade struck Candy a glancing blow to the head. She released her grip. As she did so, she enabled Betty to raise the axe and bring it down with all her might. Candy jumped out of the way. The axe hit the utility floor linoleum and bounced, inflicting a nasty cut to Candy's toe.

Once more, the two desperate women struggled for control of the axe. Finally, Candy wrenched the axe out of Betty's hands. Without hestitation, she brought the axe down on Betty's head and then continued to rain blow after blow to Betty's body. In all, 41 wounds were inflicted.

Candy looked down at the horribly mutilated body of Betty Gore. She walked into the shower and cleaned her arms and legs. Her head hurt where the flat side of the axe had made contact. Her toe throbbed. Despite all, she acted with the cunning of a desperate animal. She gathered up her purse and Alisa's bathing suit and walked out of the Gore home. She then drove to her own home, where she changed her clothing, making sure to wear clothes similar to what she had been wearing when she killed Betty. Candy returned to the church, rejoined her children and friends, and went through the remainder of the day in a routine manner.

Back at 410 Dogwood St., Betty Gore lay butchered in her utility room. Little Bethany lay crying in her crib. Candy had left behind a bloody fingerprint on the refrigerator door and a bloody footprint on the kitchen floor.

That evening, Allan Gore phoned his wife from St. Paul, Minnesota. There was no answer. After several such calls, he contacted neighbors, who entered his home and discovered Betty's body.

Initially, homicide detectives believed a psychopath had killed the Texas housewife in broad daylight in her own home. The transient appeared to have taken a shower after the murder. The undersized bloody footprint on the kitchen floor indicated that the killer had been a very small man.

Allan Gore was routinely questioned by police about his married life. He revealed that he had had a prolonged affair with Candy Montgomery. Although there was no question that Allan was in St. Paul at the time of the crime and could not have been physically involved in the killing, there was great suspicion that he and Candy had conspired to kill Betty. However, a polygraph test and the ensuing investigation proved that Allan was telling the truth. He was guilty of adultery, but had not been involved in his wife's murder.

Candy Montgomery's fingerprints were checked against the bloody fingerprint on he refrigerator door. They were identical. Candy was arrested and charged with the murder of Betty Gore. She testified in her own defence, revealing her affair with Allan. She shocked the court by admitting that she had an affair with another man after she and Allan broke up.

Candy's attorneys argued that, despite the promiscuity of their client, despite her attempts to camouflage her crime, she was not guilty of murder. They claimed that at the time of the frenzied struggle for the axe, Candy was acting in self-defence.

The Texas jury evidently believed Candy's version of the life and death struggle which had taken place in the utility room of the Gore home. They found her not guilty.

Two months after Candy's acquittal, the Montgomerys left Texas. Three months after the conclusion of Candy's murder trial, Allan Gore married a sympathetic supporter, whom he had dated during the trial.

DUTCH TREAT
Trio rehearsed murder of their pal

This is the story of four Dutch boys and how three of them deliberately planned the murder of the fourth. The three perpetrators of the crime, ranging in age from 15 to 17, were so cool and calculating that they even staged a murder rehearsal before the actual killing took place.

Theo Mastwijk, 14, was no angel. He did so poorly at the school he attended in his hometown of Soest, Holland, that there was some talk of having him transferred to our equivalent of a reform school. When a government official met with Theo's father and discussed the transfer, the boy promised to straighten out.

Theo was scared silly, but that didn't stop him from getting into more trouble. Using a borrowed motorcycle, he raced through the streets of Soest. In Holland it is against the law for anyone under the age of 16 to ride a motorcycle. Theo was picked up by police. In order to save his own skin, he told them that a buddy of his named Hendrick had stolen some paint. Theo was photographed in his loud shirt with its distinctive pattern and sent home. In the ensuing weeks, he took part in several small robberies in the area. He was suspected by police, but, as they had no proof, he was never taken into custody.

Theo had met Hendrick at a teenage snack bar in Soest.

Although Theo was two years younger than Hendrick, he was accepted as an equal by the older boy because of his reputation.

Hendrick was a bright, intelligent lad, if somewhat aloof and cold. He disliked animals and was often reprimanded for breaking the beaks of ducks. On one occasion, he strangled a cat. In the summer of 1959, his family moved two miles north of Soest to Baarn.

A hundred years earlier, when Holland was one of the chief commercial powers of the world, many wealthy Dutch industrialists built mansions in Baarn. By 1959, several of these mansions had been converted into institutions or divided into offices. Some were still partially in use as homes.

Hendrick became friends with two schoolmates, Boudewijn, 17, and his brother Evout, 15. Boudewijn and Evout lived in one of the old mansions set on five acres of well-kept grounds. The rather unattractive structure contained 30 rooms, not counting closets, bathrooms and cellars. Ten rooms had been partitioned and were in use as offices. The boys' family lived in the rest of the house, although some of the rooms were not entered for months at a time. Topping off the mansion was a small dome.

Hendrick, Boudewijn and Evout were inseparable. They attended school together. One was rarely seen without the other two. No one remembers how it started or who was the first to suggest it, but somehow the boys decided to steal for the sheer adventure of the exercise. Of course, this was old hat for Hendrick, who had often broken into warehouses.

One pleasant summer night in June, 1960, Hendrick forced open the window of a warehouse in Soest. He and Evout climbed in. Boudewijn acted as lookout. Soon the three boys were scampering away with tins of peaches, apricots and strawberries. Nothing had ever tasted as good.

Three weeks later, the police called on Hendrick. Their inquiries had nothing to do with the recent warehouse robbery. It had come to their attention that sometime earlier, a quantity of paint had been stolen. Hendrick was offended at being accused. After questioning him for an hour, the police left.

Meanwhile that summer, Theo was being harrassed by police. They were sure he was responsible for a series of minor robberies. Theo knew that it was only a matter of time before he would be picked up. He discussed the matter with friends. Everyone agreed that he should eventually try to get out of Holland. In the meantime, he should at least leave his home. Several of Theo's acquaintances were very interested in his predicament, since he made no bones about the fact that if he was picked up, his only way of staying out of jail would be to inform on friends in exchange for his freedom.

Rumors of Theo's dilemma reached Hendrick. He discussed the matter with Boudewijn and Evout. While Theo posed no threat to the brothers, they knew that he and Hendrick had taken part in burglarizing warehoues. To protect their friend, they offered to hide Theo in their parents' mansion.

On the night of June 23, the three boys escorted Theo up through the mansion to a room under the dome. The boys had equipped the room with an old mattress and a night pan. Theo, who had never before met the two brothers, was grateful. Each day the brothers would share their food with Theo or would steal food from their parents' pantry. The plan was to hide Theo until the search for him died down. He would then be smuggled across the border into Belgium. Theo was to stay in his hiding place for 40 days.

Life went on outside the mansion. The school term drew to a close. The boys took summer jobs. Sometimes, for the fun of it, they would rob a warehouse. June gave way to July.

The three boys often discussed Theo. What if their plan worked and they were successful in smuggling him into Belgium? What was to stop Theo from returning? Now Boudewijn and Evout were implicated as well. It seemed to them that more drastic measures had to be taken. They decided, plain and simple, to kill Theo Mastwijk.

An overdose of sleeping pills would be the best method. No blood, no fuss. It had to be done before Aug. 2, when the two brothers were scheduled to leave on vacation to Nauchatel with their parents. A deep grave was dug in the back-yard. Quicklime was easily stolen from a construction site. All was in readiness. An entire box of sleeping pills was dissolved in a bottle of beer. Theo was grateful as usual. The three boys left the dome. When they returned two hours later to pick up the body, they were shocked to find Theo alive and well. The pills had made him nauseous and caused him to vomit.

Why was there not a more extensive search conducted for Theo Mastwijk? It was a matter of luck. Hendrick and a friend had asked a lorry driver if they could accompany him to Antwerp for a visit. The lorry driver agreed. Before the two boys arrived in Antwerp, they quarrelled and separated. Hendrick returned to Soest alone. Police showed the lorry driver a photograph of the missing Theo Mastwijk. The lorry driver swore he was the boy he had dropped off in Antwerp. The search for Theo was called off. He had obviously left the country.

The three boys were more intent than ever on killing Theo. Hendrick obtained a piece of pink clothesline rope. He prac-tised on each brother, looping the rope over their heads from behind. They, in turn, used Hendrick as a model. It seemed easy enough.

On Aug. 1, 1960, Theo was told the time had come for him to be smuggled out of the country. He dressed rapidly, putting on the distinctive shirt he loved so well. It was mid-night. The brothers' parents were out of the mansion. Down a series of winding steps, Theo followed his friends.

Once out in the garden, Boudewijn held Theo's hands while Hendrick quickly slung the rope around Theo's neck and pulled with all his might. The rope tightened and then slipped out of his hands. Hendrick picked up a shovel and struck Theo on the head over and over until he lay still. Then he and Boudewijn lowered Theo into his grave, poured quicklime over the body and covered it with earth. Evout, who had stood watch, was delighted with the night's work. Next day, the brothers went on vacation with their parents.

Months passed. Hendrick left Baarn and obtained employment in Limberg. Boudewijn and Evout did well at school that year. Boudewijn graduated and enrolled at the University of Amsterdam.

On Oct. 27, 1961, 15 months after the murder, a plumber, repairing an underground pipe discovered the skeletal remains of Theo Mastwijk. The discovery caused a sensation throughout Holland. A small scrap of the victim's shirt found with the skeleton was the only clue police had to aid in the identification of the victim. They went back into their old files and found that Theo Mastwijk had been reported missing a year and a half earlier. He had once driven a motorcycle while underage and had been photographed by police. There, in the picture, was the boy wearing a distinctively patterned sport shirt. The shirt was identical to the scrap of shirt found with the body. According to the missing person's report, a boy named Hendrick had been the last person to see Theo alive.

Hendrick was located, questioned, and immediately confessed. Boudewijn and Evout were picked up and confessed as well. Their trial, which revealed in chilling detail the cold-blooded actions of the participants, held Holland spellbound for months. The three boys agreed to all the particulars of their deadly scheme, with one exception. Hendrick claimed that it was Boudewijn who delivered the deadly blows to Theo's head with the shovel, while Boudewijn claimed it was Hendrick who actually struck the blows. It matters little. Both boys were found equally responsible.

On April 11, 1963, sentences were passed on the three defendants. Hendrick was sentenced to nine years imprisonment, Boudewijn to nine years as well. Evout, who had been 15 at the time of the murder, was sentenced to six years imprisonment.

VELMA'S POISONOUS WAYS
First woman executed in U.S. in 24 years

Kind, generous, caring. These are the words used by acquaintances to describe Velma Barfield. Members of her own family describe her as "a wonderful mother" and "a loving grandmother". Well, folks, Velma may have been all these things. Unfortunately, she was also a cold-blooded murderer.

Margie Velma Bullard first saw the light of day in Sampson County, North Carolina on Oct. 23, 1932. Velma's daddy worked in a cotton mill, which only afforded the Bullards and their eight children the necessities of life.

When Velma was 17, she dropped out of the eleventh grade, ran away with Pepsi Cola truck driver Thomas Burke and became Mrs. Burke. Thomas was 16. The Burkes settled in the small town of Parkton (pop. 500), where Velma gave birth to her children, Kim and Ron.

For 15 years, the Burke family led a normal, happy existence. Then disaster struck and marital harmony flew out the window. Thomas lost his position with the Pepsi organization. This revolting turn of events was followed by a car accident in which Thomas received head injuries. At loose ends, without employment, Thomas took to the devil rum. Just for fun he sometimes passed the time of day by beating Velma.

Not one to let grass grow under her feet, Velma had Thomas admitted to the Dorothea Dix Hospital in Raleigh, N.C. In an attempt to hold her family together, she obtained employment in a department store in Fayetteville. When Thomas was discharged from hospital, he continued his abusive ways right up until 1969. He stopped then and with good reason.

One night he went to bed smashed to the gills. He was smoking at the time and apparently succeeded in setting the bed on fire. By the time help arrived, Thomas had swigged his last slug and puffed on his last cigarette. Many believe our Velma assisted her husband to his great reward, but we have no proof of the validity of this accusation, so we mention it only in passing. Velma always denied giving Thomas the great push.

Velma's second husband, Jennings Barfield, whom she married two years after Thomas' demise, didn't fare nearly as well as Thomas. He lasted only six months. Doctors declared that Jennings died of natural causes. His heart stopped beating. Velma always maintained that she had absolutely nothing to do with Jennings' big step to the other side.

Now, then, these untimely deaths did nothing for Velma's nerves. She began taking tranquillizers to calm herself down. What's a girl to do when the darn things fail to have their desired effect? She upped the dosage. I mean right up there until she became a bona fide pill addict.

Her two teenage children did everything to discourage Velma's self-destruction. They poured pills down sink drains, into toilets, anything to get their mother off the capsules. Velma was furious. She berated her children and found new hiding places for her stash.

Despite her consuming passion for pills, Velma had one other driving force in her life. She attended church three times a week and taught Sunday school at the First Pentacostal Holiness Church.

A steady supply of drugs doesn't come cheap. Velma was having an increasingly difficult time financing her habit. In 1974 she obtained a $1000 loan from the Commercial

Credit Corp., posing as her mother, Lillie Bullard. The fat was in the fire. Velma knew very well her 64-year-old mother would raise Cain when she learned of the deception. How to avoid a scene and very possibly a jail sentence? Simple. Velma sashayed down to the local hardware store and bought a supply of a handy little product called Ant Terro.

That very evening Velma placed a liberal quantity of the arsenic-based ant exterminator into mother's soup. For good measure, she shook a dash into mother's Coke as well. That was it. Mother didn't survive the night. Her death was attributed to natural causes.

Two years later, Velma found herself employed as a live-in maid for 85-year-old Dollie Edwards. While in Dollie's employ, Velma's star shone brightly. God fearing, churchgoing Velma took exceptional care of the elderly lady and her home. She became more a member of the Edwards family than an employee. Her kindness impressed Stuart Taylor, Dollie Edwards' nephew.

Now Stuart was something of a drinker, but under Velma's influence he swore off Johnny Barleycorn and commenced to accompany Dollie and Velma to church, not once but thrice a week. Stuart was in the process of divorcing his wife and told everloving Velma he would soon be free to marry her if she would have him. Velma said yes.

In February, 1977, Dollie Edwards felt poorly. No wonder. Velma had been up to her old tricks. This time it was a concoction called Singletary Rat Killer. Dollie took three days to die. Velma cried and cried and cried. At the cemetery she cried some more. It was touching.

Every cloud has a silver lining. The pastor of Velma's church heard that Velma was at loose ends. He highly recommended her to Mrs. Margie Lee Pittman, who was at that very moment looking for a live-in housekeeper for her parents, 80-year-old John Henry Lee and Record Lee, 75. What luck! Mrs. Pittman hired Velma.

With all this action taking place, we mustn't forget that Velma still required her pills on a daily basis. Her $75 a week salary simply didn't cover her pill purchases. One day she found a blank cheque in the Lees' home. Velma couldn't resist the temptation. She forged Mrs. Lee's name on a $50 cheque. Folks, Velma was sorry the day after she forged that cheque. Surely, old man Lee would run to the police as soon as the forgery was discovered.

Back to the cure-all — arsenic-based Ant Terro. Within a month John Henry was gone. An astute medic signed the death certificate "acute gastroenteritis". Velma was a rock. She accompanied Mrs. Lee to the cemetery.

With John Henry gone, it just wasn't the same. Velma changed jobs, accepting employment at the Lumberton United Care Rest Home, who were delighted to obtain her services.

These were exciting times for Velma. Gainfully employed, she looked forward to her upcoming marriage to Stuart Taylor. Life was coming up roses, but darn it all, a girl has to have her drugs. Velma took a chance. She forged and cashed two small cheques in Stuart's name. The first time he was mad. The second time he was furious and told Velma in no uncertain terms that if she ever forged another cheque he would turn her over to the police and that would be the end of the marriage plans. Velma couldn't live without her pills. She cashed a third cheque. Once again, someone had to die. It was Stuart Taylor's turn.

On the way home from a Rex Humbard revival meeting with Stuart, Velma dropped into a drugstore and picked up a supply of old reliable Ant Terro. That evening she spiked Stuart's beer with the poison. For three days Stuart convulsed in agony while Velma continued to feed him arsenic. On day four Stuart died. Cause of death — acute gastroenteritis.

Velma's luck didn't hold. Stuart had a family who couldn't understand how a healthy, robust man could expire in four days. They demanded an autopsy, which indicated arsenic poisoning as the cause of death.

Velma, the only person with Stuart during the last days of his life, was immediately suspected. She confided to her son that she had indeed killed Stuart. Ronnie Burke accompanied his mother to the police station. Under questioning, Velma shocked her interrogators by admitting to the murders of her mother Lillie Bullard, Dollie Edwards, John Henry Lee, and Stuart Taylor. She never did admit to poisoning husbands Thomas Burke or Jennings Barfield.

Velma stood trial for the murder of fiance Stuart Taylor, was found guilty and sentenced to death. On Nov. 2, 1984, after spending six years on Death Row, Velma Barfield was wheeled into a specially constructed chamber at Central State Prison in Raleigh, N.C., where massive quantities of procuranium bromide were pumped into her veins. She was the first woman to be executed in the U.S. in over 22 years.

GUYANA MASSACRE
Poison in the Kool-Aid

Who can forget the horrific photographs of the more than 900 corpses decomposng in the intense heat of the Guyana jungle? Almost nine years have passed since that Nov. 18, 1978 when vague news dispatches hinted at the mass suicide of some obscure religious cult in a jungle commune. The dispatches also alluded to the possible murder of a United States congressman.

The individual behind the horror story, which was soon to make headlines around the world, was the Reverend Jim Jones.

Jones was born in Lynn, Indiana in 1931. He was the son of an army veteran who was gassed in the First World War. Jones' father was an enthusiastic member of the Ku Klux Klan.

In 1951, the 20-year-old Jones attended Butler University, a school operated by the Disciples of Christ. He took courses at Butler off and on for the next 10 years, receiving his B.S. degree in education in 1961. However, in 1958, Jones founded his own interdenominational Christian Assembly of God Church. By 1960, his Peoples' Temple, located in Los Angeles, was a bona fide congregation of the Disciples of Christ, which had a membership of almost a million and a half, mostly living in the midwest states.

From 1961 to 1963, Jones performed missionary work in Brazil, organizing orphanages. There is evidence that he visited Guyana while in South America and, quite possibly, it was during this period that the seeds of his own colony in the jungle took root in his mind.

Upon his return from Brazil, Jones displayed a degree of entrepreneurial acumen by forming two non-profit organizations with headquarters in Indianapolis. The Wings of Deliverance was organized to spread the word of God, while the Jim-Lu-Mar Corp. was formed to purchase every money-making venture that was available. The latter company's elongated name was made up of his own first name as well as that of his mother, Lynette, and wife, Marceline.

During the sixties, Jones operated out of Ukiah, a small town located about 100 miles north of San Francisco. His headquarters, known simply as the Peoples' Church, became a money-making machine. The strategically located church afforded Jones and his followers the opportunity to swoop down on weekends to San Francisco and Los Angeles to spread the word, win followers, and raise hard cash.

Sometimes the group would return to headquarters richer by as much as $40,000. Members of the congregation turned over their social security cheques to Jones. As the flock grew, so did the routine amount of cash flowing into the church's coffers. Many members, completely enraptured with the charismatic Jones, turned over their entire life savings. Some cashed in their life insurance policies. Others moved into the church's dormitories to live.

Jones wasn't above slick hucksterism. Photographs of "The Father", as he was now called by his followers, were considered to have healing powers. These bogus medical aids fetched a pretty penny, as did other religious artifacts.

In 1971, Jones purchased a former synagogue and moved the centre of his operations to San Francisco. The Peoples' Temple held their opening service with much fanfare. Scores of gospel singers raised their voices in praise of the Lord. Angela Davis spoke. The Peoples' Temple appeared to be a model of what God fearing folks could achieve. It boasted a

151

day-care centre, an infirmary, a printing press, a carpentry shop and facilities to feed hundreds of the poor each day.

Soon, the devoted congregation and its dynamic leader were being lauded by the media as a fine example of an efficiently operated pure charity. Jones' photograph, depicting him handing over sizeable cheques to worthwhile causes, often appeared in the press. His now 8000-member church also became politically powerful. At the snap of a finger, Jones could muster hundreds of followers to work on a political campaign. Many dignitaries wooed the religious leader, sometimes for manpower, sometimes for substantial donations.

In 1973, Jones dispatched 20 members of the Peoples' Church to Guyana, with the express purpose of finding a site for an agricultural mission. A year later, Father Jones leased 27,000 acres in the jungle near the town of Port Kaituma from the government of Guyana. The commune was called Jonestown after its founder.

As the colony was populated, glowing reports were received by relatives back in the States. Crops were flourishing, housing was more than adequate, and above all, the individual freedom that the disciples enjoyed was lauded by all. The Minister of Foreign Affairs for Guyana reported on Jonestown, "Peace and love in action."

In 1975, Rev. Jim Jones was named one of the most outstanding clergymen in the U.S. by an interfaith organization, Religion in American Life. The following year he was named "Humanitarian of the Year" by the Los Angeles *Herald*. That same year he was appointed to the San Francisco Housing Authority by his good friend, Mayor George Moscone. In January, 1977, Jones received the annual Martin Luther King Jr. Humanitarian Award.

In the midst of this praise, there were some ominous rumblings. A few members dropped out of the congregation. Others sued, claiming they were brainwashed, beaten and stripped of their wealth. A handful of journalists made their way to Jonestown. Their stories were far from complimentary. They told of poor living conditions and disillusioned members. After their reports appeared in California papers, many of these journalists were threatened. The adverse publicity initiated an investigation of the commune by the government of Guyana. They reported "Not one confirmation of an allegation of mistreatment."

California Congressman Leo Ryan, 53, was serving his fourth term when he became interested in the Jonestown commune and reports that its members were being abused and being denied their civil rights. He decided to look into the matter.

This was not Ryan's first excursion into a high profile, well-publicized investigation. It was he who strongly and successfully petitioned for the release from prison of his constituent Patty Hearst. In 1965, he made a trip to Newfoundland and came away denouncing the hunting of seal pups. The International Wild Life Foundation named him Man of the Year for that effort.

Ryan's entourage, including aides, lawyers, a Guyanese government official, newspaper reporters and a T.V. crew from NBC landed at the closest airstrip, Port Kaituma. Only Ryan and four members of his party were allowed to proceed immediately to Jonestown. The remainder of the entourage were made to wait four hours before they too were transported over the muddy single lane road to Jonestown.

Initial impressions of the commune were favorable. Food appeared to be plentiful. The Ryan group clapped to gospel music as they finished a pleasant meal. Members of the congregation conversed with Congressman Ryan. They told him they were experiencing the happiest years of their lives. Throughout the informal introduction to Jonestown, benevolent Father Jim Jones presided, voluntering his views when asked.

Later, only Ryan and his four original party members were allowed to spend the night at the commune. The balance were transported back to Port Kaituma in a dump truck. Next morning they returned to Jonestown and were escorted around the compound by Marceline Jones. Impressive nurseries and classrooms were shown to the newsmen. Curiously, some buildings were shut tight. Newsmen were were told the inhabitants were sleeping and were not to be disturbed.

Questioned by the reporters, Jones denied the veracity of the bad press he had lately received back in the U.S. He vehemently denied the allegations by former members of his flock of poor treatment. During the questioning, word drifted down to Jones and his interrogators that several members of the commune wanted to leave with Congressman Ryan and his group. Jones flew into a rage. Tension mounted. But no one prevented the dissident members from leaving.

As Ryan talked to the disturbed Jones, a member of the commune pulled a knife and attempted to stab the congressman. While he was being disarmed, the attacker was wounded. Much blood was spilled on Ryan, who was noticeably shaken by the experience.

Finally, Ryan, his entourage of officials, newsmen and defectors, boarded the dump truck for the return trip to the airstrip at Fort Kaituma. Later, newsmen were to state that at this point they believed that Jones was an unstable character, but they were under the impression that he was sincere in his desire to do good for his fellow man. True, there were some flaws to Jonestown, but that was to be expected. Sixteen homesick dissidents out of 900 members was not out of the ordinary. No one seemed to be there against their will, no one appeared to be mistreated.

We can only surmise at the state of mind of Jim Jones. Unstable, paranoid Jones believed the adverse publicity generated by the stories the newsmen would file would spell the ruination of his colony in the jungle. He also believed that the dissidents who joined Ryan and his group were only the beginning of a wave of dissension that would sweep Jonestown. He determined to force the world to sit up and take notice.

The small planes landed at the Fort Kaituma airstrip to take the visitors home. The dump truck which had originally carried the Ryan group to the landing strip pulled up with a tractor and flatbed. The truck parked, but the tractor towing the flatbed drove up between the two aircraft. Suddenly, the men on the tractor and flatbed opened fire. Airplane tires were punctured. Jonestown defector Patricia Parks lay dead. Also killed in the rain of gunfire were San Francisco *Examiner* photographer Greg Robinson, NBC cameraman Bob Brown, NBC correspondent Don Harris, and Congressman Leo Ryan. Others were wounded, some severely.

While the Guyanese police looked on from a distance, one of the defectors pointed out that Larry Layton, posing as a defector, had opened fire on his fellow commune brothers. When uninjured Dick Dwyer, head of the U.S. Embassy in Georgetown, Guyana, and himself a member of the ill-fated mission, was told this, he insisted that the police arrest Layton on the spot.

The slow-to-react Guyanese police, together with soldiers, assisted the wounded. After a night of horror, the Ryan party was flown to safety in Georgetown.

Back in Jonestown, an unbelievable scenario was taking place. Cyanide was mixed with Kool-Aid and quickly distributed to members of the commune. Mothers forced the liquid down their children's mouths. No one refused to take the poison. Black and white, young and old, people who had fled the ghettoes and streets of America for the jungles of Guyana, were committing mass suicide. They had followed their charismatic leader, who had promised them a better life. Instead, he led them to death. All 913 died.

On Dec. 2, 1986, 41-year-old Larry Layton was convicted of conspiring to murder a U.S. congressman. He faces life imprisonment. He was the only person ever tried for the incident which took a total of 918 lives.

A WOMAN SCORNED
Mrs. Harris and the Diet Doctor

In 1965, Jean and James Harris were divorced. James later died, leaving Jean to raise two young sons.

Mrs. Harris was no ordinary woman. An honors graduate of prestigious Smith College, she embarked on a teaching career which culminated in 1977, when she was appointed headmistress of exclusive Madeira School in McLean, Virginia. Cultured, witty, pleasing to the eye, Jean Harris appeared to be the consummate career woman who had carved out a happy, interesting life for herself.

Dr. Herman Tarnower, the son of Russian-Jewish immigrants, graduated from Syracuse University to become a successful suburban physician. He owned his own medical clinic in Scarsdale, N.Y. and a large home in nearby Purchase. Two servants, Suzanne and Henri van der Vrekens, lived at the doctor's Purchase estate and took care of his day to day needs.

In 1979 Dr. Tarnower received world-wide recognition when he published his best-selling book, *The Complete Scarsdale Medical Diet*. Tarnower had been a wealthy man for years. With the acclaim his book received, he achieved celebrity status.

Back in 1966, Mrs. Harris met Dr. Tarnower at a party in New York. Soon she became lover and companion to the urbane, cultured doctor. Their relationship involved more than pillow talk. Herman Tarnower and Jean Harris travelled the world for months at a time. Jean held court as the doctor's hostess at intimate dinner parties. She often stayed at the Purchase estate for weeks.

Mrs. Harris was then and is today, by her own admission, madly in love with Hy Tarnower. The relationship over the years, while it appeared idyllic, was a fragile thing. Tarnower, a confirmed bachelor, was a completely self-centered man. Jean knew deep down that she would be his lover and companion only as long as she complied with his every whim and idiosyncrasy.

There is nothing new about the love triangle which slowly but insidiously developed. The other woman was Lynne Tryforos, a good looking nurse-secretary at Tarnower's Scarsdale Clinic.

Tarnower did little to conceal his intimacy with the younger woman. Mrs. Harris would find Lynne's nightclothes hanging in what she felt was her closet at the doctor's home. The servants would volunteer that Lynne had spent several nights with the doctor. In 1979, Dr. Tarnower vacationed with Mrs. Harris in Palm Beach. When he returned he took Lynne Tryforos on vacation to Montego Bay.

On the March night in 1980 when violence erupted to change the lives of all the members of our triangle forever, Jean Harris was 56, Lynne Tryforos was 37, and Dr. Tarnower was a healthy, vigorous 69.

There was nothing unusual about the beginning of Hy Tarnower's last evening on this good earth. Dinner was served by Suzanne van der Vrekens. Lynne and an acquaintance, Debbie Raizes, were guests. The meal broke up early and the two women left at approximately 8:30 p.m. Dr. Tarnower retired. Henri van der Vrekens, who had prepared the evening meal, also went to bed. Suzanne chose to watch television and paint a watercolor.

That afternoon, Dr. Tarnower had received a rather annoying call from Mrs. Harris in Virginia. She had asked to visit with him that very night. He tried to shake her off. "It would be more convenient if you came tomorrow." Mrs. Harris pleaded, "I can't talk to you tomorrow, Hy. Please, just this once let me say when." Tarnower replied, "Suit yourself."

Mrs. Harris left for Purchase, N.Y. in the Madeira School's blue Chrysler. It was a five hour drive. Beside her on the front seat lay a loaded .32 calibre Harrington and Richardson revolver she had purchased over a year earlier. As she drove through a storm, Mrs. Harris might have been thinking of the lengthy letter she had written Tarnower earlier that day. The letter, which belittled Lynne Tryforos in no uncertain terms, would later be used to provide motive for what was to follow.

Mrs. Harris arrived at Tarnower's Purchase estate after a tedious drive. She let herself in through a garage door which she knew was always open and made her way to the doctor's bedroom, a room she had shared with him many times over the past 14 years.

Five shots were fired. Four found their mark. Tarnower was hit in the hand, right shoulder, right arm and downward through the back, puncturing his lung and kidney.

Suzanne van der Vrekens ran to the doctor's bedroom and found him in his blood-splattered tan pyjamas. She raised the alarm, but by the time Tarnower reached a hospital, he was pronounced dead.

Mrs. Harris was arrested and stood trial for her lover's murder. Initially, as the facts of the case were revealed, there was a great deal of sympathy for the defendant. It was obvious that she had felt threatened when Tarnower turned from her in favor of a younger woman. It was also apparent that the famed doctor had treated her in a cavalier fashion.

Perhaps Mrs. Harris should not have taken the witness stand in her own defence. Many believe she was responsible for her own undoing. She stated that she had not intended to shoot the doctor. It had all been a horrible mistake. She had travelled to Purchase to see him one more time before taking her own life. As she said, "I hoped it would be a quiet, pleasant last few minutes." But it was not to be.

Tarnower was asleep when Mrs. Harris entered his bedroom. When he awakened, he was in no mood to chat. Frustrated, Mrs. Harris picked up a box of curlers and threw them through a window. Tarnower, in a rage, struck her across the face. She threw a cosmetic box. He struck her a second time. Sarcastically, she invited him to strike her again. He walked away.

Calmly, Mrs. Harris opened her purse and took out her .32 calibre revolver. She raised the gun, pointed it at her head, and pulled the trigger. At that exact moment, "Hy came at me and grabbed the gun and pushed my hand away from my head and pushed it down, and I heard the gun explode."

This first shot went through the doctor's hand. The gun dropped to the floor. Tarnower went to the bathroom to tend his hand. Mrs. Harris found the revolver on the floor, just as Tarnower reappeared. He lunged at her as she picked up the revolver. Once again, it fell to the floor. Tarnower picked it up.

Mrs. Harris then begged for the gun, "Hy, please give me the gun or shoot me yourself, but for Christ's sake let me die." He replied, "Jesus, you're crazy, get out of here."

Mrs. Harris grabbed the revolver now resting on Tarnower's lap. Tarnower jumped on her as she fell back on the bed. Mrs. Harris felt the muzzle against her stomach. She pulled the trigger but felt no pain as the gun exploded. Tarnower fell back. Mrs. Harris claimed that she placed the gun to her head, and despite continually pulling the trigger, the revolver didn't go off, although it did fire once more when she tested it away from her head.

Her wish to die was not due to Tarnower's attention to other women, Mrs. Harris claimed, but because of a deep personal and career trauma which made death more attractive than a truly exhausting life.

At her trial, prosecution attorneys stated that Mrs. Harris was the typical study of the woman scorned. Her motive was there for all the world to see in her poorly timed letter to Dr. Tarnower, in which she obviously illustrated her hatred toward her younger rival for the diet doctor's affection. She had five hours of driving with a revolver in her possession before she entered Tarnower's house, plenty of time for a calm mind to take hold of the situation.

Mrs. Harris was found guilty of second degree murder and sentenced to a minimum of 15 years imprisonment. All appeals since her conviction have failed. She is currently serving her sentence at a women's prison in Bedford Hill, N.Y.

ENOUGH IS ENOUGH
Nova Scotia housewife strikes back

Jane Stafford looked at the 280 lb. hulk of a man snoring in the cab of the family's half-ton Jeep truck, the man who had been the source of her hell on earth for five long years. Then she said to Allan, her 16-year-old son, "Get me a gun." Allan brought out a 12-gauge shotgun, passed it to his mother and returned to the house.

Jane, relating the sequence of events to me, stated, "I put the gun in the window of the cab and just fired."

It was the night of March 11, 1982 when Jane Stafford, 33, blew the head off Billy Stafford, her common-law husband. Jane didn't know that in the months to follow her case would be discussed across the nation. She didn't know that many would claim that she crystalized the plight of battered and abused women everywhere.

No — Jane knew only one thing that March evening. The beatings to herself, her family and her neighbors had to stop before Billy killed her or someone else.

Jane Stafford has not had an easy life. Born in Brooklyn, N.S., not more than 30 miles from Bangs Falls, she has rarely left the beautiful south shore area of Nova Scotia where she was born and raised. She vividly recalls her career Army father abusing her mother, so that later, when she became the victim of her second husband's abuse, she felt that this was the natural order of things.

Jane left school in Grade 9. She had married and given birth to her eldest son Allan by the time she was 15. For ten years she lived with an alcoholic husband. Her second son James was born before she obtained a divorce in 1976.

While still married, she met Big Billy Stafford, a friend of her husband's. Soon after her divorce she moved in with Billy.

For a short while, her common-law husband, a part-time fisherman and lumberman, treated her with some semblance of decency. Jane didn't know that Billy Stafford had already had two disastrous relationships with women. His first wife, Pauline, almost drowned when Billy submerged her head in a bucket of water. He terrorized their five children with lit cigarettes and knives until one day, while Billy was fishing, Pauline took off with her five children for Ontario. She never returned until after Billy's death.

Billy's next relationship with a woman fared no better. His first common-law wife left for Calgary after sampling Billy's lifestyle.

Now it was Jane's turn. Jane gave birth to Billy's son, Darren. When I met Darren, who is now six-years-old, he played hide and seek with me in the Nova Scotia Legal Aid offices.

From all outward appearances he is an attractive, normal youngster, but Darren's short life has been full of the trauma of literally having a monster for a father. When he was only two, his father would pick him up by the hair and hold him in the air before dropping the terrified child to the floor. Sometimes Billy would hold a gun to the boy's head and tell him, "I'm going to blow your head off." On other occasions he would hold a knife to the boy's throat.

Allan Ferrier, the Nova Scotia legal aid lawyer who defended Jane, told me, "Darren has received psychiatric treatment and counselling for almost two years and there is every reason to believe he will be fine. However, he shocked psychiatrists when he told them he wished he was as big as his father Billy and his father was as small as he, so that he could be mean to Billy like Billy was mean to him."

Billy directed his abuse towards Jane after Darren's birth. He had apparently wanted a girl and knew he wouldn't have one after Jane had a hysterectomy. Jane's life became a series of degrading acts and beatings.

When I met with Jane Stafford I thought one of her outstanding features was her flawless even white teeth. I mentioned this and was shocked at her reply, "Oh, they're all false. That happened when Billy kept striking me with the butt of his rifle until I was unconscious. My oldest son Allan found me on the floor and thought I was dead. The few teeth which weren't knocked out later had to be extracted by a dentist. I told the dentist I was in a car accident and struck my head on the steering wheel. I was laid up in bed for two weeks after that beating."

Coverups, such as lying to the dentist, served to isolate the life Jane was leading, but many knew the nature of the man with whom she was living. Most, if not all, were fearful for their lives if they messed around with Big Billy Stafford.

Once he forced the captain of a scallop dragger to bring his vessel to shore. Billy was charged with mutiny on that occasion, but in the end no one would testify against him. The charges were eventually dropped, but Billy found himself blacklisted by the fishing industry.

Sometimes friends would become the object of Billy's anger. For no apparent reason, he would beat them up and throw them out of his home. Once he beat up Jane's father. Soon friends stopped dropping in at the Staffords'.

Billy drank daily, used drugs, and terrorized anyone who crossed his path. Police were told to approach the Stafford home armed and with caution. They rarely did.

Just for fun Billy, who sometimes claimed he was placed on earth by the devil, would load the truck with his family and roar down the highway on the wrong side of the road. Eyes popping, mouth frothing, he laughed in the face of death while his passengers cringed in fear.

But it was against Jane that most of Billy's anger was directed.

On two occasions he fired his .22 calibre rifle at Jane, once while she was tending her garden and once while she was working in the house. Billy explained that he was just seeing how close he could come to her.

There were other, far worse, indignities and sexual abuses, some of which are so abhorrent that it is not necessary to repeat them here.

James escaped most of his stepfather's abuse as he stayed much of the time with Jane's parents. Allan was beaten up approximately once a week.

Why didn't Jane leave? Some way, somehow, taking such abuse herself and seeing her children terrorized, why didn't she simply run away?

Jane explained to me, as she earlier explained to the court, that Billy had often bragged to her that he had once murdered a man by throwing him overboard. In actual fact, a man was lost at sea while Billy was aboard, but nothing ever came of Billy's involvement. Billy assured Jane that if she ever left him he would kill her parents. Jane didn't doubt him for one minute.

Life went on. Big Billy called the shots and Jane and her children danced to his tune. There were rules. When you drove in the Jeep you were not allowed to get out before Billy. If you did, you were beaten. Some evenings Jane and Billy played cards. It was a strange game. If Jane played the wrong card she was beaten to the floor and made to struggle back onto her chair and continue playing. No Bible or prayer books were allowed in the Stafford home.

Most people knew that big Billy was in some state of drunkenness every day. They knew he got into minor scrapes with the law. Some, who asked to remain anonymous, thought that he might kill someone some day. But only Jane knew first hand the violence that was Billy Stafford.

During the last few years of her life with Billy, Jane was helped and consoled in her plight by Margaret Joudrey, an older woman who lived in a trailer adjacent to the Stafford property. For years Billy had been arguing over the boundary line between the two properties. When Margaret's common-law husband passed away without a will, it became a legal possibility that Margaret did not hold title to the property. Billy taunted his neighbor with this fact at every opportunity.

The turbulent existence that was Jane Stafford's life polarized on March 11, 1982. That morning, Billy rose early and worked in the woods with his eldest stepson, Allan, and Ronald Wamboldt, 44, an alcoholic who at that time was rooming with the Staffords. Wamboldt had often unintentionally displeased Billy, and he too had been the recipient of periodic beatings.

The men returned from the woods around noon and started drinking. By 4:30 p.m. Billy and Ron were drunk. Billy was becoming progressively wilder. They decided to visit a friend, Leona Anthony, in Charleston, five miles away. Darren and Allan were left at home. Jane drove the truck to Charleston, where the drinking continued.

By 8:30 that evening Ron Wamboldt was dead drunk. He remembers none of the events which took place that night. On the way home, Jane drove the Jeep. Ron sat next to the passenger door, while Billy was propped up in the middle. Billy bragged that once they got home he was going to burn out Margaret Joudrey. Then he would beat Allan to a pulp. No doubt it would be Jane's turn next.

Jane guided the truck onto the dirt road leading to her modest home. She pulled into the yard. Ron staggered out of the vehicle, entered the house and fell into bed. Billy was asleep in the cab. Jane hesitated before leaving the Jeep, knowing she would be breaking one of Billy's rules if she left the truck before he did.

Jane beeped the horn. When her son Allan appeared, she asked him to fetch a gun. She stepped down from the truck. Sixteen-year-old Allan gave his mother the shotgun and returned to the house. That's when Jane, by her own admission, figured, "To hell with it. I'm not going to live like this any more." She "put the gun in the window and just fired."

Billy Stafford would inflict no more indignities on his common-law wife. The shotgun blast had blown off his head.

Blood, pieces of bone, and brain fragments spattered the interior of the cab. Some blood splattered on Jane's clothing. Bits and pieces of Billy's skull lay on the cab floor.

Now in a dazed condition, Jane acted in an irrational manner. Jane Stafford, who had never harmed a living creature in her life, now shouted to her son to go to Margaret Joudrey's to phone her parents and tell them to meet her at nearby Charleston. She also told Allan to get rid of the shotgun. Without hesitation he threw it in the Medway River.

Jane jumped into the cab beside the bloody body of what had once been Billy Stafford and drove five miles to Charleston, where she met her parents. Jane merely parked the truck with its grisly cargo beside the road. She accompanied her parents to their home, changed her clothing, and had them drive her back to Bangs Falls. That night she stayed with her sons.

Next morning, a resident of the area, Carl Croft, walked past the truck and spotted the headless corpse. He contacted police. Later that day, when Jane was informed that Billy's body had been found, she fainted.

Three days after the shooting Jane Stafford was arrested and charged with first degree murder. A friend put her in touch with Allan Ferrier, a Nova Scotia legal aid lawyer.

Ferrier, 33, a graduate of Dalhousie Law School, had never been in private practice. His entire career had been spent with the province's legal aid department. The Stafford case was his second murder trial. His first defence in a murder case had resulted in an acquittal. Ferrier, a laid-back Maritimer, wears blue jeans and a t-shirt to the office. One gets the impression that the legal aid office in Bridgewater won't be able to hold bright, articulate Allan Ferrier much longer. He is a young man on the rise.

As I sat in Ferrier's office, he explained that he realized the Crown would allege that his client's life was not in danger at the time of the killing. After all, the victim was snoozing in the cab of his truck. However, Ferrier quoted Section 37 of the Criminal Code which reads, "Everyone is justified in using force to defend himself or anyone under his protection from assault, if he uses no more force than is necessary to prevent the assault or the repetition of it.'' Ferrier argued that Jane Stafford was defending her son, who was under her protection. She also had no other recourse, nowhere to turn, no one to help her.

The Nova Scotia jury of ten men and one woman had four verdicts to consider: guilty of first degree murder, guilty of second degree murder, guilty of manslaughter, or not guilty. They took 18 hours to find Jane Stafford not guilty. When the verdict was read, the crowded courtroom burst into applause. Scores of friends and spectators tried to hug Jane, slap her on the back, wish her well. It was as if abused women everywhere had won a moral victory.

Epilogue: Since her trial, Jane Stafford has taken an upgrading course with the Nova Scotia Department of Education and has received the equivalent of a Grade 12 certificate. She has also completed a nurses' assistant training course and is presently a certified nursing assistant at the Halifax County Regional Rehabilitation Centre in Dartmouth, N.S.

● ● ●

The Stafford case is no longer unique. On Dec. 8, 1982, James Clarkson, 44, of Durham Bridge, N.B. was found shot to death in his home. His wife Lana was charged with second degree murder. At Mrs. Clarkson's trial witnesses stated that the alcoholic Clarkson continually beat his wife and children. After deliberating a little over one hour, the jury found Lana Clarkson not guilty.

MIKE AND DORA
Dora strayed from the straight and narrow

Long before the Capones and the O'Banions ran the rackets in Chicago, another man, virtually unknown today, held the Windy City in the palms of his ham-like paws.

Big Mike McDonald specialized in gambling, politics and prostitution. Regardless of who actually practised these worthy pursuits, Mike skimmed off 60% of the take. Twenty percent was placed in a fund to pay off police and politicians, while the remaining 40% went into the private coffers of Big Mike McDonald.

In 1893, Mike backed Harvey Calvin for mayor of Chicago. When Calvin won, Mike became unofficial king of the city. His chain of gambling emporiums ran day and night. Mike also owned legitimate enterprises such as the extremely profitable newspaper, the Chicago *Globe*, as well as large portions of real estate in downtown Chicago.

Alas, while fortunate in the world of legitimate and illegitimate finance, Mike was unlucky in love. His first wife is a relatively unknown quantity since she was married to Mike before he rose to prominence in the rackets. We do know that she was not a faithful soul. To a man of Mike's strict Catholic background, a sin of this magnitude could not be tolerated. Before the fat fell squarely into the fire, Mrs. McDonald number one died of natural causes.

Mike married for the second time. The object of his affection was Mary Noonan, a winsome Irish colleen who immediately found herself in a pack of trouble.

The McDonalds lived in luxurious digs above one of Mike's gambling dens. One night the police, who should have known better, raided the gambling joint. A lone cop wandered upstairs into Mary's kitchen. That was a mistake. Mary shot him between the eyes without saying a word. Big Mike arranged to have Mary appear in front of a benevolent judge who stated, "The defendant was justified in killing the invader of her home."

Mary presented Mike with two fine offspring and he presented her with a huge mansion on Ashland Ave. complete with an army of servants. There would be no more nosy cops interrupting Mary while she puttered around in the kitchen.

Now, folks, you would think Mary would be content with her lot. She had everything a woman could desire, but she lacked one fulfilment which certain ladies desire. She wanted variety. Unknown to the most powerful man in Chicago, Mary was seeing minstrel singer Billy Arlington on the side.

In a moment of emotional impetuousness, Mary and Billy ran away. Initially Big Mike was devastated; then he was furious. He hired private detectives to track down the lovebirds. It didn't take long. They were found living in the Palace Hotel in San Francisco.

Mike raced to San Francisco, broke into his wife's suite, and pulled out a pistol, fully intending to kill Billy Arlington right then and there. Mary, good sport that she was, slipped between the two men and implored her husband not to do anything rash. Actually, she did more than implore. She begged and prayed. Mike saw the light, put away the pistol, gathered up the wayward Mary and returned to Chicago. All was forgiven.

Mike, a deeply religious man despite his nefarious enterprises, thought that a little religion would be good for what ailed Mary. He built her a beautiful chapel in their home and enlisted the aid of young Father Joseph Moysant to hear

Mary's rather lengthy confessions and minister to her spiritual needs each week.

Father Moysant ministered to more than Mary's spiritual needs. The pair took off and didn't stop until they reached Paris, France.

Mary and Joe lived in Paris for six years before the defrocked priest had second thoughts about the whole thing. He left Mary and entered a monastery. Mary returned home, but Mike, who had divorced her in the intervening years, refused to see her or let her see the two children. After all, enough is enough.

Mike was a glutton for punishment. He met buxom Dora Feldman and was truly smitten. There was a small problem. Dora was married to a professional baseball player named Sam Barcley. Not to worry. Mike would fix everything. He had a little chat with Sam, gave him $30,000 and told him to get a divorce. Sam said, "Right away, sir."

There is little doubt that Mike was deeply in love with Dora. In order to marry her he converted to the Jewish faith. For some time things went along just fine. Mike built a larger mansion for Dora than the one he had built for the now forgotten Mary. Furniture was imported from all over the world. Servants were hired. Dressmakers outfitted Dora with expensive gowns. A large bank account was placed at her disposal.

Would you believe that Dora wasn't the type to enjoy such luxuries? No, Dora proved to be a homebody. She shunned Chicago's night life and showed little inclination to spend money.

However, Dora was inclined in another direction. Webster Guerin was a tall blonde boy who lived down the street. He was 16. Initially, Dora inveigled the unsuspecting Webster into doing odd jobs around the McDonald mansion. It didn't take long before Webster was performing more personal tasks for Dora.

Folks, they were at it all the time. Big Mike would leave his stately home in the morning. Sneaky Webster would be in the sack with Dora before Mike was at his office. This state

170

of affairs didn't go on for a few weeks or months. No, siree, it went on for years.

Webster graduated from high school and college, all the while seeing Dora at every opportunity. When he graduated as a commercial artist, Dora put up the money for well-equipped offices for her lover.

It was a terrible blow to Dora's pride when rumors reached her ears that Webster had a girlfriend his own age whom he intended to marry. Private detectives verified her worst fears.

Dora confronted Webster. He confessed to his indiscretions but swore he would drop his girlfriend and return to Dora's side on an exclusive basis. That satisfied Dora for awhile. When once more she found out that Webster had taken up with another woman, she marched into his office on Feb. 21, 1907 and shot him twice, once in the stomach and once in the neck. Webster sunk to the floor, very dead.

Dora readily confessed to the police, not only relating details of the killing but of her lengthy affair with the victim. When news of the murder reached Big Mike, who was now 66-years-old, he was hurt beyond belief. He went to bed and stayed there for weeks. A born softie, he put up $50,000 bail for Dora, who showed up at his sickbed begging for forgiveness. Big Mike wouldn't speak to her. His condition worsened until he was taken to hospital, where he died on Aug. 9, 1907. Mike left Dora one third of his multi-million dollar estate. The balance was left to his two children.

In 1908, Dora stood trial for Webster's murder. After deliberating for over six hours the jury found her not guilty. Many believed that Big Mike's influence with judge and jury reached from the grave to bribe them into acquitting the one true love of his life, Dora Feldman McDonald.

A DUTIFUL DAUGHTER
Theresa never liked her mother

Fifteen-year-old Theresa Gresch never liked her mother. Still, that's no reason to assist in hitting her over the head with a hammer, stabbing her repeatedly and encasing her body in plaster of Paris.

Theresa's physical charms were those of a well-developed 22-year-old. She was like a frisky filly chafing at the bit to be serviced by the stallions on the other side of the fence.

Theresa's 43-year-old mother, hard-working Anna Gresch, had her own strict code of conduct. It didn't include lipstick, nylon stockings or low-cut blouses. Anna ran a tight ship. She had lost her husband some years before when Theresa was still a tyke. It wasn't easy in 1954 for a single parent to bring up a daughter in New York, particularly since Anna had to work all the time to keep the wolf from the door.

Anna put in eight hours on the assembly line at a shoe factory and worked an average of three nights a week as a charwoman in an office building. She and her daughter lived at Avenue B and 13th St. in Manhattan. It was three floors up to their cold water flat. In the half year they lived there Anna had fixed the place up and had purchased some furniture. Although it was slum living, their flat was clean and comfortable.

Although Theresa had a high I.Q. and attended high school, she had no interest in school work. Instead she craved the trappings of the mature woman. To Theresa this meant makeup, smart clothing and, above all, a boyfriend. She and her mother quarrelled over these little matters constantly.

On the night of Feb. 18, 1954, Theresa hit paydirt at a neighborhood dance. His name was Billy Snyder. Billy, an older man at 17, walked Theresa home. She poured out her tale of virginal woe. Billy understood. In fact, he could cure Theresa's particular malady for all time.

There were practical problems. Theresa's mother was between jobs in the char business and was home every night. Billy's mother was home ill, so his apartment was not available. For seven days the young couple wandered the streets of New York expressing their love for each other, but were at a complete loss as to where to consummate those sly biological urges which Theresa just had to satisfy. That sort of thing can be frustrating.

At last, Mrs. Gresch received a call to clean an office building. No sooner was she out the door than Billy scampered up those three flights of stairs into Theresa's arms and bed.

Wouldn't you know it? Mrs. Gresch finished work early. When she returned home there was Theresa, wearing nothing but a smile, in bed with Billy. Mrs. Gresch screamed, ranted and raved. Then she unceremoniously kicked Billy out of her home.

Mrs. Gresch and her wayward daughter had several heart to heart chats. It must be remembered that her daughter's welfare was the focal point of her life. When she pulled the reins too tightly, Theresa threatened to run away. A compromise was reached. Billy would be allowed in the Gresch home. In return, Theresa and Billy would refrain from doing whatever they did between the sheets.

The deal worked for exactly two weeks. On the night of March 4, Mrs. Gresch wearily dragged herself up the three flights of stairs to her home. She turned the key and walked in. This was too much. Those kids had no respect. They were at it again.

A terrific argument ensued. Billy picked up a hammer and struck Mrs. Gresch about the head several times. Blood gushing from her head, she staggered into the kitchen. Billy returned to Theresa's side in bed, but it was tough to concentrate with Mrs. Gresch moaning in the kitchen.

Annoyed, Billy jumped out of bed, surveyed the situation in the kitchen and asked for Theresa's assistance. Theresa passed Billy a knife. He proceeded to stab Anna Gresch 21 times. Together, the two teenagers mopped up the bloody floor and lifted the body into a laundry tub. Then they went to bed in peace and quiet.

Next morning, Theresa and Billy went shopping with $13 taken from Mrs. Gresch's purse. They bought a yellow light bulb to add atmosphere to their lovemaking. They also purchased some plaster of Paris, which they mistakenly thought would act as a decomposing agent if sprinkled over the body. For four consecutive nights they had friends over to the flat for dancing and a few beers. The door to the kitchen was kept closed.

On the fourth night of partying, a friend, Richie Aylward, commented that he detected a disagreeable odor coming from the kitchen. Billy explained, "It's Theresa's mother. I killed her and she's in there rotting away."

What are good friends for? Richie helped sprinkle some more plaster of Paris on the body. He told no one what he had learned that night.

On day five, Billy felt it was time to vacate the scene. He left the flat and enlisted in the Marines, stopping long enough to phone Theresa, asking her to wait for his return.

In the days which followed Theresa continued to throw the occasional party. When the urge struck her, she and good friend Richie made love. Theresa later pointed out that Richie was little more than a surrogate lover, keeping things warm, so to speak, for Billy's return.

The good times abruptly came to an end when neighbors complained to police of a disagreeable odor emanating from Apartment 3B. Investigating officers found the body of Anna Gresch, now encased in a solid layer of plaster of Paris.

Questioned by detectives, Theresa told the whole story. Billy was brought back to the Big Apple from Beaufort, South Carolina, where he was stationed with the Marines. Faced with Theresa's confession, Billy unhesitatingly told the police, "I did it." He mentioned that Theresa had passed him the knife with which he had stabbed Anna Gresch. Theresa had neglected to include this embarrassing bit of information.

While in custody, Billy wrote often to Theresa. One line is worthy of repetition. Billy wrote, "I killed your mother." Prosecuting attorneys thrill at confiscating letters like that.

The two teenagers were brought to trial. Theresa gained some measure of fame as the youngest person to be tried for murder in New York State.

Both accused repudiated their confessions, each changing pertinent details to cast the other as the true culprit. Billy now claimed that Theresa had killed her mother and had merely enlisted his help in washing the blood off the floor and encasing the body in plaster of Paris. His lawyer had a difficult time dismissing Richie Aylward's testimony and that incriminating letter.

Theresa, for her part, swore that she never passed Billy any knife. She claimed she was in bed when the dastardly deed took place in the kitchen.

Billy was found guilty of murder in the first degree, and Theresa of murder in the second degree. She was sentenced to 20 years to life in prison. After serving 14 years Theresa was released at the relatively young age of 30. Her present whereabouts are unknown.

Billy wasn't quite as fortunate. In January, 1956, after walking unassisted and chewing bubble gum, Billy Snyder was executed in Sing Sing's electric chair.

THE TEACUP PUZZLE
A not so typical tea party

On July 9, 1940, police were called to a pleasant upper middle class home in Matfield, Kent, England. The sight that greeted them was not a pleasant one. Three bodies were scattered about the garden.

Let's see, there were the occupants of the cottage, Mrs. Dorothy Fisher and her adult daughter Freda, as well as their maid, Mrs. Saunders. Mrs. Fisher and Freda had been shot while facing their attacker, while Mrs. Saunders had been mowed down from the rear. There was plenty of blood about the garden, but no sign of a weapon.

Scotland Yard detectives were called to the murder scene, where they observed a great deal of broken china and a tea tray near Mrs. Saunders' body. Each piece was gathered up and put together by the Yard's lab technicians. They ended up with four complete tea cups and saucers. A search of the garden area turned up one other clue, a woman's glove. The glove was tried on each body and did not fit.

Now, if you have been paying attention, you should by now have deduced, as Scotland Yard did, that a fourth woman had been present for tea and had shot the three victims just as tea was about to be served. Unknowingly, this fourth woman had left her glove behind.

Mrs. Fisher was separated from her husband, who lived on

a farm in Oxfordshire. He was immediately notified of his wife's death, but could offer no clue to her killer's identity. Detectives are sometimes known not to take a suspect's word at face value. They checked out Fisher's whereabouts on the day of the massacre and found that he was in his London office all that day. He could not possibly have been the killer.

They also discovered that Fisher was living with a 35-year-old widow, Mrs. Florence Ransome, but were disappointed to learn that Florence and Mrs. Fisher got along, as the British say, famously. Mrs. Ransome, who seemed to have the best of all worlds, often visited Mrs. Fisher. No one could ever remember a harsh word passing between the two women. Mrs. Ransome appeared to be in the clear.

Famed pathologist Sir Bernard Spilsbury added to the mystery by revealing that all three women had been shot with a single barrel shotgun, hardly a lady's weapon. The cunning killer, using the single action weapon, had to load and reload three times as she, or perhaps he, slew the hapless victims one by one. The killer also must have retrieved the shotgun casings, as none were found at the scene of the crime.

There you have it — broken teacups, retreived shell casings, a lady's glove, and all those bodies. In true Agatha Christie fashion, can we solve the mystery of who killed the three ladies in the garden? Let's get to it, shall we?

Detectives interviewed Mrs. Ransome. She stated quite simply that the Yard boys were barking up the wrong tree. She had been on the farm in Oxfordshire on July 9, the day of the multiple murder. She pointed out that it was impossible to travel from Oxfordshire to Matfield in one day. She tried on the glove found at the murder scene. While Mrs. Ransome thought it was decidedly small, everyone else thought it fit nicely.

Inquiries were made at the railway station. Detectives found that it was indeed quite possible to travel from Oxfordshire to Matfield and back in one day.

Things began to heat up for Mrs. Ransome. A hired hand on her farm told detectives that Mr. Fisher owned a .410

single barrel shotgun. On July 8, Mrs. Ransome had practised shooting on the farm. The next day, the all-important ninth, she was nowhere to be seen.

Mr. Fisher's shotgun was confiscated and taken back to the Yard's lab in London. Without the shotgun casings, it was impossible to ascertain if it was the murder weapon.

Detectives kept scratching and came up with a tradesman who identified Mrs. Ransome as the well-dressed lady he had seen lugging the unwieldly shotgun to the Matfield station on the day of the murder.

Motive, motive, we must have a motive. After all, what would Agatha think?

Delving deeper into Mrs. Ransome's past, those nosy Yard detectives discovered that although she appeared to be contented with her lot in life, she had confided to intimate friends that she dearly wanted to become Mrs. Fisher. As the original Mrs. Fisher was in extremely good health, she might very well have decided to kill the obstacle to her happiness.

Detectives figured Mrs. Ransome lugged the unwieldy shotgun to Mrs. Fisher's home. As all the tea party guests were well acquainted, she could have offered some excuse for having the shotgun with her, possibly taking it to a shop later for repairs.

When Mrs. Saunders brought in her tea tray, the carnage started. Mrs. Ransome had to shoot reload, shoot, reload, and shoot again. Mrs. Fisher was the prime target, but Mrs. Ransome planned to leave no witnesses. Freda and Mrs. Saunders had to die because they were there.

Mrs. Ransome then gathered up the three shotgun casings and left for her farm a Oxfordshire. She either never thought of the fourth cup on Mrs. Saunders' tray or simply didn't care. In the confusion and turmoil which must have taken place in that garden, Mrs. Ransome dropped one glove. She had to have a certain amount of guile to leave with the shotgun casings, which she probably threw off the train along with her one remaining glove on the way home.

On Nov. 8, 1940 Mrs. Ransome stood accused of multiple murder in England's famous Old Bailey. She pleaded not guilty. We have already mentioned the pertinent facts pointing to her guilt. The defence had other ideas.

Mrs. Ransome professed her innocence throughout. She claimed that she had not been in Matfield on July 9, and that the tradesman who had identified her was undoubtedly mistaken as so many eyewitnesses have been in the past. She claimed that malicious gossip of friends and neighbors was not proof of motive. Mrs. Ransome swore that she got along extremely well with Mrs. Fisher. It was true she had access to a .410 single action shotgun, but there were thousands of these guns in farmhouses throughout England.

The jury retired to reach their verdict. Surprisingly, they took only 47 minutes to find Mrs. Ransome guilty.

A panel of psychiatrists examined Mrs. Ransome and found her to be mentally ill. One might wonder why she didn't plead insanity, but it was thought by her lawyers that the act of retrieving the shell casings clearly demonstrated that she had her wits about her and knew very well at the time that what she was doing was wrong. The striker-pin marks on the casings would have definitely pointed to the murder weapon. Mrs. Ransome knew this and was intent on carrying away the casings from the scene of the crime.

Who knows, if it hadn't been for that fourth shattered teacup and the misplaced lady's glove, Scotland Yard might have concentrated their hunt on a man. Today, Mrs. Ransome might have been the second Mrs. Fisher, and at the age of 78, be a kindly little gray haired lady conducting tea parties of her own. Instead, she was detained in Broadmoor, an asylum for the criminally insane, where she died several years later.

CIRCUMSTANTIAL EVIDENCE
The killer knew his victim

It has been said that the best example of circumstantial evidence was expounded by an English judge, who pointed out that when Robinson Crusoe spotted Friday's fresh footprints in the sand on his desolate island, it was logical to assume that the island was occupied by a fellow human being. Despite the strength of circumstantial evidence, juries demand an abundance of such evidence before being convinced of a defendant's guilt.

A murder case which rested entirely on circumstantial evidence occurred in 1952 in the tiny English village of Barlaston, Staffordshire, a hamlet more famous for Wedgewood china than acts of violence.

At precisely 6:18 p.m. on Wednesday, July 16, 1952, Fred Wiltshaw, 59, returned home to find his wife Alice, 62, dead on the hall floor. The sight which greeted him was not a pleasant one. Alice was lying in a pool of her own blood. Her head had been bludgeoned beyond recognition. A bloody poker lay beside the body. A large earthen vase had been smashed to pieces. Quite possibly the vase had been brought down on the victim's head.

The Wiltshaw's hall led to the kitchen, which was in a shambles. The entire room was bloodstained. Two wooden logs lay on the floor. Both were bloodied, with tufts

180

of gray hair adhering to them. Vegetables and a broken saucepan littered the floor. A shoe print, made up of distinctive parallel lines, was visible on the kitchen floor.

Observing the scene of violence, Fred had difficulty controlling his emotions. He managed to call his immediate neighbor, Dr. Harold Browne, who was at his side in two minutes. Dr. Browne took one look, comforted Wiltshaw and called the police.

Initially there was no evidence that anything was missing from the home and thus no apparent motive for the vicious attack. Fred Wiltshaw, the respected owner of a pottery firm in Stoke, was an unlikely suspect. His activities on the day of the murder were scrupulously traced. Fred had left for his business in Stoke at 9:30 a.m. in his automobile. His gardener-chauffeur, Roy Shenton, had reported for work as usual at 8 a.m. Two daily maids, Ada Barlow and Florence Dorrell, arrived for work at 8:15 a.m.

On the day Mrs. Wiltshaw was murdered, the two maids left at 3:30 p.m., after washing the kitchen floor and placing vegetables in a saucepan for the evening meal. These were later found scattered on the kitchen floor.

Roy Shenton, who had only been employed with the Wiltshaws for ten weeks, took up his gardening duties at 8 a.m. He was around the house all day. He observed John Matthews delivering the evening paper shortly after 5 o'clock. At roughly the same time he nodded to the village constable, John Bigham, as he strolled past the Wiltshaw home. At 5:22 Shenton observed Mrs. Wiltshaw talking on the telephone. A few minutes later Shenton hopped on his bicycle and peddled home, passing the time of day with neighbors as he went.

Fred Wiltshaw left his business in Stoke at 4:15 and drove to the Trentham Golf Club near his home, where he played bridge with friends until 6:16. At 6:18 he pulled into his driveway and walked in upon the violent scene of death.

The statements of the two maids, Roy Shenton, Fred Wiltshaw, and Dr. Browne were corroborated by other individuals. In particular, the neighbor who had talked to the victim on the telephone confirmed the time of the conversation as being

5:22. Thus it was certain that Mrs. Wiltshaw had been killed between 5:22 and 6:18, a period of 56 minutes.

Who had killed Alice Wiltshaw and why? Scotland Yard was requested to enter the case and provide the answers. In their own meticulous way, they attempted to reconstruct the crime from the physical evidence in the Wiltshaw home.

They deduced that the killer had approached the house by a little-used back path. He walked through the door which was always unlocked and proceeded upstairs, where he knew some jewels were kept in a drawer. He helped himself to a few pieces which he felt would not be missed.

Downstairs, Mrs. Wiltshaw picked up her saucepan to cook the vegetables for the evening meal. Suddenly, she heard the intruder just as he was leaving the house. There was a confrontation. The thief picked up a log and struck Mrs. Wiltshaw. The saucepan and vegetables flew in the air. So did the log. He picked up a second log and struck the staggering woman again. She slumped to the floor while he made for the back door.

The realization dawned on him. Mrs. Wiltshaw had recognized him. He must be certain of her death. Desperately, he lurched into the living room and grabbed a poker from its stand. Meanwhile, Mrs. Wiltshaw had staggered out into the hall. Once again, this time with the poker, she received vicious blows to the head until she was dead. The killer dropped the poker beside the body and ran out the back door and down the secluded path without being seen.

This theory accounted for all the physical evidence, but did little to identify the killer. None of the people associated with Mrs. Wiltshaw could be the murderer. It had to be someone else.

Detectives believed that only one other person would have the intimate knowledge of the Wiltshaws' habits and would know when the servants were on the premises. This man was Leslie Green, who had been the Wiltshaws' gardener-chauffeur prior to their hiring Roy Shenton.

While attempting to trace Green, detectives found that he had left his wife and had run away with an Irish nurse. When his name and photo appeared in the press, he walked into the Longton police station and offered to clear up any misunderstanding.

Subsequent investigation into Green's activities uncovered an array of circumstantial evidence pointing to his guilt. Green knew the Wiltshaws and their habits. He and his girlfriend had spent one night in a rooming house. A few pieces of Mrs. Wiltshaw's jewelry were found hidden in their room. The shoeprint on the Wiltshaws' kitchen floor matched Green's shoe. An old raincoat belonging to Mr. Wiltshaw was found in Green's possession. It was believed that this coat was used to cover his bloodstained clothing. When Green walked into the police station he had scratches on his arms and wrists which could have been inflicted by a woman struggling for her life.

In his defence, Green claimed that his shoes were not the only ones which could have made the print on the Wiltshaws' kitchen floor. He admitted stealing Mr. Wiltshaw's raincoat before being dismissed from his job as gardener-chauffeur. Green also claimed that he had received the incriminating scratches on his arms while gardening. He could not, however, account for the stolen jewelry being in a room occupied by him and his girlfriend, except to offer the lame explanation that others had occupied the same room since the murder.

Green swore that he was drinking in the Station Hotel in Stafford, some ten miles from Barlaston, at the time the crime was committed. However, after police questioned patrons and hotel staff, Green's alibi did not stand up.

Leslie Green was tried and convicted of Mrs. Wiltshaw's murder. Green never confessed, but left notes to his wife and detectives implying that they had the right man. He was hanged on Dec. 23, 1952 without appealing either verdict or sentence.

MA BARKER
AND HER BOYS
Infamous leader of
the Barker-Karpis gang

Books, plays and movies have examined her life from every conceivable angle. Probably we will never know the exact role she played in the criminal history of the U.S. Was she the simple little hillbilly woman who stuck by her boys through good times and bad, or was she the infamous mastermind behind the most successful gang of bank robbers and killers ever to roam the U.S.?

Her real name was Arizona Donnie Clark Barker, but we know her as the notorious Ma Barker, leader of the Barker-Karpis gang which terrorized the Midwest during the early thirties.

Arrie, as she was known, was born in 1872 near Springfield, Missouri and was nurtured on the daring deeds of legendary badman Jesse James. She was ten-years-old when "that dirty little coward" Bob Ford shot Jesse in the back. Jesse James would remain Arrie Barker's hero all her life.

In 1892, at the age of 20, Arrie married farm worker George Barker. The young couple moved to Aurora, Missouri, where Arrie gave birth to her four boys, Herman, Lloyd, Doc and Freddie. All the boys turned out to be sweethearts.

The Barker clan had a difficult time coaxing a living out of the soil. When the four boys were still young, they moved to Webb City, a rough, tough mining town, where they set up housekeeping in a tarpaper shack. Despite the poverty of her surroundings, Ma scrubbed her boys' faces and hustled them off to Sunday school each week. As the boys grew up, their father George had little to do with their discipline. Ma was the authority in the family.

Gradually, each one of her sons became embroiled in minor scrapes with the law. Petty theft, assault, and carrying a concealed weapon were some of the charges. In every instance Ma was able to convince a sympathetic judge that her boys were really good boys. They were released into her custody.

When Ma ran out of sympathetic judges she moved to Tulsa, Oklahoma. By this time many of her sons' friends had landed in prison for various offences. When Freddie visited one of these friends who was soon to be released, he invited him to stop over at the Barker residence in Tulsa. Eventually Ma made a business out of providing a safe hideout for criminals on the run.

In 1922, her sons slipped over the line into serious trouble with the law. Lloyd, apprehended while attempting to hold up a post office, received a sentence of 25 years imprisonment and was stashed away in Leavenworth. A few months later Doc killed a night watchman at Johns Hospital in Tulsa while attempting to heist a drug shipment. He was sentenced to life in the Oklahoma State Penitentiary.

Four years later, Freddie received a sentence of five to ten years in Kansas State Prison in Lansing for robbing a Windfield, Kansas bank. Thus Ma Barker gained the distinction of having three of her four sons incarcerated in three different prisons at the same time.

What about Herman? He was busy too. Herman was captured while robbing a bank in Missouri. He escaped and robbed a store in Newton, Kansas. Herman bungled the job, killing the police officer J.E. Marshall along the way. Surrounded by police, Herman turned his revolver on himself, sending a slug directly into his brain. Ma Barker was down to three sons.

The years took their toll on Ma. She stood only 5 ft. 1

inch. During the years her sons were in prison she became fat. Ma left her husband and took up with a lazy alcoholic, Arthur V. Dunlop. Her lover was a natural complainer who avoided work of any kind like the plague. When Freddie was paroled in 1931, he sort of inherited Dunlop, whom he despised with a passion.

Freddie had met Canadian Alvin Karpis in prison and invited him to his mother's home. Karpis and Ma took an immediate liking to each other and for the rest of her life Ma considered old Creepy Karpis "one of her boys". Like Freddie, Karpis barely tolerated Dunlop for Ma's sake.

Freddie and Karpis went to work. They robbed a store in West Plains, Missouri. Sheriff C.R. Kelly spotted the getaway car a few days later. When he saw Freddie and Karpis in the vehicle, he stopped it to investigate. The two men shot the sheriff dead. There were no witnesses, and years later Karpis was to claim that it was not he but another hood who had been with Freddie that day. Karpis stated he was blamed because the two killers had borrowed his car.

Now hunted men, Freddie and Karpis stayed on the move. They transferred Ma and Dunlop to St. Paul, Minnesota. While drunk Dunlop talked too much of his association with the Barkers. Jack Peifer murdered Dunlop as a favor to the Barker gang. Ma understood.

Doc was granted a parole. He joined Freddie, Karpis, and Ma. The gang shifted into high gear. Together with the top gunslingers of the era, they quickly became the scourge of the FBI.

They relieved the Cloud County Bank of Concordia, Kansas of $250,000. In 1933, they knocked over banks in Kansas and Nebraska for $20,000 and $151,000 respectively. The gang turned to kidnapping, successfully snatching St. Paul brewer William A. Hamm and releasing him for $100,000 cash. This caper proved to be so successful that they kidnapped Edward C. Bremer, collecting $200,000 for their trouble. It is estimated that during their spree of kidnappings and holdups, the Barker-Karpis gang took in $3,000,000. They achieved the dubious status of being the most wanted fugitives in the United States.

By 1935 the heat was on and the gang scattered. Doc was picked up in Chicago by the FBI and sent to Alcatraz. When agents searched his room they found a map of Florida, indicating where other members of the gang were holed up. The FBI surrounded a remote resort on Lake Weir. When Ma and Freddie refused to surrender they were shot to death. Ma had over $10,000 in her handbag. By sheer accident, Karpis was out fishing mackerel at the time and so saved his life.

On June 13, 1939, Doc scampered over Alcatraz's high wall. He was spotted by tower guards, who shouted a warning. Doc chose to ignore their warnings and was gunned down, dying where he fell on the shore.

The only surviving Barker son, Lloyd, sent to Leavenworth in 1922, served every minute of his 25 year sentence. Upon his release in 1947 he obtained work in a snack shop in Colorado. Two years later, he was murdered by his wife.

Alvin Karpis was picked up by the FBI in New Orleans. He was sent to Alcatraz on Aug. 7, 1936 and remained there for 25 years, longer than any other prisoner in that famed institution's history. In 1962, he was transferred to McNeil Island, where he served a further seven years.

After spending a total of 33 years in prison, Karpis, like a ghost from the past, was released in December, 1968, and deported to Canada. He lived as a free man for 10 years before being found dead in his bed in Torremolinos, Spain, the last remaining member of the dreaded Barker-Karpis gang.

MURDER IN
SOUTH AFRICA
The triangle had one side too many

As we all know, triangles are three-cornered geometric forms. Substitute individuals for corners and you have a love triangle.

Come along with me now to Cape Town, South Africa and meet the characters who combined to produce a love triangle so hot that it erupted into bloody murder.

Marlene Lehnberg was brought up by strict religious parents. She was an excellent pupil, whose teachers were disappointed when she chose not to pursue a university education. Instead, attractive Marlene moved out of her parents' Cape Town home and moved into Stowell Lodge in nearby Rondebosch. She obtained clerical employment at the Orthopedic Workshop, an organization which outfitted, assisted, and otherwise dealt with individuals who had lost limbs.

Her boss was tall, well-preserved, 47-year-old Chistiaan van der Linde. In 1973, Chris had been married for 25 years to his 46-year-old wife, Susanna. They had three adult children. Theirs was considered to be an ideal marriage. That is, it was right up until 17-year-old Marlene began working with Chris.

Despite the 30-year age difference, Marlene fell hard for her suave employer. Chris, in turn, not only failed to put up adequate defences to ward off Marlene's advances, he actually

188

encouraged her attention. Within weeks Marlene and Chris were whipping over to Stowell Lodge at every opportunity to satisfy those oh so natural biological urges which are wont to plague us mortals.

Marlene swore undying obedience, servitude, loyalty and whatever to Chris. She urged him to tell all to his wife, obtain a divorce, marry her and live happily ever after. Chris simply didn't see it that way. Yes, he loved Marlene dearly, particularly on those occasions when they were between the sheets over at the Lodge, but he just couldn't leave his wife. Not after 25 years of marital bliss.

There matters simmered and boiled until September, 1974, when Marlene phoned Susanna for an appointment and then drove out to the van der Linde home for a meeting. She told Susanna that she was on intimate terms with Chris, that they loved each other, and asked what she intended to do about it. Susanna was understandably taken aback by the knowledge of her husband's infidelity but, in the true tradition of the wronged wife, she clearly and quite loudly told Marlene that she had no intention of giving Chris a divorce.

When Chris heard of the meeting between mistress and wife, he was furious at Marlene, but not furious enough to terminate those pleasant trysts in Marlene's room. Heavens, no.

Marlène became depressed at the hopelessness of her situation. Chris wouldn't leave his wife, Susanna wouldn't divorce him, and all the while Marlene couldn't live without her man. She thought and thought. There had to be a solution. Well, now, there was one way. Why hadn't she thought of it sooner? It was so very simple. She could kill Susanna.

With this rather positive attitude, she approached Marthinus Choegor, a 33-year-old destitute black cripple, who had lost his leg in a car accident and was an out patient at the Orthopedic Workshop where Marlene was employed. In the past Marlene had displayed some semblance of kindness toward Marthinus, who had been born to poverty and subservience to the white man in a country where blacks were treated as inferiors. Initially, Marthinus was appalled at

189

the suggestion put forth by Marlene, namely that he kill Susanna van der Linde.

To fully comprehend Marthinus' predicament, we must touch on his circumstances. Later, psychiatrists were to make much of his state of mind at the time he was approached by Marlene. He had a wife and two children who were living in squalor. Because of his crude artificial leg and use of a crutch, he could obtain only the most menial of jobs.

Marthinus' intelligence was well below average. This young white girl who had been so kind to him now offered him money, a radio and a car, riches far beyond his wildest dreams. In addition, Marlene had offered to fulfil another dream. She promised Marthinus that once the killing had taken place, she would have sex with him.

Twice Marthinus mustered up enough courage to approach the van der Linde home and twice his courage failed him. The first time he went as far as knocking on the front door, but when he saw Susanna part the drapes and look at him, he ran away. On his second attempt, police picked him up and questioned him as a vagrant before releasing him. On that occasion poor Marthinus had just enough time to get rid of the hammer he was carrying.

Marlene was furious at Marthinus' failure. In desperation, on Nov. 4, 1974, she drove her accomplice out to Susanna's house. This time the odd couple came equipped with a pistol. Marlene had no trouble gaining entrance to the home on 66 Gladstone St. Susanna let her in. Marthinus followed.

When Susanna saw Marthinus, she became frightened and ran to the telephone. Marlene crashed the pistol against Susanna's left jaw. She screamed for Marthinus to choke Susanna. Later Marthinus would say he obeyed as if hypnotized. Susanna lay on the floor being throttled when Marlene passed Marthinus a pair of scissors, at the same time commanding him to stab the now helpless Susanna. Seven times the scissors plunged into Susanna's chest. Her life's blood spilled out on her living room floor.

Marlene drove Marthinus to his corrugated tin hovel. She then drove to Johannesburg, where she had taken up residence a few days earlier in order to establish an alibi for the time of the murder.

Later that morning Chris van der Linde couldn't reach his wife by phone. He called his daughter Zelda, who drove to her mother's home and walked into the house of carnage.

It didn't take long. Police remembered detaining the distinctive derelict with the artificial leg close to Gladstone St. On the morning of the murder a neighbor had seen such a man using a crutch walk up the steps to the van der Linde residence accompanied by a white girl.

A few questions thrown at employees of the Orthopedic Workshop revealed the close relationship between the 19-year-old Marlene and her 49-year-old lover, Chris van der Linde. Marthinus and Marlene were picked up by police.

Within 24 hours both suspects confessed to the murder. Both agreed to all details except one. Marlene insisted that she had never entered the murder house but had remained outside in her car.

On March 4, 1975 the accused pair stood trial for murder. The jury chose to believe that Marlene was in the van der Linde home and took an active part in the actual murder.

Marthinus Choegor didn't get his money, radio, car or sex. He was sentenced to 15 years imprisonment.

Marlene Lehnberg didn't get the man she loved. Instead she received a sentence of 20 years in prison.

Christiaan van der Linde, who was the catalyst which caused the death of one person and ruined the life of two others, had no guilty knowledge of the murder and was never accused of any crime.

MADELINE'S MURDEROUS WAYS
The box of chocolates remained unopened

We are forever reading about beautiful young girls who make their way to Hollywood and New York to get their start in movies and plays. Their talents are discovered. Success, fame and riches follow. Rarely do we hear about the vast majority who meet with frustration, failure, and sometimes tragedy. This is the story of one such girl.

Madeline Webb graduated in the top third of her class from the Oklahoma Agricultural and Mechanics College in her hometown of Stillwater, Okla. But it wasn't only in the brains department that Madeline excelled. She was a looker with a capital L. Madeline had flaming red hair and a figure that would make the old town clock spin backwards.

Upon graduation, Madeline married her hometown sweetheart, but things simply didn't work out. Mostly it was Madeline's fault. She had a deepseated desire to become an actress and wouldn't be satisfied until she gave it her best shot. Hubby disagreed. Divorce followed.

Free to strike it rich on her own, Madeline left for Hollywood. Once there, she found out that her stunning good looks and limited singing and dancing abilities were not enough. There were thousands of beautiful girls in movieland.

Madeline decided to try New York. Again, she had difficulty breaking into the entertainment industry, but was able to obtain sporadic jobs as a model. Sometimes she caught on with the chorus of an off-Broadway play for a few months, but in general things went from bad to worse. For two years Madeline lived in sleazy hotels. When she had a half decent job she moved to a better place. When times got tough she moved on.

While employed for several months, Madeline lived at the Woodrow Hotel. It was there she met Mrs. Susan Reich, who had immigrated to the U.S. from Vienna. Mrs. Reich, a woman in her mid fifties, had once been a beauty herself and took an immediate liking to the struggling young actress. Mrs. Reich, who lived in a suite of rooms with her mother and her husband, was continually performing some kindness for Madeline. The two women became very close friends, until once again Madeline couldn't afford the comfortable hotel and moved to cheaper, less attractive accommodations.

That's where matters stood for some months until one day in March, 1942, when Mrs. Reich received a phone call from her old friend Madeline. Madeline invited the older woman to have tea with her at the elegant Hotel Sutton. She informed Mrs. Reich that she and her husband were living there. Mrs. Reich was glad to receive the call and remarked to her mother that Madeline must have married well as the Sutton was an expensive hotel.

On March 3 Mrs. Reich left her mother at the Woodrow to visit with Madeline. When she failed to return, her mother called the Sutton several times, until finally she convinced the manager that someone should look in on Room 207, where her daughter was to meet with Madeline Webb Leopold.

The manager sent a bell boy to 207 to investigate. He opened the door and gazed upon the body of Mrs. Susan Reich lying on the floor. Her arms were tied behind her back with wire and her ankles were bound with the same wire. Wide strips of adhesive tape had been placed over her mouth and a lady's scarf was wound around her neck. The body was stripped of the expensive jewelry Mrs. Reich was known to wear. Four coffee cups, several cinnamon buns, and an unopened one pound box of chocolates were on a table near the body.

The death room had been rented to Mr. and Mrs. Ted Leopold of Euclid Ave., Miami Beach. A check with Florida police revealed that the address was a vacant lot.

Mrs. Reich's mother told the police of her daughter's friendship with Madeline Webb, and was able to supply them with a picture of the aspiring actress.

The Leopolds had been living at the Sutton since Feb. 20. Detectives learned that a smalltime thief named Eli Shonbrun had stolen a valuable ring just a day before Mr. and Mrs. Leopold checked into the Sutton. A police shot of Shonbrun was shown to the employees of the hotel. They identified Shonbrun as the man they knew as Ted Leopold, husband of the beautiful Madeline.

Meanwhile, police found the store which had sold the wire used to tie Mrs. Reich' wrists and ankles. The clerk swore that Eli Shonbrun was the man who had purchased the wire.

Delving into Shonbrun's past, detectives learned that he, like Madeline, had longed for a career as a singer but had never been able to make a living at his specialty. When he met Madeline he fell deeply in love. He abandoned his wife and seven-year-old son to move in with his true love. Together they worked when they could, but more often lived by their wits and the proceeds of petty crime. For the first time in years, Madeline had someone who really cared. She loved Eli with a passion.

In the course of the investigation into Shonbrun's background, detectives came across his uncle, Harry Hirschl, who bought and sold second hand jewelry. Police tailed Hirschl. He led them to a hock shop, where he sold a ring with the diamond missing. This ring proved to be one which had been torn from Mrs. Reich's fingers.

Hirschl was picked up. To save his own skin, he sang like a canary. He told detectives that his nephew, Shonbrun, had brought him the ring, but it was too expensive an item for him to sell without raising suspicion. The two men decided to extract the diamond. They then agreed to meet soon after Hirschl sold the unmounted ring, but Shonbrun never showed up.

Hirschl admitted knowledge of the plan to lure Mrs. Reich to the Hotel Sutton, but swore it was only to rob her, not to murder her. Shonbrun and Madeline were flat broke and badly in need of money. Madeline remembered her old friend and her penchant for wearing expensive jewelry. The plan was hatched. The fourth person involved, accounting for the fourth coffee cup in the room, was an ex-con, John Cullen, a friend of Shonbrun's. Hirschl swore he wasn't in the room when the murder took place, but had been told the details when Shonbrun gave him the ring to sell.

He told police that Mrs. Reich had walked into the room. She chatted with Madeline, Shonbrun and Cullen for a few moments. Madeline excused herself and went into the bathroom. Shonbrun demanded that Mrs. Reich hand over her jewelry. The conspirators firmly believed she would do so without question. Instead, Mrs. Reich screamed. Madeline ran out of the hotel into the street. The two men slapped adhesive tape over their victim's mouth and then throttled her with Madeline's scarf.

Five days after the murder, Cullen was picked up on the streets of New York. He gave police the address of Madeline and Shonbrun. They were taken into custody without incident.

Shonbrun co-operated with the police in every way. He readily admitted his part in the murder and turned over the diamond he had removed from Mrs. Reich's ring. He insisted that Madeline knew nothing of the plot to steal Mrs. Reich's jewelry and swore she was out of the room when the attack occurred.

All three participants in the killing were brought to trial and all were found guilty of murder. Shonbrun and Cullen were executed in Sing Sing's electric chair. Madeline was sentenced to life imprisonment, eventually being paroled at the age of 54.

Oh, yes, the unopened box of chocolates found on the table beside the body. It was a gift from Mrs. Reich to her dear friend, Madeline Webb.

WHO IS THE
NATION RIVER GIRL?
Body floating in river never identified

Detective Inspector Bill MacGregor of the Ontario Provincial Police stared down at a photograph of two partial dentures taken from the unidentified body of a young woman. MacGregor, like the three previous detectives who attempted over nine long years to identify the body, is no nearer today than they were to solving the mystery of the Nation River girl.

Claude Legault was working the south section of his farm at approximately 10 a.m. on May 3, 1975 near Casselman, Ont., when he spotted what he thought was a dead animal floating in the Nation River. Upon closer inspection, he realized it was the almost nude body of a human being. Claude returned to his home and called the Casselman detachment of the OPP.

The partially decomposed body was nude from the neck down. The wrists were tied in front with a man's navy blue necktie decorated with red maple leaf emblems. The victim's ankles were tied with two neckties, one blue and gray, the other a loud red and white patterned affair. The killer had tightened a blue body shirt around her neck. A J-Cloth and an ordinary hand towel were wrapped around the dead girl's head.

A distinctive linen towel, manufactured in Ireland, was found with the body. It bore illustrations of meat, fish and drink, and was entitled Food and Drink. On the towel were printed six tips for drinking at parties. For example, number one suggested: "Eat or nibble as you drink, particularly at a cocktail party. But concentrate on protein foods that digest slowly . . . sardines, salmon, shrimp, caviar, meat and eggs."

Strangely enough, a curtain rod runner with a plastic wheel was found under the girl's left armpit. Among the crude array of materials, police found a 24-inch piece of T.V. coaxial cable. Two large sections of green cloth held the gruesome bundle in place.

Pathologist J. Hillsdon-Smith performed the autopsy. His findings confirmed that the cause of death was "strangulation by a ligature". The victim was between 25 and 35 years old. Her shoulder length dark brown hair had been dyed a reddish blond. She had had restorative dental work on her upper and lower dentures. Sometime in the past her appendix had been removed. She had never given birth. Her fingernails and toenails were painted with common pink nail polish. The Nation River girl was 5 ft. 3 in. tall and had weighed between 100 and 110 pounds.

Attempting to establish the date of death proved to be a problem for Hillsdon-Smith. The body appeared to have been in the river from one to four weeks, establishing a murder date at somewhere between April 5 and April 26. However, as temperature had a direct effect on the rate of decomposition, there was an outside chance that the victim may have been killed just before the river froze the previous fall.

Tiny bloodstains were discovered on the Nation River bridge. The quantity of blood was too small to establish a bloodtype, making it impossible to ascertain whether it was that of the victim. However, the position of the spots was compatible with someone lifting a body over the bridge railing. If investigating officers were to assume that the blood on the bridge was that of the victim, they could narrow the perimeters of the murder dates. A heavy rain had fallen on April 19, which would have obliterated the bloodstains on the bridge. It was then reasonable to assume that the girl had been tossed in the river between April 19 and April 26.

The multitude of physical clues found with the body gave OPP officials every reason to believe that the body would be readily identified and the killer apprehended. Such was not to be the case.

Initially, the victim's fingerprints were checked against all missing person's in Canada with negative results. The FBI had no record of her prints. Interpol couldn't help.

One by one the items found with the body were traced. The neckties had been manufactured in Montreal and sold in large quantities through Ontario and Quebec. The colorful towel had been imported from Ireland by Ralph Hunter Linens Co. of Toronto. They had been sold in 50 dozen lots up to 1972. The towels retailed for $1.69 and proved to be untraceable. The coaxial cable was manufactured by Amphenol Canada Ltd. and sold by hundreds of thousands of feet throughout Ontario and Quebec.

So it went with every item found with the body. All were impossible to trace. The dentures, often the means of positive identification, proved the most frustrating to the officers. The materials used in the manufacture of the dentures were of the highest quality, but the workmanship was inferior. Denturists in Toronto believed that such inferior workmanship would not be acceptable in the Toronto market, but might have been manufactured in the province of Quebec.

One by one, denturists in Ontario and Quebec were interviewed. All swore that they had not made the dentures. When it was suggested that the dentures might have been manufactured in Halifax, a member of the OPP flew there, but once again the work was not identified.

The green material wrapped around the victim's head could have been part of a curtain. With this in mind all hotels and motels for miles were canvassed to match the material, but nothing came of this avenue of the investigation.

Waitresses and entertainers who had abruptly left their places of employment were tracked down. Scores of girls, many of whom were go-go dancers in Ontario and Quebec towns, were traced and found to be alive and well.

In 1977, the Ontario Dental Association held a convention

in Toronto. Posters with an illustration and description of the dentures were distributed at the convention, but no one identified the dental work.

Det. Insp. MacGregor believes that the dentures are the key to identifying the dead girl. Prior to 1975, many dentures were being bootlegged by unlicensed techncians. Materials may have been imported from Germany and the dentures manufactured in a one man lab. When the licenced denturists were canvassed these individuals would have been missed.

I travelled to the Long Sault detachment of the OPP and watched as Cpl. Earl Bowes unsealed the small cardboard carton containing the items which were found with the victim over nine years ago.

Who once wore these neckties? Who wrapped the victim's head with the various items which must have been close at hand? These questions remain unanswered.

For years, the Nation River girl's body lay frozen in the Toronto morgue waiting to be identified. No one came forward. The unidentified body was buried in 1986.

DEATH DEALT
FINAL JUSTICE
Girl Scout camp invaded by monster

Thirty-five miles east of Tulsa, Oklahoma, lies the peaceful little town of Locust Grove. Not much ever happens in Locust Grove; yet on a rainy evening in June, 1977, one of the most horrendous crimes ever perpetrated in the U.S. took place in a Girl Scout camp located on the outskirts of the town.

It was the first day of a week-long Girl Scout outing at Camp Scott. One hundred and forty girls poured into the campground in buses, joining the 30 counsellors who had arrived a week earlier.

In the late afternoon it rained. By nightfall a thunderstorm had rolled in over the camp and the girls were delighted to be confined to their tents.

Next morning counsellor Carla Sue Wilhite decided to take a shower at the staff house before the rest of the camp awakened. As she walked along the trail, she noticed what looked like a bundle of sleeping bags. Walking closer, she couldn't believe her eyes. There, grotesquely positioned in one of the bags, was the body of a little girl.

Carla Sue screamed for help. Police were called and in a matter of minutes what had promised to be a bright fresh day at Camp Scott turned into the darkest day in the 50-year history of the camp.

Each of three sleeping bags contained the body of a little girl. The three victims had occupied tent number eight, the last tent in a semicircle. The bodies were examined, photographed and removed for post-mortems. Doris Milner, ten, had been strangled. Lori Lee Farmer, eight, and Michelle Guse, nine, had been beaten to death. All three youngsters had been raped.

Despite the fact that the tent was separated from seven other tents by only a few feet, no noise had been heard by other girls during the night. The bodies were found about 150 yards from their tent. Police found a nine volt red and white flashlight nearby. Someone had stuffed newspaper inside the flashlight, obviously to make the batteries fit snugly. The bit of paper was a portion of the April 17 issue of the Tulsa *World*.

Police organized civilian groups into a massive search party. Miles of thick woods around Camp Scott were scoured for any clues that might lead to the killer's identity. Nothing was uncovered by the organized search, but two squirrel hunters, Willis Ray Thompson and Johnny Russell Colvin, led police to a cave they had discovered about three miles from the camp. Inside the cave were two torn photographs and a portion of the April 17 issue of the Tulsa *World*.

Because of the newspaper found in the flashlight and a piece of the same issue of the paper found in the cave, detectives had every reason to believe the cave had been used by the killer.

Days passed, but nothing of a concrete nature turned up. Despite the lack of evidence, there was one prime suspect. His name was Gene Hart.

Hart, a full-blooded Cherokee Indian, as were many inhabitants of that part of Oklahoma, had a criminal record dating back ten years. In 1966, he kidnapped two pregnant women, drove them in his own car into secluded woods, where he tortured and raped them. One of the women managed to obtain Hart's licence number. Hart, 22, was picked up. Cord found in his car matched that used to tie up the two women. Hart was found guilty of two charges of kidnapping and one of rape. He received three ten year prison sentences. A little over two years later he was paroled.

Three months after his release Hart was caught red-handed with a knife burglarizing a Tulsa apartment. When his automobile was searched, the stolen property from several other apartments was recovered. Tried separately for each burglary, he received one sentence of from 30 to 90 years, another of from 40 to 120 years, a third of from 15 to 45 years, and another of a straight 50 years imprisonment, all sentences to run consecutively. Hart was placed in the Oklahoma State Penitentiary at McAlester, ostensibly for the balance of his natural life.

On April 25, 1973 Hart was transferred to the Mayes County Jail to appear at yet another court proceeding. He escaped, but was apprehended a month later. Four months later, Hart was to stand trial for escaping and being in possession of a shotgun when apprehended. Once again, he escaped. This time he remained at large. Now, four years later, his name was brought up as a man capable of raping and killing three children.

Oklahoma is Cherokee country. It is estimated that Hart had 300 relatives living within 50 miles of Camp Scott. Before his first scrape with the law, he had been something of a local high school football hero. An expert woodsman, there is little doubt that he roamed the woods while at large, living off the land. Most natives felt that Hart was innocent of all charges and had been framed by the white man. Many had assisted him with food and shelter during his four years of freedom. Now these same people believed that Gene Hart was not capable of murdering three children.

Slowly, evidence mounted against Hart. Photos found in the cave were traced to photographer Louis Lindsey. Hart had worked for Lindsey after his parole and had ready access to the photos.

As the months passed, the U.S. Army attempted to track down the wanted man. So did penitentiary officials and bounty hunters. Even medicine men had a turn at trying to locate the fugitive. All failed.

Finally, an informant gave away Hart's hideout. He was living with an old man in an isolated shack. Heavily armed police surrounded the shack and broke down the front door. Before Hart could move he was staring into the barrel of a 12-gauge shotgun. It had been two years since the Girl Scouts had been murdered. Now, after six years as a fugitive, Hart was finally taken into custody.

The shack where Hart had lived with the old man was thoroughly searched. Inside, detectives found a girl's blue mirror and a corn cob pipe. These two items were traced to Karen Mitchell, a counsellor at Camp Scott. The mirror and pipe had been stolen from her tent on the night of the murders.

Strangely enough, several funds were organized to pay for Hart's defence. In the six years he had been a fugitive, he had unbelievably become somewhat of a folk hero.

His trial, the longest in Oklahoma's history, was covered by the press of several countries. Hart's defence was based solely on the premise that the white man needed an Indian as a scapegoat to pay for the tragic murders. To the disgust of law enforcement agencies throughout the country he was found not guilty. He was returned to the Oklahoma State Prison to serve out his many other sentences.

On June 4, 1979, three months after being incarcerated, Gene Hart collapsed while jogging. He had suffered a massive heart attack and died where he fell.

DISHONEST ABE
A swindler with style

Abraham Sykowski's father was an industrious Polish immigrant who worked long and hard in his tailor shop located in New York's teeming Lower East Side. Abe's father lectured his bright son on the virtues of honesty, truthfulness and diligence. Abe didn't listen. He preferred to lie, cheat and steal.

From the age of 14, 5 ft. 5 in. Abe was in and out of trouble. He was caught stealing vegetables from tenement buildings, but was let off with a warning when his father swore his Abe would never as much as jaywalk the rest of his life.

Abe had two genuine talents. He had the natural ability to learn and speak foreign languages. He mastered six, which were to stand him in good stead in later years. Abe also learned to contort his supple body into strange shapes. That's how he found himself in vaudeville. In 1915, 20-year-old Abe was good enough to be hired by Barnum and Bailey's circus. P.T. billed him as the Human Frog.

Abe loved being the Human Frog, but longed for the big money that the frog business simply couldn't provide. He gave common theft a try, was caught and sent to prison for nine years.

While in prison Abe dreamed up a con game that was to

provide him with a minimum of $125,000 per year for the next 25 years. In good years he made $375,000. That isn't half bad when you consider that in 1930 you could purchase a hotdog and a coke for a dime. Of course, Abe did have the inconvenience of spending a couple of years in prison during that span, but then every occupation has its drawbacks.

Let's look in on Abe's scam during his salad days in the summer of 1946.

Abe, posing as Count Alexander Navarro of Madrid, Spain, checked into a luxurious suite in Montreal's Windsor Hotel. Abe was invited to Montreal's better social functions.

At one of these rather formal affairs, he let it slip that he was in dire need of a good lawyer. Someone suggested he contact 60-year-old Washington attorney Otto Dunning. Count Navarro called the lawyer, informing him that he had been given his name by a friend at a party. He required top-drawer reputable legal advice since he was about to dispose of a third of a billion dollars.

Dunning cleared his throat. He could get away immediately. There was one other little matter the Count mentioned as an afterthought. Did Dunning know anyone who would be interested in investing a piddling $125,000? The loan would be fully guaranteed, would pay a high interest rate and be payable in 90 days. Dunning thought he could dig up someone.

Count Navarro, decked out in his very best custom tailored lightweight threads, welcomed his guests into his suite of rooms. Dunning had brought along Sigmund Janas, the president of Colonial Airlines, as his investor. After offering the men two of the finest Havana stogies to accompany their Remy Martins, Count Navarro got to the point.

Faking embarrassment, the nifty little con artist explained that he was worth many millions of dollars. His face grew crimson when he admitted he had made every cent illegally as Al Capone's partner and financial advisor during that gentleman's bootlegging career.

Otto Dunning was well aware that Big Al had been stashed away because of income tax evasion. He ventured to inquire if the Count had paid income tax on his many millions.

Count Navarro responded to this query by leading the two men to a hotel safe, where he displayed a stack of letters purportedly from famed lawyer Clarence Darrow to Henry W. Morgenthau, Secretary of the Treasury of the U.S.

The letters were eight years old, having been written before Darrow died. Among the papers were cancelled cheques totalling $84 million to cover all taxes owed by the Count to the U.S. government. It was obvious that Darrow had acted as legal counsel for the Count. The last letter in the stack was from Morgenthau to Darrow, advising him that Count Navarro's tax bill was paid in full. The boys from Washington were duly impressed.

Count Navarro continued talking in that low confidential voice. He explained that he had only a year to live and planned to give his money away to charity, where it would do the most good. He also required assurances that his good works would be carried on after his demise. To start the ball rolling he wanted to donate $50 million immediately to a list of charities in case he was called away to his great reward without prior notice. In this way, Count Navarro pointed out, he could meet St. Peter with a clear conscience.

Dunning looked at Janas. Janas looked at Dunning. They were obviously in the presence of a highly moral human being. Still, business is business. Dunning gingerly inquiried as to his fee for such big time giving. The Count stated that ten percent seemed fair to him, making the rather serious point that Dunning's credentials had to check out before the deal could be consummated.

Dunning was quick with figures. He didn't need a pencil. Ten percent of $50 million dollars worked out to a cool five million. Dunning agreed that the fee seemed fair enough.

Count Navarro had a minor problem. He produced clippings from the Montreal *Star* describing the robbery of his hotel suite some two weeks previously. The Count's passport was one of the items stolen. He had to wait for a new passport from Spain, which might take months. In the meantime the third of a billion dollars was stashed away in 33 safety deposit boxes in New York City and he simply couldn't leave Canada without a passport. One of Dunning's duties back in Washington would be to pull whatever strings necessary to speed up delivery of the passport.

Navarro explained that he didn't just leave the addresses and numbers of the safety deposit boxes lying around anywhere. Naturally, the boxes had been rented under fictitious names. The Count produced a Bible. He told the two Americans that the bogus names, box numbers and locations of the banks were written in the Bible in invisible ink. A hot iron applied to the pages would reveal all.

The hook was in. The little con artist could see the greed mounting in his guests' eyes. Still sipping those Remy Martins, Janas got up enough courage to ask about the $125,000 investment. His question met with an unusual response. Navarro doubled up with laughter. Wiping tears from his eyes, he had to admit the plain truth. He was temporarily stone dead broke. He began laughing again. His two guests laughed. It was humorous, a man with a third of a billion dollars broke. When the tears cleared, Navarro explained that he required the $125,000 for incidental living expenses until he retrieved his millions from the safety deposit boxes in New York.

Janas agreed to send a cheque as soon as he returned to Washington. The Count wouldn't hear of it. There was the matter of references. He would have his people check out Dunning. After all, it was only proper. If all was in order, he would call the lawyer in Washington.

On July 2, 1946, six days after their first meeting, Dunning received the all-important phone call. He was informed that his references were impeccable. Dunning and Janas caught a plane to Montreal. They passed over a cheque for $125,000 to Count Navarro and received a promissory note due in 90 days at a whopping rate of interest. The two men returned to Washington, where Dunning was to attempt to procure a new passport for the Count.

Ten days passed. Dunning called to give his client a progress report. The Windsor Hotel informed him that Count Navarro had moved out ten days earlier. Little beads of sweat formed on Dunning's forehead. He called Janas' bank. Yes, the cheque for $125,000 had been cashed and cleared some days earlier.

The lawyer and the airline executive had been taken. Abraham Sykowski had struck again. This time Abe's luck ran out. The FBI located him four months later in Willemstead, Curacao, living in a luxurious suite with a set of blonde twins.

Brought back to New York, Abe pleaded guilty to swindling Janas and was sentenced to five years imprisonment. While in prison he had plenty of time to think about the con business. Abe made up his mind that when he was released, he would swindle King Farouk of Egypt.

• • •

In August, 1951, Abraham Sykowski, con artist extraordinaire, was released from prison. He headed for France with the express intention of conning King Farouk. Where he obtained the financial assistance to carry out his plans, no one knows. In preparation for his scam, Abe rented several safety deposit boxes in New York City banks and stuffed them with newspapers.

Abe arrived in Cannes in style, driving up to the Carlton Hotel in a white chauffeur-driven limousine. King Farouk was staying at the Carlton. His heavy Majesty dined at the same table each night. An extravagant tip to the maitre d' assured Abe of an adjoining table.

That first night, Abe walked into the dining room with three well-endowed blondes. The three ladies had been coached and well-paid to dote over Abe all through the meal. Farouk, whose appetite for bad girls was only surpassed by his penchant for good food, couldn't help but notice the action at the next table. Each evening, 59-year-old Abe repeated the performance.

Eventually His Majesty's curiosity was tweaked. He inquired as to how Abe, at his age, managed to keep three ladies so very happy, satisfied, or whatever. Abe, a master at small talk, soon became a friend of the King of Egypt.

Little by little he let the king know he had a third of a billion dollars in safety deposit boxes in New York. The money had been earned illegally. No taxes had been paid on the cash. As a result, Abe couldn't travel to New York to pick up his ill-gotten gains.

King Farouk checked out Abe's story. His investigator confirmed that Abe had indeed rented several safety deposit boxes in various New York City banks.

Farouk had a plan. If Abe signed access to the boxes over to him, he would see that Abe obtained his money under certain conditions. Faruk's fee for his services would be ten percent, or $33 million. In addition, Abe would guarantee to invest $100 million in Egyptian enterprises.

Gee, Abe told the king, His Majesty drives a hard bargain. He would have to think it over. Abe even confided to the king that he was short of cash. This was no problem to Farouk. He insisted that Abe move into the Royal Suite with him. Abe accepted. But still, a man required a certain amount of independence, say $100,000 worth of independence. Farouk had no intention of letting his pigeon off the hook because of such a paltry sum. He turned over $100,000 to Abraham Sykowski.

At that precise time in history an event took place back in Egypt over which Abe had no control. Gamal Abdel Nasser, a spoilsport army officer, was causing all sorts of unrest. The powers that be suggested that King Farouk leave the ladies alone for a while and come home. Farouk agreed, and invited Abe to accompany him. That's how the tailor's son from the Lower East Side of New York became a more or less permanent guest at Abdin Palace in Cairo. Abe had everything his heart desired. He literally lived like a king.

The good times lasted five months. In July, under Nasser's leadership, the country revolted. Large King Farouk was unceremoniously sent back to the Riviera, this time in exile.

Abe skipped. He has never been officially heard of again. However, acquaintances spotted him in a plush Paris restaurant in the mid-fifties. Abraham Sykowski was decked out in a tuxedo and was accompanied by two shapely Parisienne beauties.

THEORA
NEVER RETURNED
Dr. Snook was an unlikely suspect

Alice and Beatrice Bustin, two Ohio State University students, had reason to be concerned. Their roommate, Theora K. Hix, had left their room at the women's residence on campus at about 7 p.m. on a warm June evening in 1929. She never returned. Next day, with no word from Theora, the two sisters reported her absence to police.

When detectives read the missing persons report, they knew there was no need to search further for Theora Hix. Earlier that day her body had been found in deep grass behind a shooting range about five miles northwest of Columbus, Ohio.

The 24-year-old second year pre-medical student had been stabbed many times. She had also received several blows about the head, possibly inflicted by a ballpeen hammer. Her jugular vein and her carotid artery had been slashed. Strangely enough, three fingers on her right hand were crushed. The victim had not been sexually attacked.

Alice and Beatrice Bustin were questioned extensively, but could shed little light on their roommate's private life. Theora was a quiet girl who kept to herself. As far as they knew she had no boyfriends. However, they told detectives she had the habit of leaving their room each evening at about 5 p.m. and not returning until after 10 p.m. Knowing that Theora was a very private person, the Bustin sisters never inquired about her absences and Theora never volunteered any information.

An examination of the victim's body indicated that she had met her death sometime before a heavy rain had fallen on Thursday, the night before her body was found. The time of death was further narrowed by Constable John Guy, who was at the shooting range that Thursday evening.

Guy stated that up until 8 p.m. the shooting range was being used by two competing shooting teams. From 8 p.m. to 10 p.m. the range was deserted. At 10 p.m. Guy had concealed himself in an adjoining field in order to apprehend thieves who were stealing livestock from a nearby farm. Had the murder taken place after 10 p.m., Guy would have witnessed it.

Around 10:20 p.m., there was a heavy rainshower. Guy discontinued his surveillance. Since the victim had been killed before the rainfall, it was reasonable to assume that the murder had taken place between 8 and 10 p.m. on Thursday night.

Unknown to Theora's friends, she was keeping company with a man. This fact was revealed to authorities when a university instructor, after being promised anonymity, came forward with the information that he had often seen her driving with Dr. James Howard Snook in the doctor's blue Ford.

Dr. Snook was an unlikely suspect. The lean, balding, bespectacled 50-year-old Snook was a professor of veterinary medicine on the medical facility at Ohio State University. He was married and had an exemplary reputation.

Snook had an interesting hobby. He was an excellent pistol shot, having represented the U.S. ten years before in the 1920 Olympics. At one time he was a world champion, and on six occasions was U.S. champion.

When questioned, Snook remained aloof from his interrogators, answering all questions in a curt, brief manner. He immediately admitted having known Theora Hix for three years and volunteered that for some time he had assisted her in paying her university tuition. They often went for drives together in his car and she was an intelligent, interesting conversationalist. Dr. Snook assured detectives that there was nothing further to their relationship.

Columbus police were positive they had their man, but the good doctor was admitting nothing. Then the unexpected happened. Mrs. Smalley, an astute lady who rented furnished rooms on Hubbard Ave., saw photographs of Dr. Snook and Theora Hix in the local newspaper. She had quite a story to tell.

Four months earlier, on Feb. 11, 1929, Dr. Snook had rented a room from Mrs. Smalley, supposedly for himself and his wife. The doctor arranged with Mrs. Smalley that his wife would do the day to day cleaning of the room, while she would give the place a good cleaning once a week. In the four months Dr. Snook and Theora occupied the room, Mrs. Smalley caught a glimpse of Theora only once. She remembered her as she was impressed by the age difference between the doctor and his wife.

Mrs. Smalley went on to state that on the Friday Theora's body was found behind the firing range, Dr. Snook told her he had to leave the city immediately. His wife would be staying until Sunday to wind up their affairs. While Mrs. Smalley wished Dr. Snook good luck, Theora Hix's unidentified body lay in a Columbus funeral home.

Dr. Snook proved to be one cool cucumber. The first hint that his iron-like composure wasn't emotion free occurred when Mrs. Smalley was brought into his presence. Without hesitation she said, "Good evening, Mr. Snook." Snook replied, "Good evening, Mrs. Smalley."

It was story changing time. Dr. Snook admitted that he had set up the little love nest with Theora, but vehemently denied any involvement in her death.

Now hot on the trail, Columbus detectives discovered that Snook had taken a suit to a dry cleaning establishment on the day Theora's body was found. The suit was examined. There were bloodstains on the jacket sleeves and the knees of the trousers. The blood type was the same as Theora's.

While Mrs. Snook looked on helplessly, police raked through ashes taken from her furnace. They recovered bits of fabric, which they were able to prove came from pyjamas owned by the slain girl.

Snook weakened when faced with this overwhelming array of evidence and admitted killing his lover. It was a brief and skimpy confession, hinting that Theora had been a cocaine addict who had badgered him for money on a daily basis. However, an analysis of Theora's internal organs revealed no signs of her having been an addict.

On July 24, 1929, Dr. Snook stood trial for the murder of Theora Hix. Defence attorneys attempted to prove that his confessions had been obtained under duress and that the doctor was insane anyway. No one was buying.

Dr. Snook took the witness stand in his own defence. He told the court that he had attempted to break off his affair with Theora and return to his wife. He said Theora became incensed, cursing and striking him as he drove his car. He stopped, tried to calm her, but then in a rage rained blows to her head with a hammer. Again, no one was buying the doctor's story. The girl had been attacked with knife and hammer. Her jugular had been severed by the deliberate stroke of a knife. Dr. Snook did clear up one minor mystery. Theora had incurred the three crushed fingers when he accidentally slammed the car door on her hand.

Dr. James Howard Snook was found guilty of murder. On Feb. 28, 1930, he was executed in the electric chair, courtesy of the State of Ohio.

HORROR AT STARVED ROCK LODGE
Triple murder ends holiday

The Boy Scout troop walked carefully over the rugged terrain of an isolated portion of Starved Rock State Park. The huge Illinois recreation area was not only ideal for enthusiastic Scouts, it was also the location of Starved Rock Lodge, a plush resort frequented by wealthy guests from Chicago.

Three Scouts ventured into a small cave. The sight which greeted them on that April day in 1960 would remain forever etched in their memories. The battered bodies of three middle-aged women lay grotesquely sprawled on the floor of the cave. State police were notified and were soon on the scene.

The three women had been savagely beaten about the head. Two of the victims were tied together at the ankles and wrists with white cord. Their clothing had been pulled above their waists and their underclothes had been torn off. The third woman's clothing had not been touched.

Initially, the hideous crime was considered to be sexually motivated. The women's jewelry was intact. Small amounts of money had not been removed from their purses. A heavy, bloodstained tree branch found beside the bodies was obviously the murder weapon.

Police recovered a camera with a broken strap nearby. Film inside the camera was developed in the hope that it might contain a picture of the murderer or at least a clue to his identity. However, the photos depicted only scenic views of the area.

The three women had been guests at Starved Rock Lodge. They were readily identified as Mrs. Mildred Lindquist, 50, Mrs. Lillian Oetting, 50, and Mrs. Frances Murphy, 47. All three were the wives of prominent Chicago businessmen and had travelled the 90 miles to the park in Mrs. Murphy's station wagon. They had checked into the lodge, had lunch, and were last seen walking together through the park.

The murder scene was thoroughly studied for clues. There was little of value. The murder weapon had obviously been picked up at the spur of the moment and used as a club. The only material item the killer might have left behind were the strips of cord used to tie two of the victims.

Guests and employees of the lodge were questioned, but no one could offer any information about the murders. All employees consented to take a lie detector test. All passed without difficulty. Sexual deviates recently released from prison were interviewed. None were near the park at the time of the murders. For some time it was believed that Chicago gangsters may have fulfilled a murder contract in order to gain revenge on the husbands of the dead women. This tangent of the investigation proved fruitless.

Four months after the murders, Illinois detectives returned to square one. Using a microscope, they examined the pieces of cord used to tie the women. Most pieces of the cord were made up of 20 strands. Only one piece had 12 strands. A search of the lodge uncovered pieces of cord in almost every room. All were manufactured with 20 strands, except for pieces found in the kitchen. Some of these were composed of 12 strands.

A check of records indicated that Starved Rock Lodge purchased their cord from a Chicago store, which in turn bought it from January and Wood, a factory in Maysville, Kentucky. Factory employees identified the cord as having been manufactured at their facility. They used a distinctive white dye which they easily recognized.

Detectives felt that it was possible that an employee of the lodge had committed the crimes. They decided to conduct another series of lie detector tests. This time expert John Reid of Chicago was solicited to bring equipment to the lodge and conduct the tests under controlled conditions. All the tests indicated that the employees tested had no guilty knowledge of the murders.

It was now six months since the tragedy. Several members of the lodge staff were no longer employed there. Police located them for retesting. This tedious task brought into the sphere of the investigation a former dishwasher at the lodge, Chester Weger. Weger had taken a lie detector test previously and had passed. This time his test proved to be far from normal. The results indicated very definitely that Weger had guilty knowledge of the triple slayings.

Authorities were stumped as to how Weger had passed the previous test. They decided to set him free and keep him under constant surveillance. Meanwhile, detectives delved into Weger's past. He had once been in the U.S. Marines, where he had learned seafaring knots identical to those used to tie two of the victims.

Although he professed to have been off duty, miles from the park on the day the crime was committed, detectives now learned that he had been a substitute dishwasher for an acquaintance who wanted time off that day. Faced with this last bit of incriminating evidence, Weger stated that he had initially been in error. It was true; he was working at the lodge on the day of the crime. In fact, he was washing dishes at the time of the killings, and could not possibly have been the murderer.

Detectives had a difficult time proving or disproving Weger's claim. They tracked down every guest who had stayed at the lodge on the day of the triple murder. Weger's photograph, among others, was shown to each guest in the hope that someone had seen him outside the lodge. This was a time consuming task. Many of the guests lived hundreds of miles from the resort. One by one they were located and interviewed. Sure enough, one woman recognized

Weger as the man she had passed on one of the paths near the murder scene around the time of the murders.

Weger was taken into custody, and interrogated. Detectives played it straight. They told the pale nervous suspect every bit of evidence they had pointing to him as the guilty man. At the conclusion of the interrogation Weger blurted out, "There's no use my trying to deny anything after that — you got me cold."

Weger stated that he was a married man with two children. Heavily in debt, he realized his dishwashing job would never allow him to get out of his financial difficulties. He slipped out of the lodge unseen with the intention of snatching purses from unwary ladies along the resort's many isolated paths. He grabbed at Mrs. Murphy's camera, mistaking it for a handbag. The strap broke.

Weger claimed he then picked up the heavy branch and threatened the women. He ordered them to turn around and lie down while he tied them. The women complied. Weger stated that suddenly "the one with the camera broke loose from the string and hit me hard over the back of the head with a pair of binoculars. As she struck me, I raised my club and gave it to her. Then I hit the other two. I didn't want them telling on me."

Weger went on to say that he dragged the three women into the nearby cave. He pulled and tugged at their clothing to make it appear to be a sexually motivated crime.

How did Weger manage to beat the first lie detector test? "That was a cinch," he explained. "I stuffed myself with aspirin and Coke. I should have done that on my next test." Why did he bother to drag his victims into a cave? Weger had an answer for that one as well. At the time of the murders he observed a low flying red and white Piper Cub circling overhead. He thought the bodies would be seen from the air and decided to conceal them.

An investigation into this aspect of his confession checked out. A red and white Piper piloted by Homer Charbonneau had taken off on the day in question. Airport records verified the date and time. Charbonneau distinctly remembered circling the area several times.

Taken to Starved Rock Park, Chester Weger reenacted his senseless crime. Weger was charged with the murder of Mrs. Oetting. At his trial he repudiated his detailed confession, claiming he was innocent and had been coerced into saying what the police wanted to hear.

On the afternoon of March 4, 1961, the jury retired to reach a verdict. It was Weger's birthday. He was 22. Nine hours later the jury returned with a verdict of guilty. Weger was sentenced to life imprisonment, which was considered a victory for the defence at the time. The State had strongly urged that Weger be executed.

Chester Weger, Prisoner Number 01114, is still incarcerated at the Statesville Corectional Centre at Joliet, Ill., which has been his home for the past 26 years. Prison officials inform me that he is a quiet man who keeps to himself. He is now the longest serving inmate in the institution. Each year he is eligible for parole. Each year parole is refused.

AN UNUSUAL POISON
The doctor broke his oath

"Do you solemnly swear, that you will be loyal to the profession of medicine; that into whatever house you shall enter, it shall be for the good of the sick to the utmost of your power; that you will exercise your art solely for the cure of your patients and will give no drug, perform no operation for a criminal purpose."

Hippocratic Oath (abridged)

I am certain that Dr. Carlo Nigrisoli of Bologna, Italy, started out in the practise of medicine convinced that he would uphold every single one of old Hippocrates' tenets. After all, the good doctor came from a long line of distinguished physicians who had practised medicine in Bologna for generations. He had no reason to stray from the straight and narrow.

What went wrong? Iris Azzali, that's what.

Iris strolled into Carlo's clinic one day with a minor ailment. The doctor cured what ailed her, and other things as well. Iris was a willowy, long-legged beauty, with big brown eyes, full seductive lips, and a body that would make the Leaning Tower of Pisa stand up straight and take notice.

From that very first meeting, the older man with a wife and three children at home thought of little else but beautiful, youthful Iris. She, in turn, thought the debonair society doctor

220

so much more intelligent and mature than her regular companions.

How can one put it delicately yet retain a degree of candor? Carlo and Iris met clandestinely at her apartment where their signs of affection soon graduated to physical fulfilment. Oh, what the heck, they hit the sack at every opportunity.

Sure, there were a few anxious moments. Take the time Iris became a tad pregnant. She cried and in general carried on something fierce, but Carlo rose to the occasion. He escorted her to another city, where she obtained an abortion. Presto, her troubles were over.

Now, folks, all this intrigue did not have a good effect on Carlo's wife Ombretta. She realized that Carlo was no longer the loving husband and attentive father he had once been. When Ombretta attempted to discuss her husband's changing attitude toward her, he flew into a rage. Ombretta became nervous and distraught. Something definitely was rotten in the state of Bologna.

The unhappy couple's best friends, Anna and Carlo Frascaroli, soon became aware of the tension between Carlo and Ombretta. Frascaroli, who was also a doctor, had been approached by Carlo, who told him that Ombretta was suffering from nervous exhaustion. Dr. Frascaroli prescribed a series of injections. He began giving the injections himself, but for convenience sake both doctors agreed that Carlo Nigrisoli would continue to give them to Ombretta at their home. Of course, the Frascarolis were totally unaware of Carlo's extra-curricular activities with Iris.

Meanwhile, the affair grew warmer. Carlo and Iris couldn't stay away from each other. They took little trips together into the country. Ombretta was miserable. She was losing her husband. The father of her chilren was no longer interested. On the other hand, Carlo now regarded his wife as an obstacle standing in the way of his happiness with firecracker Iris.

The potentially dangerous triangle exploded on March 14, 1964. It was around midnight when Carlo raced from his bedroom shouting to the servants, "I must get Signora Nigrisoli to the clinic. She has had a heart attack."

Poor Ombretta was rushed to her husband's clinic, but died without regaining consciousness. Carlo explained, "I had given her a heart stimulant by injection, but it doesn't seem to have succeeded." Carlo was completely distraught, but did muster up enough presence of mind to suggest to the doctors in attendance, "Put on the death certificate that she died from coronary thrombosis." The doctors disagreed with Carlo, feeling that they did not have enough information to be certain of the cause of death.

Suddenly, Carlo extracted a neat little pistol from his inside coat pocket. Raving like a lunatic, he shouted that he would kill himself unless the doctors signed the death certificate. Instead, they calmed him down and called police. In minutes the blubbering Carlo was in a police station answering embarrassing questions. When Italian detectives found out that he had been giving his wife a series of injections, they decided to hold him until the results of the post mortem were revealed.

These results caused a sensation throughout the country. The autopsy showed that Ombretta had died from an injection of curare. Curare is not your average poison, not by a long shot. It's a rare vegetable poison derived from certain South American plants. Some South American Indian tribes treat the tips of their arrows with it for use in warfare. The poison causes paralysis of the muscles, which is quickly followed by an inability to breathe. It has been used medically as a relaxant prior to operations. Dr. Frascaroli stated definitely that he had never used nor prescribed curare for Ombretta's condition.

Dr. Carlo Nigrisoli was charged with his wife's murder. His trial began on Oct. 1, 1964. It was the first trial held in Italy where curare was used as the instrument of death. It was also Italy's first televised murder trial. Adding to the uniqueness of the proceedings, Carlo obtained permission to testify from his cell via a sound system especially set up for that purpose. At no time was he actually in the courtroom, although his voice could be heard and he could hear everything which transpired.

Iris testified, admitting to her affair with the accused man. Dr. Frascaroli related that he had prescribed a nerve tonic for Ombretta to be taken intravenously. Dr. Frascaroli dramatically added that he had instructed Carlo to discontinue the injections a few days before Ombretta died.

It was proven that Carlo continued to give the injections. The prosecution painted the cruel picture of Carlo injecting his wife with curare, which rendered her helpless. He then cleaned up the evidence of his deed and watched as his wife took 20 minutes to die. It was only then that he ran for help.

A well-known neurologist, Prof. Domenico Zanello, surprised the court when he testified that Ombretta had discovered a hidden bottle of curare in her bathroom on the day before her death. Realizing that her husband might very well be about to murder her, she visited the professor for advice. He told her to go directly to the police, but she wouldn't listen. She insisted on trying every possible method of winning back the affection of her husband. The professor did convince her to take a trip the next day in order to be out of Carlo's reach. The advice came too late. On the day following Ombretta's visit to the professor, she was dead.

On Feb. 14, 1965, the 117-day trial came to an end. Dr. Carlo Nigrisoli was found guilty of murder and sentenced to life imprisonment.

HE DIDN'T GET AWAY WITH MURDER

Former RCMP officer convicted of killing wife

On March 28, 1981, Jeanette Kelly plunged to her death from the seventeenth floor of her luxurious Palace Pier apartment overlooking Lake Ontario.

Two years later, her husband Patrick, a former RCMP undercover officer, was charged with her murder. This is the story of their lives together, culminating with Jeanette's death and with Patrick standing trial for her murder.

When Pat Kelly was still a child, his family moved from Toronto to Victoria, B.C. He attended school in Victoria, graduating from Mountain View High School after completing Grade 12.

Pat Kelly, a clean cut, bright young man, tried his hand at banking. He obtained employment with the Bank of Montreal in Port Alberni, B.C. and was soon transferred to Dawson Creek. It was only a matter of a few months before Pat knew that the regimented life of a banker was not for him. He left the bank and caught on with a logging company, but here too, a restless streak, maybe an adventurous one, made Pat look to greener pastures. What could hold more promise of adventure than the RCMP?

On Nov. 2, 1970, Pat Kelly joined the Mounties and was assigned to Regina for basic training. Six months later he graduated and was sent to Toronto, where he spent four months on duty at Pearson International Airport. Next step in Pat's law enforcement career found him stationed at the RCMP detachment at Owen Sound. Here he obtained his first taste of undercover work, becoming involved in drugs and customs investigations. A year later, he was transferred back to Toronto to enrol in a French course, which lasted 18 months. Pat was then assigned to the drug squad. Soon he was an undercover drug squad operator.

In 1974, Pat's superiors sent him to the University of Javaria in Bogota, Colombia to take part in a total immersion course in Spanish. Later, while vacationing in Acapulco with fellow RCMP officer Wayne Humby, Pat met his future wife, Jeanette Hanlon.

The daughter of an automobile dealer in Glasgow, Scotland, attractive Jeanette hit it off with Pat right from the start. She was an employee of Avianca, Colombia's national airline, and was stopping over in Acapulco on her way back to Scotland after setting up a computer program for an airline in New Zealand. Jeanette and Pat were seldom apart during the week they spent in Mexico.

Jeanette, who had a full airline pass, continued on to Scotland to visit her family. She and Pat kept in constant touch by phone for a few weeks. Then she joined him in Toronto. The lovers discussed marriage. Jeanette was smitten. She returned to Scotland, but three months later emigrated to Canada to live with Pat Kelly. Ten months after her return, on Sept. 20, 1975, Jeanette and Pat were married.

They had become good friends with another couple, Dawn Tabor and John Pinkerton Hastey, better known as Pinky. The pair had been childhood friends in Maine. A short time after they arrived in Toronto, Dawn and Pinky married. They lived at 1900 Bloor St. East in Mississauga. Pat and Jeanette lived at Applewood Towers in Mississauga. Dawn Hastey is a name to remember. Sometime later, in the tangled web of the Kellys' life, Dawn would play a starring role.

By 1976, Pat and Jeanette purchased their first home from Pat's cousin, Jack McKay, at 16 George St. in Cookstown. Jeanette discovered she had a flair for interior decorating. The young couple worked several months renovating their new home.

Once they were nicely settled, Jeanette opened a craft shop specializing in homemade quilts. She named it The Quilt Shop. Farmers' wives around Cookstown brought their homemade quilts to Jeanette, who sold them at a profit. The trendy shop gradually caught on. While it didn't produce a large profit, it did pay its own way. In the summer of 1978, the Kellys sold their shop at a small profit.

That summer of 1978, Pat was deeply involved in an RCMP undercover drug operation. It was a rather stressful time for Pat. He had been attempting to sell his home in Cookstown and purchase a condominium in the Palace Pier apartment building in the west end of Toronto. The house in Cookstown had been up for sale with no takers for over 10 months. This was of some concern, since Pat had put $3000 down on the new apartment, but required a further $5700 to close the deal toward the total price of $87,000.

Later, Pat would testify that he had several sources from whom he could have borrowed the balance of his down payment. However, all his problems appeared to evaporate when, in August, the Cookstown house burned to the ground. At the time of the fire, Pat claimed that he was at a lodge in Algonquin Park, while Jeanette was visiting her family in Glasgow. Pat phoned Jeanette, who flew back to Toronto.

Arson was strongly suspected. Jeanette was understandably shocked when Pat was charged with setting fire to the house, along with two counts of attempting to defraud the insurance companies. Their marriage deteriorated into a strained relationship. In Pat's own words, ". . . basically a platonic relationship took place. I didn't get in her way and she didn't get in mine. We would often socialize together and go to a movie perhaps or go to dinner." It was quite remarkably a congenial atmosphere considering the circumstances.

For some time after the fire took place, Pat and Jeanette lived at the Holiday Inn in Don Mills under police protection. The drug probe involving Pat had been finalized in July and the fire had taken place in August. There was a grave suspicion that Pat's life was in danger. To this day, Pat claims that criminals burned his house shortly after his cover was blown.

Others obviously had a different theory, but things took a turn for the better for the Kellys. Pat was discharged on the arson charges. He collected $60,000 in insurance for the house and $55,000 for contents, in all $115,000.

Pat and Jeanette took a holiday in Mexico. The Kellys grew much closer now that the terrible possibility of a conviction and prison sentence had been lifted from their shoulders. When they returned to Toronto, there seemed little reason not to move into the Palace Pier.

On Oct. 3, 1978, the Kellys moved into their luxurious new apartment.

• • •

Although the Kellys' domestic situation improved, there were other women in Pat Kelly's life. Let's start with Dawn Hastey.

Before Pat and Jeanette married, they made the acquaintance of Dawn Tabor and Pinky Hastey. The two couples became close friends in a short period of time. In the summer of 1975, both couples married. Five years later, when Dawn had marital difficulties, it was only natural that she discuss her problems with her close friends, the Kellys. Both Pat and Jeanette were sympathetic to her plight. They suggested that she would be welcome to stay with them should she leave her husband.

The very night this discussion took place, Dawn had a heart to heart talk with her husband. Next day, she moved into the Kellys' one bedroom apartment. Dawn slept on a pullout couch in the den.

A few weeks after Dawn moved in, Jeanette took a trip to Italy. Pat flew to Vancouver on personal business. The arrangement was working our rather well. The Kellys had an old English sheepdog, appropriately named Kelly, a 90-pound animal which took some looking after. Dawn would take care of the dog.

Pat returned from Vancouver unexpectedly at 8 o'clock the next morning. Dawn was sleeping on the pullout couch in the den. One thing led to another. Dawn had intercourse with her best friend's husband. It didn't stop there. Over a period of time, they made love again and again.

In various statements, Dawn has admitted, "It could have been ten times." On other occasions, she testified, "From the first time we made love until the last time, I don't know. I mean, I could say three times or say ten times." Obviously, it would have been too much to ask Mrs. Hastey to keep a score card. She is even on record as saying, "Probably every night when I was there."

Pat, who denies ever being intimate with Dawn, well recalls arriving at his apartment after an early morning flight from the west coast. ". . . She was sleeping in the den, and when I came in, I asked her if she wanted a coffee and I was going to make one for myself, and I made a coffee for her and took it into the den. She mentioned she hadn't slept well and asked for a back rub. I started to give her the back rub, and at one point she turned over and reached up to me and pulled me toward her to kiss her, and I said I would make another cup of coffee and got up."

There were other women in Pat Kelly's busy life. In 1978, during the course of an official investigation, Pat met librarian Jan Bradley. Every few months or so thereafter, he dropped into the library and took Jan out for coffee. For reasons of his own, he told her his name was Pat McLean. This rather casual relationship continued until January, 1981, when Pat took Jan out for dinner.

Later that month, he and Jan spent a weekend at the Briars, a resort near Sutton, Ont. They slept together for the first time. Pat informed Jan that his real name was Kelly, not McLean. She didn't take the deception well. The weekend was cut short, but the lovers made up and Jan Bradley, like Dawn Hastey, would play a large part in the future lives of the Kellys.

Pat had other diversions besides his wife, Dawn, and Jan. In the summer of 1980, he met a young lady named Cheryl.

Their relationship lasted until the Christmas season of that year. Pat claims it was a casual affair — movies, dinner, drinks, that sort of thing. Another lady, Leslie, was being courted in the same manner.

How did Patrick Kelly manage it all: an expensive car, luxurious apartment, European vacations and his constant squiring of a string of women?

In 1980, Pat left the service of the RCMP. During his career as an undercover agent with the Mounties, he made many important contacts, particularly in Colombia. Pat acted as courier for wealthy Colombians who wanted to get their money into the U.S. or Europe due to the instability of the Colombian government. Pat received healthy commissions for his services and never reported these commissions as income.

Pat, who clearly had a keen eye for turning a fast dollar, also acted in bringing seller and purchaser together for the sale of real estate in Mexico. Sellers desiring only cash for property would be put in touch with buyers who wanted to purchase properties at healthy discounts. Once the deal was consummated, Pat received commissions from both parties. Here again, Pat never declared this income.

Years earlier, Pat had attended junior high school with Victor Simpson in Victoria. The school chums kept in touch. Victor became a lawyer, while Pat became a law enforcement officer.

In 1980, Victor Simpson formed a company known as K & V Enterprises, which acted as a holding company for any type of financial transaction. In September, 1980, Pat became an employee of K & V Enterprises, with the title of executive manager. His main duties, according to Simpson, were "to investigate and locate investment opportunities for the company." Pat received a salary of $1200 a month from K & V and a car allowance of $225 per month. Pat also invested large amounts in K & V from time to time to facilitate deals which K & V consummated in French and Spanish speaking countries. In essence, almost everything funnelled into K & V came back to Kelly in wages, allowances, or loans from the company.

Apparently, Jeanette Kelly was unaware of just how her husband made his living. She did, however, know that they had collected a tidy sum in insurance after Pat had been discharged concerning the Cookstown fire. She also knew that she lived in a luxurious apartment, drove a late model Porsche and could afford to slip away to Europe whenever the fancy struck her.

In fact, in 1980, Jeanette travelled to Italy, accompanied by Dawn, who was then separated from her husband. Pat not only financed his wife's expenses, he also loaned $4000 to Dawn so that she could travel with Jeanette.

Jeanette and Dawn separated after they landed in Rome. Dawn took a room at the Holiday Inn in St. Peter's Square, while Jeanette had a liason with a friend, Marchello Rodocachi. According to Dawn's later testimony, Marchello and Jeanette were madly in love. They travelled together to Austria.

Dawn claimed Jeanette had confided in her that she had to make a decision on whether to return to Pat in Canada or stay with Marchello as his mistress in Europe.

Dawn returned to Toronto in August, a few days before Jeanette. She stayed at the Kelly apartment, but her affair with Pat had waned during her absence. Nothing happened. When Jeanette returned, Dawn noticed that she and Pat were extremely cool to each other. It was obvious to her that Jeanette was sorry to be back in Toronto. Dawn moved out of the Kelly's apartment and into a friend's home in Burlington.

Within a few weeks, Dawn and Pat discussed Jeanette's attitude. Dawn told Pat that Jeanette had mentioned divorce. Pat replied that if there was a divorce, Jeanette would end up with nothing. Jeanette was not aware of many of his debts. He had told Jeanette his feelings on the matter. According to Dawn, Jeanette told her she was concerned about her lifestyle and had decided to leave things exactly as they were. Dawn Hastey paid back the $4000 she owed Pat Kelly for the European holiday and shortly thereafter moved to the United States. In Febuary, 1981, Dawn returned to Toronto.

That winter was a hectic one for all the participants in the

Kelly affair. Pat was seeing Jan Bradley on a regular basis. They slipped away to New York for pleasant and rather expensive weekends at the Park Plaza and Algonquin Hotels. Their relationship intensified right up until March 28, when Jeanette Kelly plunged to her death from the 17th floor of the Palace Pier.

Two distinct versions exist as to how Jeanette Kelly met her death. This is the version Pat Kelly told witnesses at the time of the tragedy and which he would relate from the witness stand three years after the events took place.

The Kellys awoke around 9 a.m. that fateful day. They had tea and toast on the balcony. It was going to be a busy day for Jeanette. She was flying to Italy that evening at 6 p.m. and was busy packing. Pat helped. Then he and Jeanette slipped out for brunch at the Magic Pan in Sherway Gardens. They returned at 2 p.m.

Pat went downstairs to a storage area and carried up his wife's Samsonite luggage. They continued to clean up the apartment and packed Jeanette's clothing until around 3:15 p.m. At that time Pat suggested a pot of tea. He went into the kitchen to prepare the tea. Jeanette strolled in, mentioning something about a rattle on the balcony. She picked up a stool and walked out to the balcony.

Pat went back to preparing the tea when he heard his wife cry out. He dashed to the balcony and saw Jeanette falling. He clutched at his wife and managed to get both hands around the upper part of her legs, but as she was still in motion, he couldn't maintain his grasp and Jeanette fell away.

Pat phoned the doorman, instructing him to call an ambulance. He then ran to the elevators and was beside his wife's body in minutes. Pat felt Jeanette's pulse. There was none. Pat Kelly closed his wife's eyes. He followed the body in a separate ambulance to St. Joseph's Hospital. Pat was beside himelf with grief.

On April 1, the day Jeanette was buried, Pat demonstrated to Sgt. Michael Duchak of the Metro Police just how the accident had occurred. According to Duchak, he and Kelly stood about three feet apart. Kelly lunged at Duchak and put his arms around the police officer's waist. He put his right cheek to the right side of the police officer's chest and held on. Then Duchak states, Kelly let go and said, "She was already over the balcony, we were face to face, I remember looking at her face. I was leaning over the rail. I was too weak to hold onto her and she fell."

Prior to his wife's death, Pat claims he had arrangements to take a trip to Hawaii with Jan Bradley. Now, completely broken up over his wife's tragic death, he decided that the trip might be just what he needed to take his mind off his troubles. On April 6, 1981, eight days after his wife's untimely death, Patrick Kelly flew off to Hawaii for a holiday with Jan Bradley.

When Pat and Jan returned, Pat found it embarrassing to continually have to explain how the accident occurred. Later, witnesses were to state that Pat claimed his wife fell while hanging plants on the balcony. Others stated he told them she was attempting to fix a noisy rattle. Pat moved to Victoria for the summer.

Back in Toronto, Jan was being questioned by police. Pat sent her money and advised her to retain a lawyer. Meanwhile Pat, who apparently was never one to let grass grow under his feet, kept company with several other women. Three years later, Crown counsel would insinuate that, as a former police officer, Kelly was cunning enough to keep company with other women in order to divert suspicion from Jan Bradley. Pat, of course, claimed his involvement with other women was not serious.

Jan couldn't stand the pressure. She left her employment and flew to Victoria to discuss matters with Pat. In June, the couple vacationed in Florida. That fall, Pat decided to sell the Palace Pier condo, which held bitter memories, and move to the south of France. He could well afford the move.

In September, 1981, Pat collected life insurance from London Life Insurance Co. on three policies totalling $221,813.83. In addition to these policies, he collected $43,324.80 from Confederation Life, who covered the group plan at Canadian Pacific Airline, where Jeanette was employed. In all, the insurance proceds on Jeanette Kelly's life amounted to $271,138.83.

In December, 1981, Jan Bradley drove with her mother from Toronto to Montreal's Mirabel Airport. Pat arrived on a flight from Victoria. Together, they flew to France. Later, Mrs. Bradley would attend her daughter's wedding in the south of France.

Pat and his new wife adjusted nicely to their lifestyle. They often took pleasant junkets to the Bahamas for the weekend. Pat bought new suits by the dozen.

Meanwhile, Toronto police, who had their suspicions from the day of Jeanette Kelly's death, went about gathering evidence. An autopsy had been performed on Jeanette Kelly's body the day after the fall by Dr. John Deck, staff neuropathologist at the Toronto General Hospital. From his examination, Dr. Deck indicated that Jeanette Kelly contacted the ground in a sitting position, resulting in severe injuries to the base of the spine as well as the back of both legs. There were no major external injuries above the waist.

Dr. Deck pointed out that abrasions to the left breast, in his opinion, had not been incurred as a result of the fall. He felt the abrasions were consistent with a blow of some kind. The doctor further pointed out small scrape marks near the deceased's nose, injuries to the upper and lower lip and an abrasion over the jaw, which were not consistent with those major injuries connected to the fall. Later, in answer to prosecution counsel's question, "Are those injuries you noted to the face, the nose and the mouth consistent or inconsistent with a punch, one or more punches?", Dr. Deck replied, "I think they are quite consistent with more than one punch."

Paul Malbeuf, a member of Toronto's Metro Police Emergency Task Force, took part in an interesting experiment. An exact duplicate of the pertinent areas of Apt. 1705 were constructed. A policewoman was positioned on the stool allegedly used by Jeanette Kelly. The stool was placed beside the balcony rail. Malbeuf, an all-around athlete, was positioned in the kitchen beside the kettle, where Kelly claimed to be when his wife cried out.

When the policewoman screamed, Malbeuf, a former 100 yard dash champion, equipped with running shoes, was to race to her aid before she fell over the rail. Malbeuf extended himself, but try as he might, he never once reached the policewoman in time to grasp her before she fell, as Kelly claimed had happened with his wife. In fact, the experiment was tried several times, but Malbeuf never came close to making contact with the policewoman.

To add substance to the results of Officer Malbeuf's experiments, Eric Krueger of Toronto's Centre of Forensic Sciences, an expert in velocity, stated that Jeanette could not have fallen from the balcony as Pat Kelly claims. Krueger takes into account that from balcony to street level in 140 feet, Jeanette Kelly, 5 ft. 3 in. tall and weighing 132 pounds, would have been on the ground in three seconds. The fastest a runner could make it to her side was four seconds. Besides, according to Krueger, if Jeanette accidentally lost her balance, she would not have landed on her spine.

On a visit to Canada in 1982, Patrick Kelly was arrested on three charges of credit card fraud involving $125,000. He was then charged with his wife's murder.

Much of evidence related here came from expert testimony and from witnesses who observed Pat Kelly's guilty actions. But the Crown's star witness was not an expert. Dawn Tabor/Hastey/Bragg, the Kellys' dear friend, claimed to be an eyewitness to Jeanette Kelly's murder. By the time Pat came to trial, Dawn had married for the second time.

Dawn Bragg stated she was in Apt. 1705 on the day of Jeanette Kelly's death. On March 29, 1981, Dawn drove up to the Palace Pier and entered the building via a back door, using keys given to her by Jeanette some months earlier. Both Pat and Jeanette were in. They were arguing. Dawn offered to give Jeanette a lift to the airport.

Meanwhile, she was asked to take a seat in the den. She could hear her friends arguing about a divorce. Jeanette was adamant about refusing to grant Pat a divorce. The Kellys raised their voices. Suddenly, Jeanette screamed. Dawn walked out of the den to find her friend Jeanette on the floor. Pat picked up the limp form of his wife. He carried her over to the balcony and opened the doors. From the witness stand, Dawn Bragg would state, "He took Jeanette out to the balcony and dropped her over the edge."

Dawn went out to the balcony, looked down and collapsed. In an instant Pat was at her side, consoling her, telling her everything would be all right, telling her he loved her. Pat hurried Dawn to the elevators. They went up a few floors. All the while, Pat told Dawn to be quiet, to go out the back way and to go home. She listened and did as she was told. After all, she and Pat had been lovers.

Dawn remembered well one night at the Palace Pier Club when Pat had discussed taking care of Jeanette. He had said he would take Dawn to France. He told her he was in love. He also told her there was no way anyone could tell how a person fell off a balcony.

According to Dawn, Pat had previously confided to her how he set fire to his home in Cookstown. He took Dawn to the lodge where he supposedly was when his house burned. He explained how he went to bed that night, got up and drove to Cookstown. He spread gasoline throughout the house and lit it. Then he drove back to the lodge without being seen.

The day after Jeanette fell to her death, Dawn Bragg was in a dilemma. Three years later, as the Crown's star witness in the murder trial of Pat Kelly, she attempted to explain when she was asked, "What were your feelings on March 30?"

"I was afraid," Dawn answered. "Afraid of what I had seen and I was afraid of Pat. I was afraid I knew too much." A couple of days after Jeanette's funeral, Pat called Dawn. He told her he was going away alone and would call her if he needed her.

Dawn Bragg's story was fascinating. If true, it branded Pat Kelly a cold-blooded killer. Yet, there were doubts concerning her testimony. Why did she wait two years to inform police that she was a witness to Jeanette's death? Quite possibly Dawn Bragg felt she could be charged with conspiracy to commit murder. Given the promise by Metro Police Sgt. Ed Stewart that any statement she might give would not be used against her, she decided to reveal to police that she was in Apt. 1705 when Jeanette was killed. Sgt. Stewart, who had doggedly gathered evidence for close to three years, would later earn a commendation for his relentless work on the Kelly case.

Defence Counsel Earl Levy pleaded that much of the prosecution evidence was theatrical and circumstantial. If Dawn Bragg, an admitted liar, was still lying when she claimed to be an eyewitness to the murder, then the prosecution's case was without merit.

Crown Counsel L. Budzinsky contended that even without Dawn Bragg's testimony, the circumstantial evidence against Kelly was overwhelming. If her evidence was taken at face value, Pat Kelly was guilty of first degree murder.

The jury agreed with the Crown. Pat Kelly was found guilty of murder in the first degree. He was sentenced to life imprisonment with no possibility of parole for 25 years.

Kelly appealed his conviction. The Ontario Court of Appeal upheld the conviction. Mr. Justice Bert MacKinnon stated on behalf of the three man court, "There was no miscarriage of justice."

SHE WASN'T
A GOOD MOTHER
Her children died mysteriously

Can a woman murder eight of her nine children over a period of 14 years and go undetected? That's what the 70,000 citizens of the factory city of Schenectady, N.Y. are asking themselves.

Mary Beth Tinning, 44, was born in the area back in the war years when the local General Electric plants employed 45,000 workers churning out strategic war materials. That large figure has steadily declined, and today 12,000 are gainfully employed at G.E., still the largest industry by far in Schenectady. The town, adjacent to Albany, has seen better days.

Joe Tinning works at General Electric as a systems analyst. He and Mary Beth have moved frequently over the years. No one gave it much thought. The area around Albany, the state capital, is surrounded by villages and towns. It is difficult to ascertain where one stops and the next one begins. There was one thing different about the Tinnings. They suffered tragic misfortune with their children — all nine of them.

On Jan. 3, 1972, the Tinnings' new baby, Jennifer, died while still in hospital. She was eight days old. Jennifer is the only Tinning death not considered to be suspicious. Seventeen days later, on Jan. 20, two-year-old Joseph died. Understandably, the Tinnings were devastated. But there was more to come. On March 2, 1972, four-year-old Barbara died.

What a horrible experience for any family to endure. In two months less a day all three Tinning children were dead. Their deaths were attributed to natural causes. Those who knew the Tinnings offered their sympathy. It happens. There was little anyone could do.

Nine months later, Mary Beth gave birth to a son, Timothy. On Dec. 10, 1973, 14 days after his birth, Timothy died. The cause of death noted on the death certificate is SIDS (Sudden Infant Death Syndrome). In its purest sense, SIDS is not a cause of death. It really means that the cause of death is unknown.

With Timothy's death occurring so soon after being taken home from hospital, rumors spread among the Tinnings' few acquaintances. Was it possible that there was something wrong with the Tinnings' genes, some imperfection which caused their offspring to die suddenly?

Just under two year's after this tragedy, five-month-old Nathan died. His death was attributed to acute pulmonary edema. When Nathan died on Sept. 2, 1975, various individuals in official capacities, such as doctors and social service workers, became somewhat suspicious. However, it must be pointed out that the same doctors and social workers were not necessarily involved in all the deaths. Autopsies were performed on all the Tinning children. The results were always the same. Death was attributed to natural causes.

Dr. Robert Sullivan, the Schenectady County Medical Examiner, admits that when Nathan died, he was aware of the earlier deaths. Nathan's death was thoroughly investigated, but no evidence of foul play was found. Dr. Sullivan reveals, "The parents were doing nothing wrong. They were initiating examinations into the deaths of the children."

Joe Tinning had a responsible position at the G.E. plant. He is an avid bowler. Over the years, Mary Beth often worked as a waitress to supplement the family's income. Sometimes she served as a volunteer ambulance driver. There was absolutely nothing to distinguish the Tinnings from their neighbors.

238

Absolutely nothing except the inexplicable deaths of their children.

After Nathan's death, three and a half years passed before Mary Beth gave birth to another child, a daughter, Mary Frances. The beat continued. Mary Frances died at age three and a half months.

Ten months later, Mary Beth had a little boy, Jonathan. He died three months later, on March 24, 1980. That same year, the Tinnings adopted a son, Michael. He died a year after Jonathan, on March 2, 1981.

Michael's death put an end to the theory that some kind of black genetic evil was at work causing the strange deaths of the Tinning children. After all, he was adopted. An autopsy was performed. The official cause of death was listed as viral pneumonia. Now, suspicions ran rampant. Although there was no proof of any wrongdoing, pediatricians and social workers advised police that should any further Tinning children die, a forensic pathologist should be called in immediately.

Eight children were dead. It seems unbelievable that, despite an extensive investigation into some of the deaths, nothing more than dark suspicions were cast in Mrs. Tinning's direction. The bodies of Timothy and Nathan were exhumed, but nothing new was found.

Over three years passed. Mary Beth became pregnant for the eighth time. She gave birth to Tami Lynne, who died four months later, on Dec. 20, 1985. This ninth death initiated a massive investigation. I have been unable to unearth just what, if anything, investigating officers uncovered. Evidently, a tip concerning Tami's death came from someone attached to the Schenectady County Social Services Department's Child Protective Unit.

On Feb. 4, 1986, Mary Beth was picked up by detectives and taken to the nearby State Police Headquarters at Loudonville. Under intensive questioning, which lasted a total of 10 hours, Mary Berth admitted killing three of her children, Timothy, Nathan and Tami.

She was duly arrested, lodged in jail and charged with two counts of second degree murder concerning Tami's death.

More specifically, she was charged with one count of "having intentionally caused her daughter's death by smothering her with a pillow", and in the other count "with showing depraved indifference to human life by engaging in conduct which caused Tami Lynne's death." The maximum penalty for second degree murder in New York state is life imprisonment. The minimum penalty is from 15 to 25 years.

On March 19, after spending a month and a half in jail, Mary Beth Tinning was released on $100,000 bail. She immediately instituted court proceedings to have her confession deemed inadmissable evidence at her impending murder trial.

Mary Beth professed that her constitutional rights had been violated when the confessions were obtained. The suppression hearing into this charge was concluded in April. As a result, the details of what was said on the night Mary Beth confessed to detectives can now be made public.

The first statement, given in narrative form, describes how Mary Beth smothered Timothy, Nathan and Tami, "With a pillow, because I'm not a good mother. I'm not a good mother because of the other children." She also said, "I did not do anything to Jennifer, Joseph, Barbara, Michael, Mary Frances or Jonathan."

In a second question and answer session with detectives, Mary Beth gave more details of Tami's death. She arrived home that night, five days before Christmas in 1985, at about 8:35 p.m., after being out shopping with a friend. Her mother-in-law and father-in-law had been baby sitting four-month-old Tami. They, as well as her friend, left at about 9:30 p.m. Mary Beth sat in a recliner chair with Tami on her lap. After a while she put the baby to bed.

Mary Beth related, "I tried to give her a bottle, but she didn't want it. She fussed and cried for about a half hour. She finally went to sleep. I then went to bed." Joe came home at 11 p.m. They chatted for a few moments.

"I was about to doze off when Tami woke up and started to cry. I got up and went to the crib and tried to do something with her to get her to stop crying. I finally used the pillow from my bed and put it over her head. I did it until she stopped crying.'' Mary Beth went on, ''When I finally lifted the pillow off Tami, she wasn't moving. I put the pillow on the couch and then screamed for Joe and he woke up and I told Joe Tami wasn't breathing.''

It was this chilling recital that Mary Beth attempted to suppress. However, a county court judge ruled that her statements would be admissable at her upcoming murder trial. He also ruled that they had been given willingly and voluntarily.

While awaiting her murder trial, Mary Beth and her faithful husband Joe have moved to Ballston Spa, a tiny community about 25 miles outside Schenectady. The prosecution's case is being prepared by District Attorney John Poersch. He is quick to point out, ''Mrs. Tinning's rights must be protected. She is only being tried for the murder of one daughter, Tami. Joe Tinning is not a suspect in the case.''

In a city where two murders a year is the average, the Tinning case is the main topic of conversation. One almost forgets that Mary Beth has not yet been tried. District Attorney Poersch guards what he says, but as I left his office he assured me, ''The Grand Jury made a proper indictment and I'm sure we will gain a conviction.''

I drove to the Most Holy Redeemer Cemetery and removed the snow from the tiny markers indicating the final resting place of the Tinning children. None of them reached five years of age.

Epilogue: On July 19, 1987, Mary Beth Tinning was found guilty of second degree murder in the case of her infant daughter Tami. She was sentenced to life imprisonment.